↠ Additional Praise for *The Gardner Heist*

"An enjoyable true-crime tale accessible to lovers of art and whodunits alike."
　　　　　　　　　　　　　　　　　　　　　　—*Kirkus*

"This riveting, wonderfully vivid account takes you into the underworld of obsessed art detectives, con men, and thieves, tantalizing leads and dead ends."　　　　　　—Jonathan Harr, author of *The Lost Painting*

"The book is a thrill . . . the mystery remains unsolved, but the case is reinvigorated in its retelling by a man who fully appreciates the value of the masterpieces and the magnitude of the criminal conspiracy that carried them away in the night."　　　　　　　　—*The Guardian*

"A fascinating, well-researched investigation . . . [a] police-eye-view of an unsolved crime—the solution for which may be just around the corner."
　　　　　　　　　　—Noah Charney, director of the Association
　　　　　　　　　　　　for Research into Crimes Against Art
　　　　　　　　　　　　　　and author of *The Art Thief*

"Boser's carefully researched and brilliantly written of the twentieth century's greatest art heist is too stunningly fascinating to miss."
　　　　　　　　　　　　　　　—Phyllis Karas, author of
　　　　　　　　　　　　Brutal: The Untold Story of My Life
　　　　　　　　　　　　　Inside Whitey Bulger's Irish Mob

"Ulrich Boser presents his solution to the [Gardner] mystery."
　　　　　　　　　　　　　　　　　　　　—*Washington Post*

"The theft has roiled many imaginations, including that of Ulrich Boser."　　　　　　　　　　　　　　　　　—*New York Times*

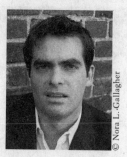
© Nora L. Gallagher

✈ About the Author

ULRICH BOSER has written for the *New York Times*, the *Washington Post, Smithsonian* magazine, *Slate,* and many other publications. He has served as a contributing editor at *U.S. News and World Report* and is the founding editor of *The Open Case,* a crime magazine and web community. He lives in Washington, D.C.

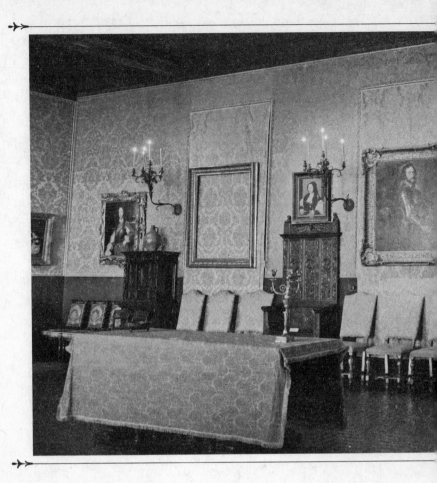

The True Story of the World's Largest Unsolved Art Theft

⊙ Smithsonian Books

HARPER

NEW YORK • LONDON • TORONTO • SYDNEY

ULRICH BOSER

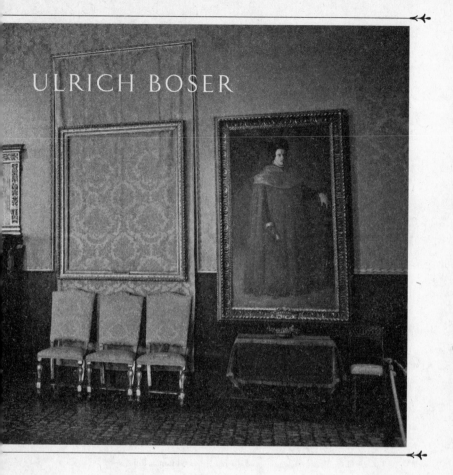

THE GARDNER HEIST

HARPER

A hardcover edition of this book was published in 2009 by Collins.

THE GARDNER HEIST. Copyright © 2009 by Ulrich Boser. All rights reserved. Printed in the United States of America. No part of this book may be used or reproduced in any manner whatsoever without written permission except in the case of brief quotations embodied in critical articles and reviews. For information address HarperCollins Publishers, 10 East 53rd Street, New York, NY 10022.

HarperCollins books may be purchased for educational, business, or sales promotional use. For information please write: Special Markets Department, HarperCollins Publishers, 10 East 53rd Street, New York, NY 10022.

FIRST HARPER PAPERBACK PUBLISHED 2010.

Designed by Kate Nichols

The Library of Congress has catalogued the hardcover edition as follows:

Boser, Ulrich.
    The Gardner heist : the true story of the world's largest unsolved art theft / Ulrich Boser. — 1st ed.
        p. cm.
    Includes bibliographical references.
    ISBN: 978-0-06-145183-6   1. Art thefts—Massachusetts—Boston. 2. Theft from museums—Massachusetts—Boston. 3. Isabella Stewart Gardner Museum. I. Title.
    NB795.3.M4.B67 2009
    364.16'287599492–dc22

                                                                                    2008038803

ISBN 978-0-06-145184-3 (pbk.)

    11 12 13 14 OV/RRD 10 9 8 7 6

For *Nora, Leila, and Sonja*

CONTENTS

AUTHOR'S NOTE

THIS IS A WORK of fact. In some places, I have relied on outside sources—books, newspapers, films, wiretaps—for quotes and other factual information. In order to make the story more readable, I did not always cite these outside sources within the text; they are all referenced in the notes. I also changed the names and certain details of some individuals to protect their anonymity; this is also indicated within the notes. Quotes were altered as little as possible for grammar and clarity.

1. THE STORM ON THE SEA OF GALILEE

A Disturbance in the Courtyard

Boston, Massachusetts
Around 12:30 a.m.
March 18, 1990

ON THE EAST SIDE of Palace Road, just beyond the harsh glare of a sodium streetlight, two men sit in a small, gray hatchback. The man in the driver's seat is stocky and broad shouldered, with round cheeks and squinty, James Dean eyes. The other man is shorter, standing just under five foot ten. He has the worn, craggy face of a hard-working longshoreman. A pair of square, gold-framed glasses perch on his nose. Both men are dressed as police officers, and they look the part, dark blue uniforms, eight-point service caps, and the nylon, knee-length coats that beat cops use to stay dry on wet New England nights.

A light rain fell earlier in the day. Water beads on the window of the hatchback. Across the street, a few late-night revelers spill out of an apartment building. They're young—seniors in high school—and just left a college-dorm party because the beer ran out. Now they linger on the street, talking and laughing, their voices thick and boozy. It's late on one of the biggest nights of the year, St. Patrick's Day. They have to go somewhere, one of the revelers says. Should they try and sneak into a bar on Huntington Avenue? Or pick up a case of beer and head to someone's house? Jerry Stratberg jokes with one of his friends, pulling her onto his back and wobbling her piggyback style south along Palace Road. He seesaws down the sidewalk for a few yards. She taps him on the shoulder. "Watch out, there's a cop in that car over there," she says.

Stratberg sees the broad-shouldered man in the driver's seat of the hatchback and steps toward him. Through the thin fog, they stare at each other, the broad-shouldered man giving Stratberg a flinty look that says back off, go home. Stratberg notices the man's unusual eyes—they look almost Asian—and then spots the Boston police patch on his shoulder.

What are the cops doing here? Looking for thieves? Drug dealers? There have been a spate of muggings in the area, and in October, a gunman shot and killed a pregnant woman waiting at a stoplight a few blocks away. Still, Stratberg thinks, nothing good can come from this. He's under the legal drinking age, a few months away from his high school diploma. "Let's go back and tell the others," he says. His friend slips from his shoulders. The two soberly cross the street. They whisper quietly with the group, before they all hop in a car and roar off.

The street falls silent. Some oak trees quiver in the wind. Then, shortly after 1 a.m., the two men step onto the sidewalk, the Isabella Stewart Gardner Museum looming above them like a castle. The nineteenth-century heiress Isabella Stewart Gardner designed the four-story building as a replica of a Renaissance-era Venetian palazzo, with soaring balconies, stone stylobates, and a blooming courtyard brimming with lofty palms and hothouse jasmines. Art was Gardner's passion, and she built a world-class collection, packing her museum with tens of thousands of treasures, including works by Titian, Velazquez, Raphael, Manet, and Botticelli. The museum also contains the only Cellini bronze in the country, the first Matisse acquired by an American museum, and Michelangelo's tragically moving *Pieta*.

Flamboyant, imperious, with a deep belief in the redemptive power of art, Gardner built intimate galleries for her masterworks, each room extolling a different theme, each one its own creative stew. There's a quiet, calming Chinese Loggia; a Gothic Room that recalls a medieval chapel; a Yellow Room lined with pastel-toned paintings by J. M. W. Turner and Edgar Degas. In her will, Gardner forbade any changes to her museum. She wanted her work of art to always remain her work of art. Nothing could be added or taken away. Not a Chippendale chair, not a Rembrandt canvas, not a bamboo window shade. Everything must remain in the same Victorian patchwork of wood-paneled corners and draped alcoves, or the trustees would be required to sell off the collection and donate the profits to Harvard University. And from Gardner's death in 1924 until that March 1990 evening, it was a wish faithfully kept.

The two men move to the side entrance. Next to the large wooden door is a white buzzer. One of the men presses it.

Through an intercom, a security guard answers.

"Police. Let us in," the man says. "We heard about a disturbance in the courtyard."

Inside the museum, sitting in front of a console of four large video screens, Ray Abell thinks for a moment. He's short and gangly, with a long mop of curly hair that cascades over his shoulders. A student at the Berklee College of Music, he wears one of his favorite hats, a large, wide-brimmed Stetson. For him the job is little more than a rest between rock shows, and he will often gig with his band at a local bar before he strolls into the museum just before midnight. The third shift can be hauntingly spooky. Late at night, the floorboards squeak and moan, bats dash around the Italianate courtyard, their wings softly fluttering in the night air. But the job doesn't require much work, and Abell will usually wile away the hours in the way that most guards wile away the hours, reading magazines, playing cribbage, waiting for the moment when the sun comes up and filters though the courtyard in a rosy haze of light.

Abell stares at the video screen images of the two men. Tonight's shift has already been too busy for his liking. Thirty minutes earlier, while he was doing his rounds, a fire alarm went off in the conservation lab on the fourth floor. He ran up the wooden stairs and into the room, the bright lights of the alarm strobing the walls. But there was nothing. Then, some ten minutes later, the alarm rang in the carriage house. He sprinted outside, and with the beam of a flashlight he must have speared the darkness, looking flames, smoke, any signs of fire. Again, nothing.

And on the video screens in front of Abell, the men look like cops. They have police patches on their shoulders. Insignia dot their lapels. Maybe someone managed to get into the courtyard? Or there was someone in the carriage house? Despite orders never to let anyone into the museum, Abell buzzes the men inside.

It's 1:24 a.m. The shorter intruder, the one with the glasses, steps up to the watch desk and asks if there are any other guards in the building.

Just one, Abell replies.

"Get him down here," he says.

Abell calls his partner, Ralph Helman, on his walkie-talkie. "Will you please come to the desk?"

The man with the glasses peers at Abell. "You look familiar," he says. "I think we have a default warrant out on you. Come out here and show us some identification."

Abell is nervous. He moves out of the booth and away from the panic button—the only direct connection to the outside world—and hands over his driver's license and Berklee student ID. There are some things that could get him into trouble. Sometimes he needed a way to come down after a gig, ease into the mood of sitting around an empty museum all night, and so he'd smoke some marijuana and come to work high. And then there was the Christmas party. A few months earlier, he and another guard snuck some friends in through the side entrance and drank a few bottles of wine in the Dutch Room. They didn't damage anything, just stood and gaped at the paintings. It seemed like harmless fun at the time.

The second security guard, Ralph Helman, appears in the doorway. He's tall and thin, with a wispy, brown beard, and such a dedicated trombone player that he brought his horn with him to work that evening. It's a few days before his twenty-eighth birthday, and this is one of the first times that Helman has ever worked third shift. He had received a frantic call early that afternoon. Could he work tonight? A guard had fallen ill. He agreed, and now in front of the watch desk, the taller thief thrusts him against the wall and spread-eagles his arms and legs.

"Why are you arresting me?" Helman asks, as the handcuffs click over his wrists.

The other intruder shoves Abell against the wall, and as he pinches Abell's arms together, Abell has a sinking thought—they never frisked me. Even in late-night TV cop shows, they frisk suspects before they arrest them.

"This is a robbery," one of the men says. "Don't give us any problems, and you won't get hurt."

"Don't worry," Helman mutters, "they don't pay me enough to get hurt."

The thieves wrap strip after strip of duct tape around the eyes and mouths of the guards, swaddling their heads until they look like mummies. Then they steer the men down a set of stairs and into the basement. Using a second set of handcuffs, they secure Helman to a workbench. Then they walk Abell down a long, dark hallway and bind him to a steam pipe. Before they leave, one of the thieves takes their wallets. "We know where you live," he says. "Do as I say and no harm will come to you. Don't tell them anything and in about a year you will get a reward."

The men move back up to the first floor. The museum is now as helpless as an upended turtle. There are no other defenses—no secret wires, no hidden video cameras, no other guards. There's no other way for the police to know that the museum has been taken over by thieves. For all intents and purposes, the intruders now own the Gardner museum—and they begin to act like it, padding up the marble steps of the grand staircase and striding into the Dutch Room.

It's 1:48 a.m. A streetlamp sprawls a rectangle of yellow light across the floor of the room, and in the artificial twilight, the thieves move toward the south wall. They hope to seize the large Rembrandts first, but as they step toward the artworks, a piercing alarm sounds, ringing loudly in the empty room. The intruders must have been surprised. Are the police outside? Did the guards escape? This wasn't supposed to happen. A thief sees the source of the noise—a motion detector that goes off when visitors get too close to the art. With a swift, powerful boot, he kicks the buzzer silent.

The intruders step in front of the silk-draped south wall, moving in front of their target, Rembrandt's *The Storm on the Sea of Galilee*. The

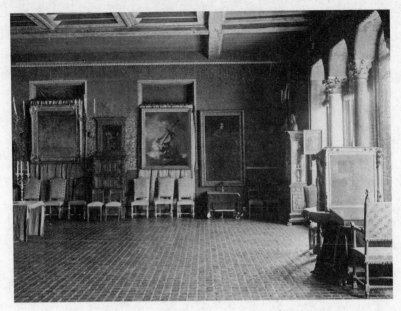

*The Dutch Room of the Isabella Stewart Gardner Museum
before the 1990 theft.*

painting presents a dramatic interpretation of a famous biblical tale—Jesus and his apostles fighting a savage thunderstorm, their small, unsteady boat cresting a massive breaker. An early Rembrandt, the work shows all of the artist's unbound audacity, and he slipped a small self-portrait into the canvas, painting himself as one of the disciples, looking straight out at the viewer. *Look at me*, he seems to say, *Can you see what I can do?* The painting has been hailed as one of the best examples of chiaroscuro—the dramatic contrasting of light and shadow—ever created. It is the Dutch master's only seascape.

But the thieves don't seem to know this—or they don't care. They haul the work down from the wall and smash the painting out of its frame. Then one of the thieves pulls out a blade and knifes the canvas. He cuts along the edge, slicing the painting from its stretcher, leaving behind stitches of canvas and flakes of paint. The intruders then pull down Rembrandt's *A Lady and Gentleman in Black*, painted in 1633 for one of the artist's Dutch patrons. With its exquisite lighting and balanced structure, the work would be any lesser artist's masterpiece. But again the thieves break the picture from its frame and slash the work out of its stretcher. Again, they litter the floor with bits of canvas, flecks of paint, and the dreams of countless art lovers.

The men then move toward the window, where a small table holds Vermeer's *The Concert*. The thieves must be grinning as they lift the painting from the stand. Rarely has taking something so precious been so easy, and in one quick moment, the men become owners of one of the most valuable artworks in the world. Created by Johannes Vermeer in the late 1650s, the painting depicts a man and two women playing music. Bathed in a soft, late-day light, the work exudes a subtle loneliness, each person working his own instrument, a quiet, immutable moment captured forever in a four-hundred-year-old canvas. The oil is one of only thirty-six surviving works by Vermeer, and some dealers estimate its price to be as high as $300 million. In other words, each square inch of the canvas might be worth more than a quarter of a million dollars.

With their biggest treasures in hand—and the police nowhere in sight—the thieves become bolder, more ravenous, as if the experience of stealing the works somehow intoxicates them. They swipe Govaert Flinck's *Landscape with an Obelisk*. They pocket a third Rembrandt, a postage stamp–sized self portrait. They remove another large Rembrandt from the wall and then abandon the work on the floor, leaning the painting against a cabinet like a visitor's forgotten umbrella. Before the men move out of the room, they also grab a bronze Chinese beaker from the Shang era. Called a ku, the foot-tall goblet dates back to 1200 BCE, and even this item, seemingly nothing more than a passing afterthought for the looters, is a prized artifact, worth thousands of dollars, one of the oldest pieces in the museum's collection.

At 1:51 a.m., one of the thieves dashes across the museum, passing the courtyard, moving along walls filled with masterpieces by Bellini, Raphael, and Rubens. A few minutes later his partner joins him, and they enter into the Short Gallery. Named for its small size, the room is little more than a narrow hallway, and as the intruders step inside, they're greeted by the silent image of the founder of the museum, Isabella Stewart Gardner. Painted by Anders Zorn, the small oil sketch hangs across from the entrance and shows Gardner joyfully pushing open a set of glass doors, a fireworks display rocketing off behind her in the evening sky. Bold and graceful, Gardner seems to almost float from the painting, her gaze focusing directly on the viewer, a vision of elegant, artful enthusiasm.

But the looters ignore the portrait and pull down five Degas sketches from a wooden door. Created in the late 1880s, the works are rough and unfinished, some of them nothing more than doodles of men dancing with their lovers. The intruders snap the pictures out of their frames, and as the wood and glass clatters to the ground, the image of Isabella Stewart Gardner gazes down at the intruders, looking wry and mocking, as if she wonders why the thieves seem so painfully amateurish. Why do they treat her works so poorly? Why haven't they stolen the more impressive drawings like the Michelangelo that hangs nearby? Or the Titian upstairs? Why are they robbing her museum at all?

The questions remain unanswered, as the robbery devolves into a felonious orgy, as if the men have grown totteringly drunk from all the rare treasures that have become theirs for the taking. In the corner of the Short Gallery, one of the thieves clambers on top of a narrow French cabinet. Above him is a gilded battle flag from Napoleon's Imperial Guard. The silk banner is yarned together with gilt sequins and bosses, and the thief starts to unscrew the glass casing that protects the flag, undoing metal screw by metal screw. He gets a half-dozen out, but then he decides to simply rip the eagle finial from the top of the flagstaff and pocket that item instead.

Back on the ground level, the thieves nab their last spoil, Edouard Manet's *Chez Tortoni,* a powerful portrait of a gentlemen sitting in a French café. They also check again on the security guards who remain bound and blindfolded in the basement, trussed among the thick steam pipes and clanking sounds of the boiler. To calm himself, Abell hums Bob Dylan's mournful ballad, "I Shall Be Released." Helman listens to the loud thumping noises upstairs and wonders if the thieves will burn down the museum, if they will kill him. But when the thieves visit the guards, they seem almost solicitous. "Are you comfortable?" they ask. "Handcuffs too tight?" The frightened guards don't say much—their mouths are taped shut.

The thieves have one last piece of business to attend to. They move to the first floor and kick open the security director's office. Inside, they rip open the video recorders that filmed their entrance and seize the cassettes. They will leave behind no visual record of their faces. The intruders also grab the data print-outs from the motion detector equipment, which recorded their movements through the galleries. They appear not to realize, though, that the data is also stored on the hard drive of the device. And before they leave, the men place the empty frame of the Manet on the security director's chair, a sneering taunt to the museum, the police, and all those art world snobs.

At 2:41 a.m., the thieves step out of the museum's side door and hurry across the sidewalk with their loot. They almost certainly have a van or truck waiting for them in the street—and it takes two trips for the men to get everything out of the museum. The side door to the Gardner closes for the last time at 2:45. The thieves were inside for a total of eighty-one minutes and nabbed thirteen works of art, valued today at over $500 million. They've just pulled off the largest robbery in history. In the wet, empty streets, the thieves and their faceless associates start up their cars and speed down Palace Road, and as their taillights disappear into the night, so do the Gardner masterpieces.

2. CHEZ TORTONI

The Art Detective

TANDING IN THE MIDDLE of Manhattan's Grand Central Terminal, Harold Smith checked again to make sure his nose wasn't missing. He hated when things went missing.

It was January 2005. Smith was seventy-eight years old. Over the past five decades, cancer had gnawed away his nose, his right eye, parts of his skull, much of his stomach, and almost all of his right lung. To cover up the ravenous damage to his body, Smith wore a derby hat, eye patch, and prosthetic nose. The fake nose had fallen off before—the glue weakens over the course of a day—and Smith often rubbed the plastic flange along the side of his face to make sure that the prosthetic was still attached to his cheeks.

As I pushed through the throng of commuters, I recognized his derby over the crowd. "Harold Smith?" I asked. It was our first meeting, and while I had seen pictures, it hadn't prepared me for the moment when he turned around. His prosthetic nose was large and rubbery, like a clown's; thin scars crisscrossed his face, twisting his left eye and snarling his upper lip. Dotting his face, neck, and hands were thick, leaking wounds covered by pieces of gauze. It seemed like his derby hat was the only thing keeping his head together—later that day a homeless man would bang on his car window and ask him if he was the undead monster Freddy Krueger from the *A Nightmare on Elm Street* films.

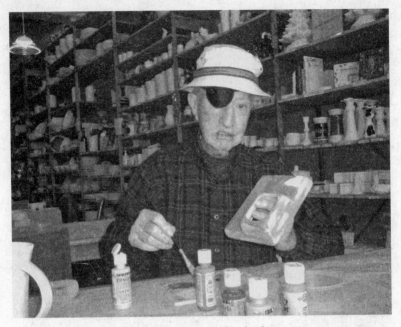

Harold Smith shortly before his death in 2005.

Smith smiled as broadly as his plasticine mouth would allow and shook my hand. Though he was nattily dressed—charcoal suit, blue shirt, silk tie—I found myself staring at his face, disgusted, entranced.

"Did you fly in from Washington?" he deadpanned. "Your arms must be tired."

I laughed. I learned later that this was classic Smith. He often eased social tensions with goofy riddles, little brainteasers, and some very bad knock-knock jokes. At that moment, though, I didn't have much time to think about his disfigured face or sugary humor. Smith hustled me into his waiting Volvo, explaining that we were late for our first appointment, a meeting with a well-known art dealer. He eased into the passenger seat; I sat in the back. Smith's son, a large, quiet man, drove the car. We dashed up Park Avenue, and at the corner of Fifty-seventh and Park, we stopped at a red light. Smith gestured toward a large jewelry store that was one block over on Madison.

"That place, right there," he said, pointing. "The thieves drove a pickup right through the window." The truck ripped a wide gash in the facade of the store, Smith explained, and two men dashed inside and stole hundreds of pieces of jewelry, diamond earrings, silver brooches, expensive rings. The loot was worth well over a half million dollars. "It was a Yugoslavian gang that did it," he said. "They cleaned out the whole place."

The light flashed green, and we continued north. At the corner of Seventy-ninth Street, Smith motioned again down toward Madison.

"The Soufer Gallery is over there. A few years ago, a man walked up to the entrance and snatched a Maurice Utrillo right out of the window. His car was idling outside, and he just drove right off." Smith's tone was quiet and slightly amused, a teenager discussing the hijinks of the class clown. He explained that the gallery's security camera had recorded the thief's license plate—and the man had been careless enough to drive his own car. "We found him in Brooklyn, a Hungarian guy, and he had another million dollars worth of stolen paintings in his house."

While it was hard to tell immediately—Smith said it all with such an easy nonchalance—he knew about these thefts because he'd solved them and hundreds of other cases of stolen art and jewelry. Smith was an independent fine arts claims adjuster, the long-winded name for an art sleuth who works for insurance companies, and he was among the best in the world. Over his five-decade career, he had recovered lost Renoirs, exposed forged Da Vincis, and tracked down stolen Matisses. He had rescued a missing Stradivarius violin in Japan, hunted down the famous Janiece Christner collection of Faberge eggs, and when Dade County police set up a sting to recover some stolen Monets a few months before we met, it was Smith who pushed—and paid—for the undercover cop to rent a Rolls-Royce for a meeting with the thieves in Miami. It was the detail that made the case. The art was recovered that afternoon.

But there was one case that haunted Smith, one case that he had yet to crack—the Isabella Stewart Gardner theft. Smith had been searching for the missing masterpieces for years. He hopscotched the globe to meet with sources. He spent hundreds of thousands of his own money on leads. He started his own toll-free tips line and established a Gardner theft website and swore to everyone that he met that he wouldn't stop working the case until the art hung again on the walls of the museum. And as the car motored up Park Avenue, I asked Smith why the lost paintings were so important to him. He looked at the long line of traffic in front of us for a moment and then threw his arm over the seat and stared at me. It gave me a jolt—his blue eye afire, the eye patch hanging loosely on his face, a modern-day Captain Ahab. "There are hundreds of thousands of people who would be deprived of seeing that art. Losing that art is like losing our history, our culture," he said. "I want it back."

I CONTACTED SMITH after reading a short magazine article about how he had recovered a Dali painting that had been missing since 1974. The article praised Smith as the Colombo of the international art scene, and I wanted to learn more and perhaps write a feature story about him. But what I didn't know—what I couldn't have known—was that Smith would be dead within weeks of our meeting and that I would soon pick up where he left off. My search for the Gardner art would take me to four countries, a dozen states, and more cities and towns than I care to count. I would develop a deep and consuming zeal for the case. I would chase countless leads, stake out suspected thieves, and fly thousands of miles to interview underworld figures who swore that they could return the lost paintings. My life would be threatened more than once. And while I would unravel some of the biggest puzzles of the heist, I would eventually discover that the Gardner case wasn't a mystery like the ones in movie theaters and Saturday afternoon TV specials, a cozy whodunit that wrapped up neatly at the end like an algebra problem. It was more like a mystery with a capital M, the sort of enigma that you find in church pews or philosophy lectures or on the canvas of an Old Master painting, something clear and compelling but also abstruse and obscure, something essentially unknowable.

But on that crisp winter morning I knew little about the Gardner museum or the lost art. I was simply following Smith as he did his daily detective work, interviewing art collectors, lunching with insurance brokers, calling on museum officials. Early in the afternoon, Smith dropped in on an art restorer on the Upper West Side to discuss a canvas that had been sent in for some minor repairs. The conservator was highly secretive, and I had to sign a nondisclosure agreement that prevented me from discussing what I saw there. I couldn't describe the artworks that littered the studio or detail how teams of conservators restored the canvases. There was no way to mention that stacks of paintings lined the storage room, hundreds of canvases leaning frame to frame like books crammed into a shelf, not that they necessarily were. The problem, Smith explained as we got back in the car, is that even the slightest whisper of damage can reduce the price of an artwork by millions. A painting by a modern artist that suffers as much as a pinprick can become completely worthless. "Art is about image, it has a certain mystique. It's not like owning a Cadillac," Smith told me. "It's a status symbol of the highest order."

Smith introduced me to art dealer Frederick Berry Hill. A portly man with an Otto Von Bismarck mustache, he greeted us in the marbled foyer of his Upper East Side gallery. He wore a silk ascot and a blue blazer with brass buttons the size of nickels. "Ah, Mr. Smith," he said, with a heavy shaking of the investigator's hands. After glancing at the other visitors, a group of bejeweled women—potential buyers, in other words—he escorted us into his private showing area. The room looked like the library of a robber baron, with club chairs, thick velvet curtains, and Oriental rugs plush enough to sleep on.

Then, looking around to make sure that no one overheard us, Hill quietly told Smith that he had recently discovered that a security guard had swiped a small painting from his warehouse. "It must have happened a few years ago, but I just figured it out recently as I was going through my inventory," Hill said sotto voce. "I was looking around one day and said, 'oh my God,' that painting is gone. It was a small piece, somewhere in the back of our warehouse, and now, I don't know."

Smith asked a few questions. Where was the guard today? Did he want to file a insurance claim? Did he contact police? But Hill didn't want to disclose any specifics, nor did he want to mention the name of the painting or the whereabouts of the guard or even how the heist might have occurred. He was worried that the news might mar his reputation, that he might be seen as anything but a careful custodian of cultural treasures. "We're the premier dealers of nineteenth-century American art in this country," he said.

But it turned out that Hill had much bigger problems. Soon after our meeting, Christie's auction house accused him of shilling, bidding on his own works at an auction in order to boost the sale price. While the exact details are murky, it appears that Hill told Christie's that he was selling forty-three paintings that belonged to a divorcing couple. The disclosure allowed the gallery to bid on the works since he might be buying the pieces back for either the husband or wife. But, according to Christie's, there was no divorcing couple—Hill had put offers on twenty-one of his own paintings in order to drive up the prices—and the auction house refused to give any of the paintings back to Hill. Christie's also demanded that Hill immediately pay back millions in debts, and while no charges were filed in the case, Hill's gallery eventually declared bankruptcy and had to sell off much of its stock of nineteenth-century American masterpieces.

It seemed as if Smith might have known what would happen to Hill. As we left his gallery that day, Smith explained that when it came to fine art, the boundaries between right and wrong, rich and poor, beautiful and ugly often become thin and hazy. Some of the art world's most famous personalities have been some of its least savory characters. Vincent Van Gogh sold only one work during his lifetime; now his paintings regularly go for a million dollars or more. While art dealer Joseph Duveen helped create the National Gallery of Art in Washington, he instructed his employees to scrape the ancient patina off the Elgin Marbles in order to boost the selling price of the precious sculptures. Rembrandt ran art scams, stole from his son's inheritance, and once had a mistress imprisoned in a mental institution rather than pay her alimony. For Smith, this aspect of the art world was part of its fascination. "It's what I love about the business. There is no rule book, nothing that tells you what to do," he told me. "Everyday is a surprise."

Riding the train home that night, I felt a little like Alice coming out of the rabbit hole. I flipped through my notes, my mind dazed and jumbled. So much seemed to be a mirage of its self; nothing was quite what it appeared. I recalled a moment early that afternoon. Smith and I were striding through the Jewish Museum when we stopped in front of a dark canvas titled *Kiev 1919*. Created by Ukrainian modernist Abraham Manievich, the painting shows the town exploding into a pogrom, a tall, angular pile of collapsing homes and buildings, painted in sharp reds and angry browns. While piercing flames lick the sky of the canvas, a lone boxy goat stands in the middle of the empty streets, staring out with haunting eyes. The caption noted that Manievich's own son died in the town's ethnic cleansing. For a moment, Smith and I stared at the painting, not saying a word. Then our eyes met. We both nodded.

The moment put the day in perspective—because art is powerful. That is its definition, an expression of creativity that moves people, that pushes them beyond themselves. The effects can be strong and savage. The ancient Israelites found a sculpture of a golden calf so impressive that they worshipped it like a god. Louis XVI lost his throne largely because of his court's uncontrolled spending on paintings and sculptures. Stephen Breitwieser's binge started in March 1995 when he was alone in a small Swiss museum and spied an eighteenth-century portrait. "I was fascinated by her beauty, by the qualities of the woman in the portrait and by her eyes," he said, and within a moment, he pried the work from the wall and strolled out of the museum. Over the following six years, Breitwieser stole hundreds of artworks, eventually collecting a hoard of paintings and sculptures worth an estimated $1 billion. He never sold a single piece. "Whether it was worth a thousand euros or millions, it was the beauty of the work of art that interested me."

Art's inspiration can be raw and painful. It can be a sort of sickness. The Louisiana Museum of Modern Art once had to remove a sculpture by Ed Kienholz because visitors would vomit when they saw the work. Philosopher Richard Wollheim made three trips to Germany to view the Isenheim Altarpiece, Matthias Grünewald's sixteenth-century masterwork, but each time he looked at the canvas, he found it unbearable and had to turn away. There is a book dedicated to people who cry in front of paintings, and a disease called Stendhal's Syndrome, where extensive exposure to Old Master paintings can cause dizziness, confusion, and hallucinations. Graziella Magherini, the head of psychiatry at Santa Maria Nuova Hospital in Florence, Italy, identified the syndrome in 1989 and has devoted much of her life to curing it. In addition to intensive therapy, she prescribes tranquilizers, bed rest—and time away from art.

HAROLD SMITH NEVER PLANNED on becoming an art detective. Born in the South Bronx in 1926, he attended Catholic schools, rooted for the Yankees, and aside from drawing doodles in the margins of his textbooks, he had little interest in paintings or sculpture. After high school, he enrolled in the Merchant Marine Academy, served a short stint in the South Pacific, and then signed up as a claims adjuster. Smith took the job because a friend told him that the money was good and that he could take Friday afternoons off to go to the Jersey shore with his family. "I just knew that I couldn't have a job where I would be chained to a desk," he told me.

Over the years, Smith began specializing in fine art losses, usually on assignment for insurance giant Lloyd's of London. It wasn't the beautiful paintings or glittering diamonds that attracted him as much as the complex nature of the cases. In a typical property claim, an insurance adjuster has a fairly straightforward job. If nothing has been faked or forged, the adjuster simply needs to figure out the value of the loss and then pay the client. If, for example, a 1982 red Corvette is stolen, the adjuster has to calculate the current value of a 1982 red Corvette and then write a check. The process is pretty much the same for anything from a $20 radio to a $200 million yacht. But art is different. If a painting or sculpture goes missing, there is no replacement, and that's what fascinated Smith. If a thief stole a work of art, Smith needed to find the original. If a child kicked a hole in a painting, he needed to enter into a delicate negotiation over its lost value. And art lovers can become desperate. Because collectors purchase works for their emotional power, for the way it touches their very being, they're often devastated when a work is damaged or stolen. Even a few tiny nicks can set off a collector.

Once, a few years ago, Smith consoled an heiress because a few grains of sand fell from her Anselm Kiefer multimedia installation during shipping. "She cried so much that I had Anselm himself come to her house and tell her that it was OK," Smith chuckled.

Smith did not have an art historian's expertise. While he could tell a Monet from a Manet, a Renoir from a Rembrandt, he couldn't do his work without help from his extensive Rolodex of art historians, restorers, and curators. He was a missing artifacts broker—he understood the art world and how people operated within it. Lose an Art Nouveau necklace? Smith knew a downtown dealer who had a stockpile but, be careful, he loves to bargain. Did a fire damage your Morris Louis canvas? Conservator Sandra Amann has restored dozens—and she is remarkably easy to work with. When a member of the Rockefeller family lost her string of pearls, Smith knew the jeweler who could build her a new necklace that would match the color of her teeth just like the old one did.

With his bad jokes and easy style, Smith developed friendships with some of the most famous artists of the last century—Mark Rothko, Dale Chihuly—and he would call on them to help repair damaged works or get him out of a knotty insurance problem. Smith once visited Salvador Dali at his mansion outside of Barcelona to discuss a painting that had been stolen from the artist's New York gallery. At the end of the meeting, Dali's wife, Gala, asked Smith if he wanted to dance, and after she accidentally kicked him in the shins, she pressed a lollipop and a glass of champagne into his hands. "The Dalis offered for me to stay for the night," Smith told me, shaking his head as if to say, those were some weird people. "But I drove back the most dangerous mountain road that you can imagine to get back to my hotel in Barcelona."

If Smith had a deep skill, it was dedication, and he proudly told people that he wanted to die while working on a case on behalf of Lloyd's. If he had an area of expertise, it was human nature. He understood what made people paint, what made them steal, and what made people steal from the people who painted. Both talents would be tested frequently. In 1983 Lloyd's tapped Smith to investigate the theft of sixty-three gold artifacts from the Houston Museum of Fine Arts.

Someone had nabbed the works from a storage cabinet and made off with more than $3 million worth of African ceremonial items. Smith arrived at the museum the day after the theft and soon suspected an inside job, perhaps a guard or a curator. The locked storage cabinet had not been forced open, and the museum was closed at the time of the heist.

Smith's biggest concern as an adjuster was not the whodunit. In art insurance, the business is focused on servicing clients—and recovering the art—not capturing crooks, and so Smith first went to the media, lobbying the *Houston Chronicle* to run an article advertising a $25,000 reward for the sculptures. Smith also thought that the thief might melt the gold artifacts to sell as bullion, and he pushed the local papers to run stories about how the artifacts were more valuable if they were left intact. "Since the [melted] gold value is $5,000 and we're offering $25,000, [you may be enticing] someone who has been asked to melt the gold to return it," Smith told a reporter. At the same time, Smith turned up the heat on the museum staff, telling the guards that they would all be required to take a polygraph test. The day before the exam, one of the guards came forward, saying that he had discovered the artifacts lying in a hallway and had taken them home to protect them. Police raided his house that night and found the set of artworks tucked behind a bathroom mirror, and within two weeks Smith was able to return the artifacts, unharmed, to their owner.

Smith was not typically successful. Despite a decade-long investigation, he never figured out what happened to the Christner collection of Faberge eggs swiped from a Dallas mansion in 1978. Nor was he ever able to catch art broker Michel Cohen. Investigators believe Cohen swindled more than a dozen art dealers—including Sotheby's—out of more than $50 million by repeatedly selling a set of paintings by Picasso and Marc Chagall, and while Smith worked closely with the FBI and Interpol, he never managed to put the art broker behind bars for good. At the end of the day, Smith only had an art theft recovery rate of 15 percent, and while it sounds low, the number was impressive for the field, where the average is about 5 percent. Smith found it difficult to make recoveries for countless reasons. Thieves will steal an object in this country and then sell it in China or Russia, where loose property laws makes it hard to track the item down, or crooks will warehouse a stolen painting, waiting a decade or more before selling it to a fence. Sometimes a thief will develop a rapt passion for an artwork and keep the canvas secreted under his bed, swooning over the painting late at night, after the world has gone to bed. Or, if the criminals are professionals, they might tweak the signature—make a Franz Hals into a School of Hals—and then ease the canvas back into the legitimate market. "What happens to fine art, I don't always know," Smith told me. "It could be anywhere."

Whatever case, the large number of thefts—and the increasing value of fine art—has made stolen art a booming criminal industry. Smith estimated the current value of the stolen art trade to be between $4 and $6 billion, making it one of the largest black markets in the world. Most of the heists don't make headlines. An intruder will swipe a scroll of Tang Dynasty calligraphy from a Florida antiques barn, or some drunken teenagers might carry a post-Expressionist painting out of an empty country house. The looted items are worth a few thousand dollars, and the hometown newspaper might not even find it worthy of an inch of newsprint. But once every few months, a group of criminals will stage a spectacular score, swiping a Cranach or a Van Eyck or some other work of inestimable historical value, and the Art Loss Register's database of stolen art has swelled over the years to include 609 Picassos, 181 Rembrandts, 173 Warhols, and Caravaggio's priceless masterpiece *Nativity with San Lorenzo and San Francesco*. In fact, if a museum were filled with all of the world's stolen artworks, it would be the most impressive collection ever created. It would have far more Baroque sculptures, much better Surrealist paintings, and the best Greek antiquities of any known institution. A gallery of stolen art would make the Louvre seem like a small-town art gallery in comparison. Experts call it the Lost Museum.

SMITH WAS NOT a tough guy. He didn't carry a gun or threaten violence. No one could remember a time when he raised his voice at a suspect. His disposition was fundamentally trusting. He was the type of person who would pick up hitchhikers on rural roads and then drive an extra ten miles to make sure that they arrived safely at their destination. But in his investigative work, Smith had some advantages over law enforcement. His firm, Smith International Adjusters Inc., was never larger than a dozen people and could move quickly, scoring interviews and tracking down leads faster than most police departments. Smith could also tap criminals that might not want to talk with law enforcement because they would be afraid of being branded as snitches, and Smith's underworld network was so developed that he would sometimes know about heists before even the owners. When Smith heard from an informant that five paintings, including a Van Gogh, had been swiped from the basement of the prestigious Hammer Galleries in New York, he called the head of the FBI art theft team Tom McShane. "That's news to me," McShane replied. McShane then called the galleries, and they didn't know about the theft either. It turned out that an employee had walked out of the service entrance with the paintings a few weeks earlier, and no one had noticed.

But perhaps the best weapon in Smith's arsenal was money, and Lloyd's of London gave Smith carte blanche to post a reward of 10 percent of the insured value of any stolen item. This was not cash that was paid to the thieves. Smith believed that encouraged crime, and he steadfastly opposed anyone involved in an art heist landing any insurance bounty. "If it became known to the common thief that all you had to do was steal a painting and call the insurance company, you wouldn't have a painting left on any wall in the United States, or the world, for that matter," Smith explained. Rather, the reward money would go to a friend, a lover, anyone who could offer a tip that would break the case and bring back the art. "There's very little that happens in this world that some other party doesn't know about," he told me, "and everyone likes money."

It was a lot of money—and seven years of tireless work—that helped Smith crack the largest gold heist in history. The caper began early on a February evening in 1987. It was just before closing time when two men burst through the front door of a Miami jewelry factory called the Golden Door. After hog-tying the owner and his two employees, the gunmen opened the safes and robbed the factory of its entire inventory of gold. The haul was nothing short of spectacular and included hundreds of gold bars along with a king-sized heaping of rings, pendants, bracelets, necklaces, and brooches. Valued at an estimated $13 million, the theft was immediately hailed as the largest gold heist in the country's history.

Smith flew to Miami the next day, and he knew almost immediately that owner Sandy Credin staged the heist. It was obvious, really. There were just too many coincidences. The security alarm had been turned off; the front door of the factory was left unlocked; the guard at the entrance of the industrial park had gone home early; and not one of the employees heard the gunmen removing the nine hundred pounds of gold—about the weight of a cow—from the safes. But Smith needed hard evidence, and so he posted a $100,000 reward for any information leading to the arrest of the thieves. Smith received hundreds of tips; he spent weeks sorting through the myriad of leads. He heard from a man who said that Cuban leader Fidel Castro had been behind the theft. Another caller was imprisoned in Leavenworth and said that he was friends with Credin, and, by the way, could Smith get a doctor to remove the Q-tip stuck in his ear canal?

Then, late one afternoon, about six weeks after the theft, Smith got a phone call.

"I know how that scam went down in Miami and I can save your insurance company all that money," the man told him.

"That's great," Smith said. "How do you know?"

"Never mind how," he said. "I bet you the safes were left unlocked, they weren't opened all the way. I'll bet you that manager never worked after five o'clock in a whole year."

Smith interrupted. "How can we get together?"

The man's name was Eddie Hollock, and he was an enforcer for the Canadian mob. Smith met him in a hotel in downtown Montreal, and in exchange for $100,000, Hollock told Smith what happened: Credin had sold the factory's gold to pay off almost a million dollars in gambling debts, and in order to cover up the loss, he hired Hollock to set up a heist of the factory. But on the night that Hollock was supposed to rob the Golden Door, a security guard followed him into the factory parking lot, and he quit the job. A few weeks later, Credin paid two of Hollock's friends to do the theft.

While the information made the case, Hollock refused to testify. The enforcer believed that the mob would kill him for being a snitch, and Smith spent six months cajoling Hollock into submitting a sworn affidavit. Smith also gave Hollock another $500,000, paid for plastic surgery and bodyguards, until finally the mobster agreed to testify. But by then, Credin had left the country, and it took Smith another five years of grueling detective work to track him down. Credin went to New York, then Panama, then Israel, before he was finally nabbed outside of a restaurant in Wiesbaden, Germany. Before the case went to trial, Credin pled guilty. He told the judge that he had sold all of the stolen gold—he didn't keep a single ring or bracelet. He was given five years for defrauding Lloyd's of London.

Smith was standing in his office in midtown Manhattan, right off of Times Square, when a co-worker told him the news of Credin's arrest. Smith hugged him, saying, "This is the greatest news I've heard in many, many years." Then, after working the case for seven years, talking to hundreds of sources, visiting dozens of cities, traveling to three different countries, Smith called an underwriter at Lloyd's of London. He wanted to get started on his next case.

IN 2000 SMITH sold his company to his youngest son, Greg, and became an adjuster for his firm. The arrangement allowed Smith to focus on what he did best—working fine art and jewelry cases—and reduce his office hours. He was seventy-four years old and exhausted. For years he had been working twelve-hour days, six days a week, all while trying to stay involved in the lives of his eight children. Smith's home life was complicated by the fact that two of his children were disabled. Because of a drug given to his wife during her pregnancy, they were born mentally handicapped and needed help with everything from eating dinner to tying their shoes. Smith and his wife decided early on that their disabled children would not grow up in an institution, and the couple cared for them along with the rest of their baseball team–sized family.

The situation could sometimes be overwhelming. "It could be hard. I mean really hard," said Smith's youngest daughter, Tara. She recalled one evening when one of the disabled children threatened her father with a knife because she had become so frustrated with her limitations. For the most part, though, the Smith household was a happy, bustling place. "We had a lot of fun growing up. My parents had a lot of love to give," Tara said, "and I think we became really tight because we didn't have time to fight over who got a blue sweater and who got a red one. We had more important things to worry about."

One of those more important things to worry about was Smith's murderous case of skin cancer. He acquired the disease while serving in the Merchant Marines. A doctor discovered that he had ichyosis, a genetic disorder that caused dry, scaly skin, and tapped him for an experimental skin treatment in which Smith would lie under a high-intensity UV lamp for a few hours each morning. It turned out to be the equivalent of tanning under a nuclear sun, and within three years of the experiment, almost every inch of Smith's skin had become cancerous.

When Smith was in his twenties and thirties, doctors could keep the disease under control. Small tumors and lesions would sprout up on his arms and face, and dermatologists would remove them with a scalpel or a batch of acid. It was painful and time-consuming but not debilitating. As Smith grew older, the cancer grew more virulent. It chewed deep into his body, and by the time Smith was in his fifties, he would check into the hospital every few weeks. The surgeries would be long and agonizing, and it would sometimes take ten hours or more for doctors to remove all the malignant growths. The disease eventually spread to Smith's internal organs, and surgeons had to remove pieces of his stomach, bits of his skull, as well as parts of his neck.

It wasn't clear what was the worst—losing his right eye or losing his nose. The eye came first. Doctors removed it during a lengthy surgery, and Smith had to relearn how to drive a car and balance himself. Then, when Smith was seventy-four, his dermatologist told him that his nose had to go too. He would lose his ability to smell anything—not a cup of coffee, not his wife's perfume, not yesterday's trash. To cover the massive scar in the middle of his face, Duke University Medical School built an artificial nose for Smith that attached to his cheeks with a special glue. Smith took a gleeful pleasure in telling the story about the time that his nose fell off. It was a few weeks after his surgery, and he was lunching with some business partners from Lloyd's. He was eating some chicken soup when the steam loosened the special glue, and without his realizing it, the nose slipped off his cheeks and dropped onto the table with a soft plonk. "You should have seen them. Can you imagine their surprise?" Smith told me with a laugh, pausing for the punch line. "My nose was on the table and so were their jaws."

Smith didn't complain about the pains of his personal life. When he wrote a letter to his lawyer about a potential lawsuit against the Merchant Marines because of his skin cancer, he barely described the agony of all his surgeries. He detailed his medical history and noted his suffering in a single sentence. "Suffice it to say that this has been an unpleasant experience of blood, pain, [and] disfigurement," he wrote. Instead, he'd make light of the disease. "God is just taking me away

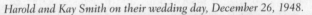

Harold and Kay Smith on their wedding day, December 26, 1948.

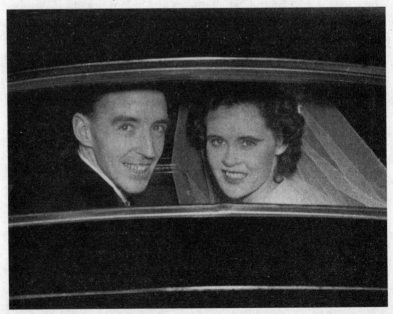

piece by piece," he'd joke. Or he'd recount the time that he was in an airport and a young boy mistook him for a pirate. "Now that was funny! The little kid pointing at me and telling his mommy that I was Captain Cook."

Smith wasn't a stoic. He would express his emotions and fears, usually by saying in his nasally voice, "Now that doesn't make you feel like a million dollars." But he viewed his suffering as a redemptive act. A deeply spiritual Catholic, Smith understood pain as a fundamental part of being human. He believed that his sacrifice allowed him to communicate with God, to reconcile his humanity with heaven, and in his last years, when it took more than thirty minutes for him to put on all his bandages each morning, he pushed on with his life. He worked for his son's insurance firm, went golfing with his wife, and babysat his grandchildren. He visited the local homeless shelter, taught Sunday school, and won an award from the North Carolina Knights of Columbus for his work helping impoverished families in the area. In his office, over his desk, in a small wooden frame, Smith kept a quote from Winston Churchill, and he would often repeat the sentence to friends and family. "We make a living by what we get, but we make a life by what we give."

WHEN NEWS OF THE GARDNER THEFT broke on the morning of March 18, 1990, Smith knew that he would not be asked to work the robbery. The museum did not have any indemnity on the paintings, so it would not be hiring an insurance investigator. Still, Smith followed the case. He called friends in the FBI to learn about leads; he read newspaper stories about the latest suspects. A few weeks after the heist, he sent a letter to the director to express his sympathies. "I would keep a positive attitude, since some very strange things have happened in the history of art theft," he wrote. "A million dollar incentive, plus little bit of luck and human frailties, might combine to bring these valued paintings back."

In the years after the caper, Smith watched as the FBI ran down thousands of tips, clues, and angles, investigating South American drug lords, ex-museum guards, and Japanese underworld figures. The evidence all led to the same place—a dead end—and that was why Smith first decided to get involved. He couldn't bear the idea that the paintings were forever missing. There was a long list of other, more personal reasons. Smith felt a powerful kinship with the museum's founder, Isabella Stewart Gardner, a woman who had also suffered severe personal hardships and shared his belief in the redemptive power of art. Smith also understood how much a heist might be a smear on a city, perhaps nowhere more than Boston, a place where the tension between high and low, upstairs and downstairs, might be one of its most enduring traits. And if Smith recovered the lost masterpieces, it would be the perfect capstone to an impressive career as the world's foremost art detective. The heist was the largest burglary in American history. No other robbery—art or otherwise—has ever been as costly.

In spite of all of Smith's troubles—or perhaps because of them—he never stopped working the case. Even as a septuagenarian, his body covered with cancers, he toiled on leads for nine or ten hours a day. It would take dozens of trips, hundreds of interviews, years of research, everything that I lay out in this book, for me to fully grasp Smith's dedication. But by that time he was dead. On February 19, 2005, twelve days after his seventy-ninth birthday, he passed away in a hospital in Raleigh, North Carolina. He worked the Gardner case up until his last week, emailing with an informant a few days before he went into the hospital. He never stopped telling silly riddles and corny stumpers, either, and in his hospice room, he left a plastic cockroach on his bedside table just to give the nurses a laugh. Smith died with more than a dozen family members in his room, the theme from *Love Story* playing on the stereo, and when he passed, he left the Gardner case behind, the paintings as lost and gone as his dead body.

3. A LADY AND GENTLEMAN IN BLACK

It Was a Passion

IT'S A GREAT PAINTING," a voice rumbled over my shoulder.

It was a few months after Harold Smith's death, and I was standing in the offices of Greg Smith, staring at a reproduction of Vermeer's *The Concert*. The framed poster hung in the center of the lobby, right over the secretary's desk, and I had become so enthralled by its details that I didn't hear Greg come up behind me. I turned around and was confronted by a bear of a man with a beer-keg chest and large, brawny arms. Dressed in a conservative suit, dark tie, and white Oxford shirt, he exuded the calm authority of a Secret Service bodyguard. "It was my Dad's copy," Greg said, gesturing toward the poster. "We keep it here, because it keeps us honest, tells us we're in the business of protecting fine art and jewelry."

I had come to New York to talk to Greg about his father, art theft, and the Gardner case. Greg joined the family business shortly after graduating from college, and within a few years, he cracked his first big case, helping his father solve a $2 million heist from the Walters Art Museum in Baltimore. The caper started curiously—a curator went away on a two-week vacation and when he returned, he noticed that an eighteenth-century, Chinese peach bloom vase had gone missing. After the museum staff began looking for the porcelain, they discovered that the vase had been pocketed along with at least eighty other objects, including antique pistols, bejeweled daggers, and ancient Chinese snuff bottles. The thief had stolen the works from the museum's showcases along with the exhibition labels, as if he wanted to remove every last trace of the works, and no one could say with any precision when the heist had occurred. Last week, last year, no one had any idea.

Greg and Harold Smith questioned the staff, and one of the guards told them that he recalled seeing the security director praying in front of a glass showcase late one evening. While the museum's registrar said that nothing was missing from that particular vitrine, Greg noticed indentations on the silky material at the bottom of the case as if artifacts had recently been removed, and he asked the registrar to recheck their files. It turned out that an artwork had been pocketed from that particular showcase—and the clue broke open the case. The FBI searched the security director's home and found all of the missing artworks, carefully wrapped in paper and cloth, in his basement. The thief soon confessed, explaining that he would steal the objects from the showcases late at night and then rearrange the remaining items so that no one would notice anything amiss. Later, museum staff would admit that visitors told them that the vitrines looked better with fewer artifacts—the showcases seemed less busy.

The Walters theft occurred in 1988, and since then Greg Smith has worked thousands of other art heists, scams, and losses. He's uncovered fake Caravaggios, hunted down a stash of stolen Milton Avery paintings, and recovered a Lichtenstein sculpture buried in the rubble of the World Trade Center. When casino magnate Steve Wynn accidentally put his elbow through Picasso's *Le Rêve*, Lloyd's of London sent Greg out to investigate. The painting is a world-renowned masterpiece, worth an estimated $139 million, and as part of the case, Greg evaluated the loss, compensated Wynn, and oversaw the $90,000 restoration project. And since Greg has taken over the family business, it has stayed very much a family business. At the time of my visit, the firm employed one of Harold Smith's daughters, a daughter-in-law, and a grandson.

Greg brought me into his office. It was a large, windowless room with almost every available horizontal space covered by files. The desk, the floor, the heating unit in the corner, all were buried in a snowfall of court proceedings, art auction records, and provenance certificates. The reason for the paperwork soon became clear—Greg had his hands full with the running of the company. His father had brought in much of the new business, and his death was a major blow to the firm. And when I asked about the Gardner heist, he shook his head. He was far too busy to put any time into the case. "It would be a great thing for us to return those works. At the very least, you'd see a smile up in heaven. But I have to feed my family." We talked for another hour, and before I left, I asked Greg if I could take a look at his father's Gardner files. "Go for it," he said. "Maybe you can do something with them."

IT TOOK ME some time to collect what was left of Harold Smith's Gardner files. After Smith died, his house in Sanford, North Carolina, was sold, and most of his files were thrown out. But some of Smith's most important papers were saved, including interview transcripts, police reports, and newspaper clippings, along with some leads that he never had a chance to pursue. I kept the files in my office, and I'd read through them periodically, always impressed by Smith's work. Long after the public had forgotten about the heist, Smith kept the stolen artworks in the headlines, landing stories about the caper in the *New York Times*, *Reader's Digest*, and various Boston television stations.

Smith also inspired documentary filmmaker Rebecca Dreyfus to make a film about his hunt. Dreyfus had long been passionate about the case. She had visited the Gardner as a teenager and been captivated by Vermeer's *The Concert*. "When I stood in front of that painting for the first time, it was very intense. A transcendent thing," she told me. "The theft left me speechless. I couldn't believe it. I didn't think that anyone would ever dare take that painting." And after Dreyfus contacted Smith for an expert interview, he began calling her almost every day. He believed that the publicity surrounding her movie could inspire the return of the paintings, and Dreyfus and her producer, Susannah Ludwig, worked with Smith for more than three years, filming him as he tracked down leads, spoke to sources, and interviewed suspects. The movie, titled *Stolen*, aired first on CourtTV, and then a slightly different version hit the independent film circuit, earning admiring reviews and a number of prestigious awards.

Smith saw his media outreach efforts as central to his Gardner investigation. He was sure that a third party knew the whereabouts of the lost paintings. Maybe it was a resentful employee or a spurned friend or perhaps someone had glimpsed a cobwebbed Old Master canvas in an attic. If Smith could make that person aware of the museum's $5 million reward, he was sure he would recover the missing art. He believed that the case was ready for a big break. When Smith started his investigation, it was some ten years after the theft, and he thought that the passage of time would make people more inclined to come forward, that the ties that bound people to the stolen art would have been loosened. "Wives become ex-wives. Girlfriends become ex-girlfriends. Maids become ex-maids," Smith told the *New York Times*. "Maybe the person who engineered this is facing mortality and wants to clean up his act."

Smith knew an informant would not come forward easily. A tipster might get spooked by the police or worry what would happen when his name became public, and so Smith presented himself as the art underworld's middleman. If someone had information about the stolen paintings, he would help them collect the bounty—and keep them clear of both the cops and the robbers. Smith promised total anonymity and advised anyone who wanted to keep their information secret to seal their letters with tape in order to keep police from recovering any DNA or send him emails from a public computer so that the IP address couldn't be traced.

Smith had served as a stolen art mediator in dozens of other cases. He once investigated a Los Angeles jewelry dealer who claimed that a man had knocked her unconscious, hog-tied her foot-to-head with wire, and then robbed her of more than $2 million worth of diamonds. A few days into the investigation, Smith interviewed the dealer's niece, Sarah Yu, and she told him that there was no thief. Her aunt had made up the story. But Yu wouldn't go to the cops. Smith futilely tried to convince her—he pushed her for weeks without success. Then he found out that Yu was a devout Christian, and so he brought her to her church and held a meeting with her pastor. The brash gambit worked—Yu gave a statement, the aunt was sent to jail, and Smith recovered many of the diamonds.

As part of his effort to publicize the Gardner theft, Smith created a toll-free number and a website, and he received hundreds of tips over the years. Most of them were duds. The callers would be senile or mentally unstable or just weird. One woman said that she had seen the ghost of Isabella Stewart Gardner and that the paintings were tucked into a hollow door in a house in Scotland. A cleaning lady claimed that she had caught a glimpse of the artworks in a closet, but she couldn't remember where. Another caller said that her previous employer had put the paintings in the trunk of a car that was buried under a mountain of dirt and only she knew where it was. Many of the callers wanted money. They needed cash in order to retrieve the artworks, or they wanted a couple of thousand dollars to pay off the current owner. Still others delivered ominous warnings. "There is no man alive that knows the whereabouts of the artworks. . . . A man who masterminded the theft . . . was led to an untimely death," read one note. "We pray for you."

No matter what the message, Smith would ask his secretary to transcribe it for his files. If the call seemed promising, he would phone the person and ask for more details. What was on the back of the paintings? Did you see any dealer's stickers? Unusual markings? Smith used the particulars as a litmus test to separate the worthwhile leads from the hoaxes. It wasn't that Smith didn't like a good prank, and as I rummaged through his art theft files, I'd often find goofy little puzzles. In one folder, a brain teaser accompanied an account of a jewelry store holdup. In another, a stumper lay next to a graceful description of a stolen artwork. Smith loved the experience of unraveling a riddle, and before business meetings, he'd often pull out a deck of cards and ask his co-workers to figure out his newest sleight of hand. (He typically used a variation of the glide, a technique that made it look like he was dealing the bottom card of the deck.) Or he would make a packet of sugar disappear in his hand, then press his friends about how exactly he did it. (He used a fake thumb.)

These weren't just games for Smith—this was how he approached the world. There were mysteries, there were clues, and if you put enough work into a problem, you could figure out the answer. He didn't use intuition or instinct. He would roll his eyes at any mention of sixth sense. He believed that almost any problem could be solved with a bit of intelligence, some hard work, and a lot of deductive reasoning. The Gardner case was no different. Smith pulled together as many leads as he could, studied them closely, and then tried to work out an answer, and when he wasn't successful, he tried harder. "The longer the case goes on, the more interested I become," Smith told me. "I wake up at two in the morning wondering what happened to those paintings."

IF ART IS DEFINED by its emotional power, by how it affects people, then perhaps the Gardner heist might be considered its own sort of masterpiece. The heist haunted Smith along with innumerable others. Since the night of the robbery, millions have visited the museum to view the empty frames, thousands have called in leads, hundreds of detectives have thrown themselves at the case. The caper stands among the nation's most compelling unsolved crimes, an epic whodunit on par with the disappearance of Amelia Earhart and the murder of Jimmy Hoffa. Countless newspaper articles, untold magazine stories, along with novels, screenplays, poems, movies, drawings, plays, and paintings have all been dedicated to its mystery. It's hard to explain the exact draw of the Gardner heist, to describe why it maintains such a firm hold on the American imagination, but at the root of it is the art.

Lost is Manet's masterpiece, *Chez Tortoni*. Perhaps the first modernist, Manet used turn-of-the-century Paris as his muse, and he painted hundreds of detailed street scenes. Women drinking coffee, friends listening to music, young couples flirting, and in *Chez Tortoni* he profiles a man sitting at a café table. At first glance, the work seems to be an uncomplicated portrait. But then one notices the man's hard stare, his half-finished beer, the painting's loose brush strokes; the artwork appears to be an examination of the fleeting nature of images, a snapshot of modern urban life.

Missing are three works by Rembrandt, one of the world's most powerful artists. Goethe described him as the Shakespeare of painting. Kenneth Clark dubbed him "one of the great prophets of civilization." Like Napoleon and Jesus, he belongs to that fraternity of famous persons where last names are unnecessary—and certainly Rembrandt would have wanted it that way. As a young man, he dreamed of becoming rich and renowned, and he used his first name exclusively as a way to build his reputation. His full name was Rembrandt Harmenszoon van Rijn, and he was born in July 1606 in the Dutch town of Leiden. His parents hoped that he would become a civil servant. But Rembrandt wanted to become an artist, and he painted constantly, he drew on everything, sometimes even sketching on the back of funeral notices. After he finished his schooling, success came quick, and within a few years Rembrandt was considered one of the most talented painters in Northern Europe, famous for his lush, graphic portraits of Holland's high society.

But Rembrandt's interests lay far beyond fawning profiles of Europe's moneyed classes. He wanted to display the grit and gravity of existence, to show the world without sugarcoating, without condescension or praise—life as it really was. And in his late twenties, he began painting intimate portraits of ugly prostitutes, crippled maids, and arthritic beggars. In his paintings, babies piss on floors, dogs shit on sidewalks, women have fat breasts, dimpled thighs, and sagging bellies. Even the Virgin Mary is drawn fully mortal, and when Rembrandt shows her pulling a suckling baby Jesus from her breast, her nipple glistens with thick drops of milk. Perhaps the most talented artist to ever probe the human spirit, Rembrandt showed uncanny psychological insight, as if he could limn the complete essence of his subjects. He honed this skill on himself, examining his own soul—or at least his own face—more than any other painter in history. At least ninety of his self-portraits exist today, and he may have made hundreds more. Most of the works are etchings, simple drawings of a feeling or an expression. In one, he draws himself as angry—his forehead is down, his lips are pursed, his eyes flash and burn. Later, he shows himself shouting, frowning, sneering, a clown, a king, a jester. The stamp-sized etching ripped from the walls of the Gardner was part of this series, and in the work Rembrandt shows his face deep in cogitation. His mane of hair bristles in all directions, his eyes are perfectly black. He can see out, but you can't see in. It is titled, simply, *Self-Portrait*.

As Rembrandt grew older, he moved farther away from late seventeenth-century artistic fashion. Instead of the smooth portraits the patrons loved, he began creating smaller, darker works, using heavy paints and earthy colors. The canvases didn't sell, clients stopped calling, and in 1656, at the age of fifty, he went bankrupt. But he never stopped striving to be the ultimate painter of the human condition, and when the city council commissioned Rembrandt to create a portrait of the Dutch war hero Claudius Civilis, he gave them a work of raw power in wild hues of eerie green and glowing yellows, the paint slathered in cake-like layers. In the past, artists had always showed Civilis in profile as a matter of respect—the war hero had only one good eye. Rembrandt showed the general boldly facing the viewer, the war hero's bad eye nothing more than a smudge. It was Rembrandt telling the guardians of taste one last time—you might not like it, but this is what the world is really

Rembrandt, Self-Portrait.

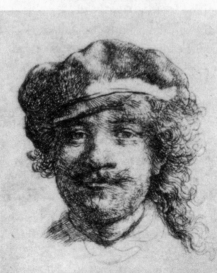

like. The council didn't enjoy the message. The painting came down, and Rembrandt died penniless, buried in an unmarked grave.

Gone from the Gardner is Vermeer's *The Concert*. The painting might be the most expensive, the most rare, the most moving artwork ever stolen. Critics call Vermeer the "Sphinx of Delft," his intrigue heightened by the fact that historians don't know much about him. He left no writings, no diaries or letters. The basic facts of his life have been gleaned only through legal documents. He was born in 1632 in the Dutch town of Delft; his father owned an inn and occasionally dealt in art. Little is known about his mother. During his teenage years, Vermeer worked as an apprentice to a more experienced painter, but scholars have never been able to figure out the identity of his mentor. Vermeer probably had a patron who supported his artistic work. No one knows for sure.

What's clear, though, is that Vermeer's life was troubled, filled with disappointments and debts. His wife gave birth to fifteen children, four of whom died young. He earned such little income that he and his family had to move in with his mother-in-law. In his early thirties, Vermeer was voted president of the local artists' guild, but he never found much fame outside of his hometown of Delft. Part of the problem was that Vermeer was painfully meticulous, a complete perfectionist. He would spend months working on a single canvas, and he is believed to have completed no more than sixty artworks in his lifetime. In contrast, contemporaries like Frans Hals would paint a new work almost every week. Vermeer and his family lived a fragile sort of financial existence until 1672, when France invaded Holland. The economy bottomed out, and he couldn't sell any of his paintings. He went deeper into debt. "He had lapsed into such decay and decadence . . . as if he had fallen into a frenzy," his wife told a bankruptcy court. "In a day or day and a half he had gone from being healthy to being dead." Vermeer was forty-three.

Because of the chaos that must have reigned over Vermeer's life, or despite it, almost all of his artworks present quiet, domestic scenes. A housewife reading a letter, a young maid sleeping in the kitchen, the moment infused with a deep sense of reflection. As a silvery light spears through an open window, a woman silently gazes across the room, her unstated thoughts hovering in the air like a curl of smoke. Art historians often refer to Vermeers as still lifes with people, and the paintings are all executed with mathematical precision, showing every glimmer of light, every loose hair, down to the tiny, round beads of water pearling on the outside of a wine glass.

Vermeer's works, though, are ultimately mysteries. For all the artistic detail, he presented elusive narratives, compelling yet unknowable dramas, domestic moments transformed into scenes that are at once real and unreal, ordinary and extraordinary, and he would often return to works and paint out symbols to make an image more ambiguous, to stymie any simple sort of interpretation. At the center of *The Concert* is a chair filled with a large, square-shouldered man playing the zither. There's a woman on either side of him—one sings, the other plays the harpsichord. The man appears to be a wealthy soldier or aristocrat—a sword hangs at his side, a finely woven vestment hangs over his shoulder. Money must have come easy for the women too. They're dressed in a shimmer of glossy blouses and fur-lined coats, the singer's pearl earring glitters like a sun-filled dewdrop. Although the man hulks in the middle of the canvas, drawing the viewer's eyes with his presence, the women throw not a glance in his direction. They seem to be completely absorbed in song. The singer's mouth is just about to open; her hand arches over her chest. The harpsichordist focuses on the keyboard, the high airy notes breezing along on the velveteen light.

But something darker lurks within the canvas. Long shadows spill across the room, a cello lies in the middle of the floor as if someone just left. What happened before they started playing music? What is the relationship between the man and these two women? While never revealing anything definitive, Vermeer offers some suggestive hints. Above the singer, he drew a reproduction of another work, Dirck Van Baburen's *Procuress*. Vermeer knew the painting well—his mother-in-law owned the artwork—and the oil depicts a bordello scene, with a raunchy drunk trying to hustle a young woman into bed. It's unclear why Vermeer included the painting-within-the-painting. Perhaps he wanted to emphasize the contrast between the low life and the high life, to show how art could blur the hazy line between the smart and seedy set. But maybe he doesn't. The women's faces remain intense and focused. There is a second painting on the wall, a lush landscape. *The Concert* remains a narrative unknown.

BUT THE LOST ART—even the missing Vermeer—doesn't fully explain the full power of the Gardner case, why so many visit the museum to see the empty frames, why dozens of authors, artists, and academics have thrown themselves at the caper's mystery. When I spoke to Gardner obsessives, they couldn't quite explain it either; they always talked about the theft as something intensely personal, often reaching for metaphors in the way that people do when they want to comprehend something that is incomprehensible. Some say the theft is like having something ripped from their soul. Others compare the burglary to the death of a family member. "Imagine you can never hear a Verdi *Requiem* or a Beethoven symphony again. Just erased. Imagine Shakespeare's *Hamlet*. Erased," the director of the museum told me. One afternoon a few weeks after the theft, a woman walked into the museum with a large bouquet of yellow tulips. She was smartly dressed in a dark pantsuit and spoke with a European accent. She pushed the flowers into the arms of an employee and said, "Yellow is for hope."

Even after almost twenty years, many can still recall the moment when they first learned about the robbery. Journalist Roger Atwood was standing in a post office in Lima, Peru. "It was a letter from my mother, and I thought my heart was going to break," he told me. "I got very angry about it, I mean like muttering to myself in anger as I walked out of the post office." Another woman got the call on the morning of the theft—and immediately began sobbing as she tried to recall the missing canvases. A few have been so devastated that they can no longer visit the Gardner. They view the robbery as an unholy tragedy, a monstrous corruption of beauty, and they refuse to even set foot in the building. "I had a woman come up to me a few nights ago and say that it was the first time she had made it back to the museum since the theft," one staff member told me. "What happened was still very much alive for her."

The effort to recover the works has completely consumed some investigators. There was Harold Smith, of course, along with dozens of reformed thieves, private detectives, amateur sleuths, and retired gumshoes. "At the start, I would walk home, grab a bite, and some sleep and then go right back," FBI agent Dan Falzon once told a reporter. "I literally worked day and night. It wasn't a task; it was a passion, and it still is." People have been hurt, murdered, and thrown in jail because of the missing masterpieces. Smuggler Joe Murray was killed in 1992, shortly after telling an ex-FBI agent that he had information on the lost paintings. That same year, mob associate Bobby Donati was found in the trunk of his Cadillac, stabbed twenty-eight times, his throat slit—it was widely rumored that he was going to talk to authorities about the theft. Even law enforcement hasn't been safe from the Gardner curse. FBI agent Neil Cronin worked the heist for more than ten years, believed that he had uncovered the identities of the thieves, and then, late one evening, a tractor trailer slammed into his Toyota Camry and killed him instantly. "You should have a sticker put on your book like they put on cigarettes. 'Warning. The Gardner case is highly addictive and could be dangerous to your health,'" one of Smith's informants once told me.

If such a label were produced, it should appear on much more than this book. After my meeting with Smith, I began to collect examples of creative works that featured the theft. I read the political potboiler that used the Gardner art as its MacGuffin, I watched the animated art house video whose final scene features the thieves throwing the lost canvases onto a pyre and setting them aflame. For the most part, the works meditate on the senselessness of the loss—and dream about the paintings soon being returned. Pulitzer Prize–winning author John Updike once wrote a poem that wonders how it would feel to be one of the stolen paintings, brooding over how bored the works must get, wrapped in brown paper, hidden in a wooden crate somewhere outside of Boston. For her photo-and-text series *Last Seen,* Sophie Calle interviewed the staff of the Gardner museum about their memories of the lost paintings and displayed their responses next to photographs of the empty frames. In the panel devoted to Rembrandt's *The Storm on the Sea of Galilee,* Calle presents a series of wistful memories:

It was Rembrandt's only seascape, a very luscious painting that always enlivened me. It just felt like your adrenaline picked up when you looked at the picture. The tumultuousness and the chaos were very contagious. I don't remember the painting as color. Action, not color.

When I was a youngster, one Christmas, a dear family friend gave me a five-pound box of candy in a tin box. And on the lid was *The Storm on the Sea of Galilee*. It was the first time I'd ever seen it. It was my prized possession. I loved it, absolutely loved it.

Calle's artwork—all of the heist-themed works, really—raise a simple question: If a sculpture doesn't stand in a courtyard, if a painting appears only as an image in an art history textbook, does it even matter? To Calle, to any serious art lover, the answer is no. Every work of art is singular, unique, and when a creation goes missing, there is nothing left behind but inadequate facsimiles—and fading memories. If a painting is stolen, if it's gone missing, it cannot be replaced. Lost art is lost forever.

WHEN I FIRST saw Rembrandt's *The Storm on the Sea of Galilee,* I believe that I was sitting in Sunday school. I was eleven or twelve years old. It was early afternoon. An autumn light sliced through the window and splashed on the floor in a large pool. At the front of the room, a pear-shaped nun paced back and forth, talking about God and evil and Jesus, and as I aimlessly leafed through my textbook, my eyes caught on a small dark-hued reproduction of *The Storm*. An excited breath, a pulsing chest, I splayed out the book and studied the painting, the wall of water ramming the boat, the ocher hues of the sky, foam jetting into the air like a massive geyser. I was familiar with the basics of the biblical narrative—the apostles waking Jesus from a deep sleep, asking him to save them from a terrible thunderstorm. "Peace, be still," Jesus says, calming the waters. Rembrandt chose the most dramatic, white-knuckle moment for the work, sailors lunging across the boat to secure the twisted rigging, men pulling on thick oars in a vain attempt to steady the boat. One man leans over the stern and vomits into the sea, his life passing him by in the hammering whitecaps. When I looked up again, it seemed as if days had passed.

One evening, decades later, I was sitting in my office. It was late, just before midnight, my wife and daughter were in bed. The house was hushed and still. Only the noise of the dishwasher purred through the night. In front of me were Smith's files, spread out over my desk like an unfolded road map. I stared at the pile of papers and recalled the first time that I saw *The Storm*, how the canvas smoldered in my chest, made me feel like I was standing on a pebbly shoreline watching a storm lob around a small fishing boat. And right there, sitting in my office, I decided to try and recover the Gardner masterpieces. While the notion had been lingering in my mind for weeks, the conclusion came suddenly—I would pick up where Smith left off. I would meet with his sources; I would run down unfinished leads; I would post an updated website and investigate all and any new tips.

My chances for success were undoubtedly slim. Smith hadn't recovered the works, and what did I know about the art underworld? But I knew that Smith's story—and the tale behind the lost masterpieces—needed to be told. I understood even then that the Gardner caper was like the seed of a fruit. It looked small and dirty, but then you planted it and it grew into something big and poignant, with deep roots and intricate blossoms, something beautiful and a little dangerous. And like Smith, I didn't want to sit around while *The Storm* languished in the bottom of an old packing case. I didn't want to do nothing as the Vermeer was tossed into the cold depths of Boston's Charles River. I felt the tug of the missing paintings; I had been hooked by the lure of the lost Gardner art.

4. THE CONCERT

The Picture Habit

THE ART ITCH can start early, and even as a young woman, Isabella Stewart Gardner dreamed of becoming a collector. After visiting the masterpieces that hung in the grand estates and soaring cathedrals of Europe, the self-assured teenager wrote to a friend stating that if she ever had the money, she would "have a house . . . like the one in Milan filled with beautiful pictures and objects of art, for people to come and enjoy." It took more than fifty years, but her teenage dream came true. In the Back Bay neighborhood of Boston, she built a four-story palazzo and filled it with more than three hundred paintings, nearly four hundred sculptures, along with thousands of prints, drawings, manuscripts, and pieces of antiquity. "It's the only institution designed and named after a woman," Gardner biographer Douglass Shand-Tucci told me. "It's a palace dedicated to the idea of beauty and really the country's first great art collection."

Born in New York City in April 1840, Isabella Stewart was the daughter of a wealthy businessman who made his fortune in steel. Educated at elite private schools in New York, she showed her gritty spirit—and passion for the exotic—at an early age. She loved to play pranks and walk around barefoot and when the traveling circus came to town one summer, she begged her parents to take her. They refused, and so she set out alone. When her grandmother noticed her absence, she sent

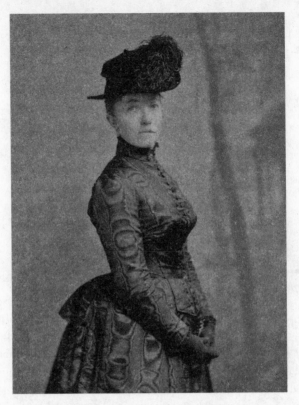

Isabella Stewart Gardner in 1888.

the family butler to chase Isabella down. The child saw him and began running as fast as her little legs would allow. He caught her by the ankles just as she was crawling under the circus tent and walked her home as she howled with rage.

In her teens, Isabella met John Lowell "Jack" Gardner at a family gathering in Europe. He was the grandson of one of the wealthiest men in the country, a member of one of New England's most prominent families. Quiet and reserved, he was a full-blooded Boston Brahmin, the type that always left the house with a silver-topped cane and a top hat and a diary in which he noted every penny that he spent over the course of a day. When he met potential female partners, they were usually distant cousins or the stiff-necked daughters of his mother's friends. No woman like Isabella had really crossed his path before. She wasn't beautiful. She had plain brown hair and a long face, but she loved to talk and dance and sometimes hijack horse-drawn sleighs and career them around Boston Common. Jack courted her for months, and their wedding, a massive affair, was in the summer of 1860.

Isabella soon gave birth to a child, John III, nicknamed Jackie. Two years later, the boy fell ill and died suddenly of pneumonia. Swept away by grief, she refused to let anyone go near the child's body. She prepared it for the funeral herself, dressing him one last time. A year later, doctors discovered that Isabella could have no more children. The news shattered her already delicate spirit, and for more than a year she did not leave the house. She took various remedies and elixirs, while doctors hovered around her bed. Friends whispered about a nervous breakdown. Then, at the urging of a family physician, she and Jack went to Europe for a three-month vacation. They visited Saint Basil's Cathedral in Moscow and waltzed in Vienna and saw the displays at the French exposition in Paris. Gardner felt rejuvenated, and they soon returned home, the first of many occasions that she would turn to art as a way to jump-start her soul.

Back in Boston, Gardner began attending charity dances and formal events in slim Parisian dresses. Created by the haute-couture designer Charles Worth, the post-Civil War outfits did not have hoops. Instead, the gowns flowed directly over her hips, and the modish dresses soon made the gossip-column headlines. According to one newspaper, Isabella was coming up the stairs at a party when an older man said to her: "Pray, who undressed you!"

"Worth," Gardner replied. "Didn't he do it well?"

The incident became Boston legend. Gardner had moved to perhaps the most high-minded city in the country. A hundred years earlier, the state's first governor, John Winthrop, called the bustling harbor town the "shining city on the hill," the American Jerusalem, and Isabella had married into the Gardner, Lowell, and Peabody clans, all certified First Families. She was expected to behave like one of the Brahmins, one of the Cold Roast set. But Gardner refused to conform to their puritan expectations. She enjoyed being brash and extravagant, and with unsaddled pride she wore pearl necklaces as thick as sailing ropes and a diamond tiara called the Rajah. Unlike the tight-lipped, corseted ladies of her time, she threw herself into anything that smacked of adventure. She traveled to Asia and rode an elephant through the jungles of Cambodia. She raced cars and once staged a boxing match in her living room. "Win as though you were used to it and lose as if you like it," she'd say as she gambled on horses at the local racetrack.

The Boston press reveled in Isabella's exploits, and she became a gossip-column staple, a steady source of tabloid news. "Mrs. Jack Gardner is one of the seven wonders of Boston," wrote one reporter. "She is a millionaire bohemian. She is eccentric and has the courage of eccentricity. She is the leader of the smart set but often leads where none dare follow." But the local media was not usually so kind. "It looks like this woman has gone crazy," the newspaper *Town Topics* wrote. The occasion was the Boston Red Sox championship win over the New York Giants in 1912, and Gardner had showed up at the Boston Symphony wearing a headband with the words "Oh, you Red Sox" to celebrate. "With this band bound like a fillet around her auburn hair, she appeared in her conspicuous seat at a recent Saturday night Symphony Concert, almost causing a panic among those in the audience who discovered the ornamentation."

Gardner reveled in her myth. She kept a scrapbook of her media mentions and didn't complain when the papers printed trumped up stories about how she greeted guests while perched in a palm tree or walked a pair of lions down Tremont Street. "Don't spoil a good story by telling the truth," she said. And when she was thirty-seven, she commissioned one of the most revered painters of the time, John Singer Sargent, to paint her portrait. It was a difficult process for the artist—Gardner never liked to sit still. But after eight attempts, he delivered a final work. In thick brush strokes and radiant colors, Sargent showed Gardner in a black, low-cut dress, a string of pearls wrapped suggestively around her waist. Encased by a Byzantine-style gold penumbra, Gardner seems to hover over the canvas, her face calm and focused, her mouth slightly open, a spirited, stylized woman determined to make her mark in the world.

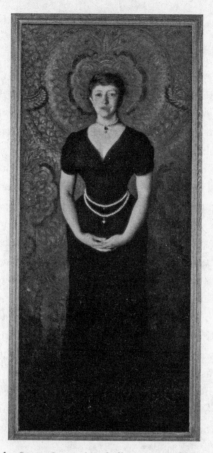

John Singer Sargent's Isabella Stewart Gardner.

Gardner's husband made his wife promise to never publicly show the work. He thought it was salacious and ungodly and vowed to horse-whip anyone telling the joke going around the men's clubs about how Sargent had painted Gardner "down to Crawford's Notch," the name of a New Hampshire resort and a pun on the name of one of his wife's hangers-on, Francis Crawford. But after her husband's death, Gardner hung the painting in the museum's Gothic Room. It is there today, sur-rounded by altar pieces and golden chalices, Gardner inserting herself into the world of religious worship, presenting herself as a secular saint, a pagan deity.

ISABELLA GARDNER was deeply devoted to the arts. As a young woman, she read Shakespeare and practiced landscape painting. In her thirties, she studied Latin at Harvard with Professor Charles Norton and worked to establish the Boston Symphony Orchestra. With her snappy wit and eager mind, she became close friends with some of the most revered artists and intellectuals of her time, novelist Henry James, painter James Whistler, the writer Henry Adams. John Singer Sargent painted Gardner dozens of times over the course of her life, including a tragically beautiful watercolor just months before her death.

Well before Gardner had the plans—or even the money—to build a world-class museum, she purchased artworks and antiques for her five-story mansion on Beacon Street. In 1892, while in Paris on a month-long vacation, she visited the auction house Drouot with her friend, the painter Ralph Curtis, and saw Vermeer's *The Concert* for sale. At the time, Vermeer was an artworld unknown. His paintings were attributed to other Old Masters; they moldered in dusty Dutch attics. In 1816 one of Vermeer's canvases, *Head of Girl*, was auctioned off in Rotterdam for three florins, the equivalent of about $15 in today's terms. It was unclear how the Dutch artist even spelled his name—was it Vermeer or van der Meer?

But Gardner was enthralled by the canvas and immediately decided to purchase the painting. She loved music, especially trios, and the luxurious setting looked like a room from her own Boston home. The attraction must have more than the familiar, though—like the women in the painting, Gardner understood how fluid the boundaries were between saint and sinner, how beautiful art could lead to ugly offenses. Later, she would ask her art dealer to smuggle newly purchased paintings out of Europe in order to avoid paying import taxes, reveling in the details of the bootlegging, how her artworks would be tucked into the false bottom of a wooden trunk hidden under toys, dolls, and other trinkets.

On that afternoon in 1892, Gardner and Curtis didn't linger in front of the Vermeer. Gardner knew that she would be bidding on the work, and she told Curtis that if they stayed too long, they might arouse the suspicions of other buyers. Gardner went back to the auction house a few days later. She sat in the back of the room, not wanting anyone to know she was interested in the canvas. Her art dealer, M. Fernand Robert, would bid on her behalf, and she told him to put in offers in 200-franc increments as long as she kept her handkerchief up to her face. Robert followed her directions, placing bids as the price climbed past 25,000 francs, then 26,000, then 27,000, then 28,000. Any more takers?

Gardner stayed in the back of the room, her kerchief hovered over her mouth. Robert now bid 29,000, and the gavel went down. The painting belonged to the Boston heiress. Later, Gardner said that she learned that both the Louvre in Paris and the National Gallery in London had tried to buy the painting and were displeased to find that they had been outmaneuvered by a private individual, an American woman no less. It made Gardner all the more proud. Vermeer was one of her first discoveries, and she had scored the painting just like the artist created his art—with a touch of mystery.

WHEN GARDNER was fifty-one, her father died and left her with $2.1 million, about $40 million in today's dollars. She decided to spend the money on art. Gardner was a true believer in art's redemptive power, she found it deeply spiritual, something incorporeal and otherworldly, and she said, without a touch of irony, that truth and beauty would bring her greater dividends than stocks or bonds. Late in life, after she had amassed her treasures, she penned a note to a friend about her collection. "I look out as I write and see the rain puddling the snow and man and beast wallowing!" she said. "Downstairs, I feel, are all these glories I could look at if I wanted to! Think of that. I can see that *Europa*, that Rembrandt, that Bonifazio, that Velazquez, et al.—anytime I want to. There's richness for you."

Gardner knew that building a world-class collection would be difficult work. She would have to compete with the robber barons, J. P. Morgan, Henry Clay Frick, Andrew Mellon, or "the squillionaires," as she called them. These men, and they were all men, had much more money. Morgan's fortune was at least thirty times larger than Gardner's—and they were just as passionate about art. Mellon more or less gave up his career to collect paintings. So did Frick. In his diary, the oil magnate J. Paul Getty refers to himself as "incurably hooked" and an "addict" of collecting art and antiques. On one afternoon, he writes: "I should stop buying pictures. My mind is set. I'm not going to change it." Then, on the very next day, his diary entry leads with the words, "the best laid schemes . . ."

Gardner would also have to endure the treacheries of the art market and steer clear of the scores of well-executed counterfeits that floated around Europe waiting for an innocent millionaire. She and her husband had been duped before. During a trip to Italy in 1888 they bought a fake Rossellino relief. In 1892 they purchased forged antiques from a duplicitous Venetian vendor. The imitations were artful and convincing and could seduce the most knowledgeable experts. In 1895 a critic visited an exhibition of Venetian art at a London museum and declared that only one of the thirty-three Titians on display was authentic. A few years later, the American Impressionist painter Mary Cassatt accompanied sugar heiress Louisine Havemeyer on a European collecting trip, and Havemeyer spent an exorbitant amount of money on canvases by Titian, Veronese, and Raphael. The paintings all turned out to have been created by much lesser artists.

Gardner soon enlisted the help of Bernard Berenson. Born to an impoverished Jewish family in 1865, Berenson went onto become one of the most influential art critics of his time. He helped define the modern notion of art connoisseurship. His books on the Italian Renaissance were considered beyond reproach. For decades, there was not an art historian who did not have at least one of his tomes on his shelf. Lithe, handsome, and always impeccably dressed, he was a world-famous aesthete. He dined with Jacqueline Kennedy, corresponded with Ernest Hemingway, and had a not-so secret affair with the scholar Belle da Costa Greene. Harry Truman once came for tea at his villa in the hills outside of Florence.

But when Gardner and Berenson began corresponding in 1894, the art historian was young and penniless, and it was Gardner who had much to offer. She had the money, and more importantly, the opportunity for Berenson to make his name as a man of taste and influence. Gardner had known Berenson from his days as a Harvard undergraduate, and after they exchanged a few letters, Berenson boldly asked: "How much do you want a Botticelli? Lord Ashburnham has a great one—one of the greatest: *A Death of Lucretia*." Gardner wrote back immediately. She would buy the work—the Italian Renaissance painter was among her favorites.

Berenson worked as Gardner's art advisor for more than fifty years. His authentications were considered unassailable; he had pitch-perfect taste. He suggested Gardner buy works like Titian's *Rape of Europa* and Rembrandt's *Self-Portrait*, which experts still consider to be some of the finest paintings in existence. Indeed, Boston Museum of Fine Arts curator Peter Sutton once called the Titian "arguably the greatest painting in America." Peter Paul Rubens pronounced it "the greatest painting in the world." Berenson also recommended most of the works stolen in the 1990 heist. He urged Gardner to purchase the Degas sketches, the Manet, and the Flinck. And when Rembrandt's *A Lady and Gentleman in Black* and *The Storm* came up for sale, Berenson sent a letter to Gardner the next day. "A glance at the [two paintings] together gives one a marvelous idea of Rembrandt's range," he wrote. "The one picture represents, as you will see, a couple, quiet, refined people, limned in a dignified, distinguished way. If in this canvas you see [Rembrandt] at his height as a portrait-painter, in the other you see him as the profound interpreter and poet." Gardner later hung the works in a way that echoed Berenson's remarks, placing them at either end of a gallery with a Rubens in between.

Over the years, Gardner and Berenson developed an intimate relationship. She relished the ins and outs of the art market, the chance to build a masterful collection. "Let us aim awfully high," she wrote to him in 1896. "If you don't aim, you can't get there." Then a few weeks later: "I've got the picture habit. It's as bad as the whiskey habit!" Berenson responded with equal enthusiasm, not hesitating to tell Gardner to empty her pockets for a beautiful work. "You know that Gainsborough is one of the world's painters. So of course you must have it," he wrote. "I advise you to borrow, to do anything, but get that picture."

Like any good salesman, Berenson would flatter Gardner, telling her of all his hard work. "It will require cunning angling to bring that beauty to land. A bait of less than $100,000 will be out of the question. All my subterranean efforts have not succeeded thus far in settling a definite price." But Berenson did not protect Gardner from all of the art market's darkest corners. In a practice considered unethical even by the cut-throat standards of nineteenth-century art dealers, he would double dip—taking a 5 percent commission from Gardner while also earning a stipend from the seller.

Jack Gardner was the first to learn of Berenson's deceitful business practices, and he asked his wife to find a new art dealer. Isabella dashed off a set of venomous letters to Berenson. "Tell me exactly what you paid for the Holbeins. I have a most singular letter from the former owners," she wrote. "I think this is a matter for the law courts." But ultimately she decided to keep Berenson. She wanted only the best—and he knew how to find them.

ON DECEMBER 10, 1898, a stroke killed Jack Gardner. He was sixty-one years old. For decades, he had served as his wife's emotional counterbalance, the reasoned calm to her creative storm, and in a state of grief she did not eat or drink for a week. But instead of continuing her mourning, Gardner threw herself into her legacy—her museum—and within weeks of his death, she purchased a plot of land, hired an architect, and drew up architectural plans. Inspired by visits to Venice, Gardner modeled the building after the Grand Canal's Palazzo Barbaro, and she knitted various design elements directly into the walls. But her brilliant architectural twist was to turn the palazzo design inside out, so that the arches and columns that usually overlook the Venetian streets face a courtyard filled with greenery.

Gardner was an exacting client. She visited the construction site every day and frequently battled with workmen over minor details, once climbing a ladder to show the plasterers how to redo the salmon-colored stucco so that it recalled the sun-dappled walls of Venice. "Never do anything you are not ordered to," she barked. She often changed her mind: she had the façade altered, the foundation bricks moved, the main staircase put up and then taken down. But her willful efforts paid off. After walking through a narrow entrance, visitors step into a tall, airy courtyard steeped in sparkling light and flashes of color. Italianate arches, ornate balustrades, lion stylobates surround the space; the garden overflows with greenery, jasmine trees, white azaleas, freesia, cineraria, orchids. The graceful, atmospheric space is one of the architectural gems of Boston, often cited as one of the most romantically beautiful places in the city.

After the building was finished, Gardner spent another year installing her collection. She wanted her museum to be a place where stunning paintings and powerful sculptures inspired the deepest feelings of being human, a venue where art would be celebrated above all else, and she surrounded the garden with small, intimate rooms, each gallery aiming to transport the viewer, to fully reveal an artistic moment. In the Raphael Room, the Venetian master's *Count Tommasso Inghirami* doesn't hang in the middle of a cold, white wall lit by spotlights. Instead, the painting is tucked next to a large window so that natural light can show off the painting's tight brushwork and crisp tones. The oil is surrounded with period items, Italian Renaissance tables, chairs, vases. A firecracker-red wallpaper reflects the painting's vibrant undertone, giving the Count a dense, knowing energy.

Gardner pondered the location of every single item, the lock of Robert Browning's hair, Bellini's *Christ Bearing the Cross*, and the museum stands as its own work of art, an imaginative performance piece in its entirety. Within galleries, across rooms, she juxtaposed pieces to highlight a common style or spark a conversation between artworks, regardless of their history or medium. In the Early Italian Room, a pair of simple Chinese Han Dynasty bears stare at Piero della Francesca's masterpiece *Hercules*, echoing the fresco's direct style and earthy colors. An Art Deco sculpture sits on top of a High Renaissance Venetian dresser, each artwork showing off its own period's fascination with visual twists and turns. It can make for an intense, wunderkammer experience, with bric-a-brac next to a magnum opus, Whistler's bamboo wand knuckled behind a Raphael, a plaster cast of Franz Liszt's hand sitting across from a Botticelli.

Gardner called her museum Fenway Court—it was renamed the Isabella Stewart Gardner Museum after her death—and she lived on the fourth floor of the building for another decade. She charged a dollar entrance fee in order to keep out the curious and required guards to be "young men whose business is ushering." Still, Gardner worried about the safety of her collection and would prowl the galleries on visiting days. When Gardner once discovered an elderly woman poking at some of her treasures, she cursed her, bellowing, "Jesus Christ, madam, this is no menagerie!" It makes it easy to see why some observers suggest that if she had lived another few decades after her death in July 1924, she might have prevented the heist of her beloved masterpieces—or at least have recovered them by now. "She was dreadfully afraid of a robbery, and it just wouldn't have been successful," biographer Shand-Tucci told me, "because, really, she valued the contents of her museum above all else, even herself."

THE DUTCH ROOM is the largest, most austere, most visited gallery in the museum. Located at the top of the main staircase, the room resembles a seventeenth-century Dutch guildhall. Well-worn ceramic tiles cover the floor; intricately carved wood panels hang from the ceiling. A silk, green-gold fabric decorates the space giving it a soft, emerald-like glow. Along the walls are various period furnishings—an elaborate fireplace, late sixteenth-century tapestries, an ornate breadbox—and dozens of extraordinary paintings. A Dürer etching, two pendant Van Dykes, some Holbeins, and a dramatic Rubens titled *Portrait of Thomas Howard*, which stares out into the room with wizened eyes.

On a bright spring morning, I walked up the museum's grand staircase and stepped into the Dutch Room, and the first thing I noticed—the first thing anyone notices—is the large, hollow frame on the south wall. Rembrandt's *The Storm on the Sea of Galilee* once filled the gilded frame; now it showed only the silk fabric behind it. In her will, Gardner

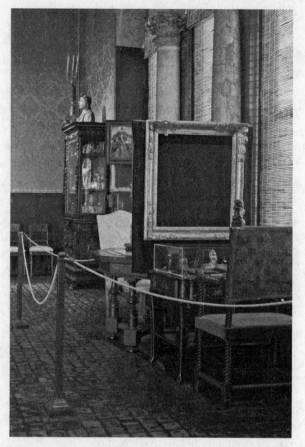

The hollow frame of Vermeer's The Concert *in the Dutch Room of the Isabella Stewart Gardner Museum.*

stipulated that nothing in her museum could ever be altered, and after the heist, the staff placed the empty frames of *The Storm* and *A Lady and Gentleman in Black* back up on the south wall; they returned the hollow frames of the Vermeer and the Flinck to their easel-like tables next to the windows. The missing paintings provide a deeply mournful spectacle. The room feels sad and haunted. When Gardner created her museum, she positioned a high-backed, upholstered Victorian chair in front of the Vermeer and the Flinck, hoping that visitors would sit down in front of the works and appreciate their mastery. Now the empty chairs face the only thing that's left of the canvases—a silhouette of brown velvet.

When I stepped into the Dutch Room that morning, it was almost twenty years after the robbery, but the heist still felt fresh and raw, as if the police had just pulled down the crime tape. Next to the doorway was a curved seventeenth-century oak chest with intricate groves and flutes, and on the side of the bureau, there were four tiny holes, remnants of the screws that once secured the tiny Rembrandt self-portrait. When the thieves wrenched the finial from the Napoleonic battle flag in the Short Gallery, they chipped the wall above the glass casing. It was a small mark—no larger than a quarter—and it still marred the plaster.

I stayed in front of the frame of *The Storm on the Sea of Galilee* for a while that morning, as visitors filtered past me, gathering in front of the lost paintings, searching, it seemed, for some sort of explanation. "Some really rich guy must have them," a woman told her friends. She came into the room as part of a tour and had a pair of large plastic sunglasses pushed back on her head, holding back a thick mane of black hair. "He must, you know, go down into his basement and look at them every night with a glass of wine."

A woman with cherry red lipstick and a set of oversized pearls stared at the gilded setting of *The Storm*. "Some weirdo has the paintings," she told a man standing next to her.

He peered through tumbler-sized eyeglasses and frowned. "Nah," he replied with bald certainty, "they're in China."

The Gardner guards are not supposed to discuss the theft. But like the visitors, they can't seem to help themselves, and they gossip about the caper like servants in a castle. "I watch the *America's Most Wanted* show dedicated to the theft every year it comes on," a guard told me. "It's cool to see the guards wearing our uniforms and everything."

We turned to face the empty frames. The guard and I stood in silence for a moment. A tall, gangly young man moved past us and positioned himself in front of the settings and said to no one in particular: "Man, that is spooky."

I CAME TO THE GARDNER to experience the scene of the crime and talk to any remaining witnesses. But landing interviews proved difficult. When I sent my request to the museum's public relations director, she emailed me back and said simply: "We have to decline access." If I needed quotes, I could get a written statement from the director or interview the head of security. I wasn't really surprised. Much of the staff had become sick of the caper. They had seen thousands of leads come and go. They had received countless calls from kooks, wackos, and a-third-man-shot-Kennedy-type weirdos. It had been almost twenty years, and they had grown tired of all the media queries, the letters from charlatans, the solicitations from low-grade shamuses. The museum's heist fatigue was apparent in little things. On the anniversary of the robbery, the Gardner's public relations staff would sometimes put out almost the exact same press release as they had in the previous year, with the same limp quote from the director: "We remain confident that these rare and important treasures will be returned to the Gardner Museum where they can be enjoyed by the public, and society at large."

The Gardner, as a museum, has always been rather circumspect. Soon after the death of its founder, the board became dominated by a group of Boston blue bloods, men like Malcolm Perkins, John Gardner III, and Frank Hatch, scions from old patrician families, and in a famously conservative town, they helped turn the museum into a famously conservative institution. For years, the trustees battled bitterly over replacing candlelight with electricity—the pro-electricity camp finally won out in the late 1930s. It seemed as if asking people for money was beneath them, too, and in 1984 they collected only eleven major donations, just under $300,000, almost nothing for a museum of the Gardner's size and stature. Even the current director, Anne Hawley, who has smartly instituted management reforms and fund-raises millions annually, still shows some of the old school ways. She once denounced "overzealous museum staff who pushed too far, too fast."

The Gardner's orthodoxy has long been its charm, of course. But when it came to the heist, it occasionally made the museum willing to cut off its nose to spite its handsome face. Six weeks after the theft, the FBI had to strong-arm the Gardner into allowing the highly successful

TV program *America's Most Wanted* to devote an episode to the caper. The museum didn't explain their apprehension, but it seemed that they didn't approve of the show's tawdry reenactments. "It was hard for them, but they did it," an FBI agent told the *Globe*. The museum also refused interview requests from Harold Smith and the documentary filmmakers. The movie went on to feature in almost a hundred theaters around the country and has been shown more than one thousand times on PBS stations here and abroad.

The Gardner's reticence wasn't unusual. Most museums are loath to discuss art thefts. They want to be seen as the vigilant protectors of treasures—they fear that news of a robbery might lead to an erosion in public trust, that a heist might taint their reputation, make the gallery seem vulnerable, irresponsible, negligent. The Gardner in fact might be more open than most: experts believe that as many as half of all art heists never even get reported, that institutions will hush up an art crime before the public finds out about it. When the Museum of Modern Art put together their 1989 Andy Warhol retrospective, the Andy Warhol Foundation sent forty-five drawings to the museum. But when the paintings went missing, the Museum of Modern Art did not contact the authorities or issue any sort of public explanation. The insurers paid out for the loss, and while a few reporters eventually learned about the missing paintings, what exactly happened to the art is still a mystery.

The Gardner wanted their masterpieces back. Since the night of the heist, the staff has put in endless hours working leads and running down suspects. They have hired private detectives and paid out to informants and met with tipsters in downtown hotel rooms. The recovery efforts are expensive. The institution often will spend more than $50,000 a year just on private investigative services. But most important, the museum continues to offer a $5 million reward for any information on the whereabouts of the missing masterpieces. The sum is believed to be the biggest bounty ever offered by a private institution. (The reward posted by the Lindbergh family for information on the kidnapping of their child is believed to be the second largest reward—tipsters on the 1932 crime could earn $75,000, or $1.1 million, in today's dollars.) The Gardner's reward is exceeded only by the federal govern-ment's $25 million for Osama bin Laden.

For the past few years, security director Anthony Amore has led the Gardner's recovery efforts. He goes everywhere—grocery stores, restau-rants—with a memory stick filled with his investigation files hanging around his neck. He talks about recovering the art so much that his daughters recently drew a copy of *The Storm* for him to hang in his office. "I think they just wanted me to shut up about the paintings," he said. "Because, really, aside from my daughters, I don't think about any-thing more than those missing paintings. When I go to sleep at night, when I wake up in the morning, I'm thinking about the paintings. I'm not somewhat obsessed. I'm wildly obsessed. No matter where my life leads me, I'll never be able to stop thinking about the missing art."

Amore and I were standing in the Dutch Room at the time. It was early evening, the museum was empty, the visitors had all gone home. A reddish light filtered in through the windows and gave the room a chest-nut glow. Amore pointed at the frames on the wall. Covered in long shadows, they looked like portals to some distant place. "It's those frames that get me. Because with those frames just hanging up there, you can't say, 'I'm not coming into work today.' Every time I come in here, I think I have to get back in my office and start chasing those paintings down. Something clearly belongs in those rectangles."

Over the following weeks, I pleaded with the Gardner for more access, and the museum soon relented. I think they saw that my effort was serious, that I had a deep interest in returning the art, and they gave me permission to use their archives, they provided images of the stolen art, they offered me the opportunity to interview key staff, includ-ing curators, conservators, and the director. And so it was on a warm fall day that I found myself in director Anne Hawley's office. It is a sumptuous parlor, really, with fifteen-foot ceilings, Persian rugs, and a grand piano. Hawley's desk—an antique escritoire—stood next to the window, decorated with a large white orchid and a Venetian party mask. Hawley is tall and thin, with high cheekbones and a small, flared nose. Although we were meeting for the first time, she raised her arms as if we hadn't seen each other in years. "You must be Ulrich. Come in, come in," she said in a well-accented voice. "You're in the drawing room of Isabella Stewart Gardner. The chandelier is original, which came from France. Obviously Napoleonic or Napoleonic inspired."

Hawley settled down in one of the Victorian chairs and began recalling the theft with vivid clarity. On the day of the heist, she had been at a conference and flew back to Boston early that evening. Her husband picked her up at Logan airport and took her to dinner at a small restaurant on Beacon Hill. After the meal she wanted to go to the Gardner to pick up some papers but her husband dissuaded her. "I wish we had come to the museum. I was married to a very tall and husky Australian who, I was always convinced, would have done the thieves in," she said. "But the FBI told me that we probably would have just been shot."

The next morning, Hawley was in the kitchen of her Brookline home when the phone rang. Some friends were supposed to come by for brunch, and she was at the stove making breakfast. On the line was then-director of security Lyle Grindle. There has been a theft, he said, the police are at the museum. She hung up and drove to the Gardner as fast as she could, rushing into the galleries to figure out what had been stolen. "It was just hell after that. The problem is not just the theft. It's dealing with the investigation. You've got the FBI. You've got other criminals calling you to negotiate a deal. You've got the press killing you because you let it happen. People called making bomb threats," Hawley said, shaking her head.

An assistant brought Hawley some tea, and she pinched the handle of the cup with her forefinger and thumb and sipped from the white china as she began talking about the missing art. She discussed the Rembrandt *Self-Portrait* ("The painting seems to say 'look at me, I'm really cool!'") and the Degas sketches ("He was just such a complex thinker!"), and the Manet painting ("It's just a wonderful little joie de vivre"). For Hawley, the Vermeer was the biggest loss, and as she talked about the canvas, recalling the painting in her mind's eye, her voice grew softer, her eyes widened. She imitated the singer arching her right hand, and for a brief moment, I felt like I was talking with Isabella Stewart Gardner herself, recalling a letter that the Boston heiress wrote to Berenson about Titian's *Europa* shortly after receiving the painting: "I am breathless after a two days' orgy, drinking myself drunk with Europa, thinking and dreaming about her."

Hawley stopped and pursed her lips and blew out a deep breath. She thinks about the stolen paintings every day; the memory of the missing artworks still pains her. At a press conference a few days after the robbery, Hawley nearly broke down in tears as she spoke to the assembled reporters. "The theft was a violent act. It was a murder, a death," she told me. Still, she wanted to make sure that the robbery never overshadowed the museum itself, and after the heist she pushed new initiatives to invigorate the museum. She began an artist-in-residency program to bring more contemporary artists into the museum and established a partnership between the Gardner and nearby elementary schools. A few of the programs have been controversial—some members complained about the sound therapy lessons in the Chinese Loggia—but the initiatives have boosted revenue and made for record attendance levels. At least in the public eye, Hawley has made the museum far more than the site of the biggest art theft in history.

After an hour, an assistant glided into the office with a speakerphone. It was the signal that our meeting was over. Earlier, the public relations director told me that some topics were off limits. I wasn't allowed to ask Hawley directly about the investigation or query her about any specific attempts to recover the art. But before I left, I asked if she thought that the paintings would ever be returned. She looked at me with her saucer-sized eyes and raised her palms to emphasize her point. "I live in hope. I dwell in possibility, as Emily Dickinson says," she told me. "I just have to believe that the stolen paintings are still out there."

5. CORTEGE AUX ENVIRONS DE FLORENCE

The Art of the Theft

THE JEWISH MUSEUM in New York City looks like a massive French Gothic chateau, with marble ceilings and ogee-arched windows and herringboned floors. For decades, the seven-story, 1908 mansion served as the Warburg family estate, and almost everything about it seems rich and opulent. Drip moldings line the lobby, light floods through stained-glass windows, a steep mansard roof caps the building. It's easy to imagine the servants of the original owners floating along the hallways with silver platters brimming with rare champagnes and heapings of fresh caviar.

"A Chagall was stolen from here a few years ago," Smith told me. It was late on a Wednesday afternoon; we were standing in one of the second-floor galleries. Smith explained that the museum was holding a Jewish singles event on the night of the robbery, and while waiters served kosher hors d'oeuvres to some three hundred guests, someone ripped Chagall's *Study for 'Over Vitebsk'* from the wall. The painting was small—about the size of a manila folder—and showed an angular snow-covered cityscape, with a man dressed in old, raggedy clothes floating over the rooftops. On loan for a special exhibition on the artist, the canvas was valued at over $1 million.

No one realized that the painting was missing until the next morning when a cleaning lady heard a loose bolt rattle into her vacuum cleaner. Smith was called into the case later that day. He interviewed a few suspects, ran down some leads, put out a $25,000 reward. Nothing. Then, a few weeks later, someone mailed a typewritten letter to the museum. The author claimed to represent the International Committee for Art and Peace and said that the painting would be returned only after Israel and Palestine had signed a peace accord. The author said that the Chagall was "being taken care of" and apologized to the museum for swiping the canvas.

"It's not as crazy as it sounds. Sometimes the robbers are terrorists and have some political agenda," Smith told me as we stood in the gallery. In 1911 an Italian patriot stole the *Mona Lisa*, and the thief later claimed that the heist was an effort to return the artwork to his homeland. In 1971 an intruder sneaked into the Palais des Beaux-Arts in Brussels, cut a Vermeer out of its frame, and then disappeared over a balcony. A few days later, a man called a local magazine with a ransom request—he wanted $4 million paid to a relief organization for East Pakistani refugees. But before any money was paid for the canvas, police bagged the thief at a highway rest stop, and the painting was found in his home, hidden under his bed. But Smith told me that no one had ever heard of the International Committee for Art and Peace. Nor was it exactly clear whose side of the Middle Eastern conflict the author of the letter supported. "It was also possible that the man was a little cuckoo." Smith shrugged.

Smith was sure from the letter that the robber wasn't an expert burglar, or even a professional terrorist, or he would have asked for a hefty ransom. Smith also believed that the person was someone close to the museum, perhaps an employee or a guard, or he would not have apologized to the institution. The clues were enough for the art detective to start narrowing his list of suspects, and after some more sleuthing, he believed that he uncovered the culprit. While the evidence was not strong enough for a criminal prosecution, Smith told the man that he was a suspect and the police began interviewing his friends and family. "The person who did this, he really started to feel the heat," Smith told me.

Then, a few weeks later, the painting was recovered at a post office in Topeka, Kansas. Smith believed that the investigative pressure forced the thief's hand, and he mailed the artwork as a dead letter in an effort to rid himself of the painting. "We were lucky. The man in charge of opening the mail that day decided that this thing might actually be something important," Smith said. "He saw the dealer's marks and checked the Internet, and what do you know, the painting turned out to be stolen."

"So was it your guy?"

"I'm not 100 percent sure," Smith said, his face creased with a wry smile. "But we got the painting back."

THERE IS NO PROFILE of an art thief—people swipe paintings and sculptures for countless reasons. Some steal for the insurance money; some steal to impress their friends; some steal out of a haunting fixation with art. Smith worked the case of John Quentin Feller, the art world's Robin Hood. A widely published scholar on Chinese porcelains, Feller pocketed ceramic artifacts from institutions that he believed did not sufficiently appreciate the works, and once told a reporter that he just couldn't restrain himself when he saw the Van Goghs of the porcelain field kept in dusty storage areas, out of the public's view. Feller stole from almost a dozen museums, pilfering more than a hundred objects, and he would frequently donate his spoils to other institutions, ones that promised to display them. Feller eventually gave so many artworks to the Peabody Essex Museum that they made him a trustee because of his felonious generosity. After getting caught, Feller confessed—and resigned from his position at the Peabody.

There are some art theft professionals. They usually specialize in lesser-known works that can be eased back into the legitimate trade, taking advantage of the fact that the art market is the largest unregulated business in the world. There are no standardized forms or databases. Government agencies have a hands-off attitude, and so knowledgeable crooks will filch mid-level canvases and sell them to buyers who are oblivious to the illicit nature of their purchase. Smith once investigated two burglars who focused on Ming Dynasty vases. After thoroughly casing a museum, they would stroll inside on a bustling Saturday afternoon, and while one man diverted the guard's attention, the other would unscrew a vitrine, remove a vase or two, and then saunter out the door. The men stole ancient Chinese porcelains because only an expert can tell one from another, making it easier to sell the stolen ones. Before police pinched the thieves, they had looted almost $4 million worth of art from more than a dozen different galleries. "Right in broad daylight, they were going into museums and things were disappearing. Not from storerooms—from the busiest part of the museum at the busiest time of the day!" Smith explained, shaking his head with admiration. "They were so fast no one noticed."

Such polished heists are rare, the headline-grabbing minority, and the vast majority of art thieves are inexperienced, low-grade rogues: Ex-cons looking to pay the rent, pickpockets looking for a simple score, drug dealers on parole. They're in it for the money. They don't know or care about the art. While swiping a Bauhaus print, the burglars might break a canvas from its setting, or they will crack an Egyptian urn in their rush to leave a gallery. Smith once tracked down a gang that would hijack copper sculptures from college campuses and corporate headquarters in order to sell as scrap metal. In 2005 Charles McDougal swiped a painting from a shed while doing some electrical work on a home in Waterford, Connecticut. He sold the canvas to an antiques dealer for $100 and later told investigators he was hoping to just make a few bucks. Within weeks the dealer had the canvas appraised at $150,000 and the painting eventually sold for $1 million to a wealthy Dutch collector. French Realist artist Henri Fantin-Latour had painted the canvas—the robbery was one of the largest ever committed in the state.

MOST ART CROOKS are motivated by the lure of easy money and, relative to their size, top-notch paintings represent some of the most valuable items on the planet. A minor Picasso or Van Gogh carries a bigger price tag than the finest diamonds or the purest gold, and a major canvas by an Old Master might have the value of a Gulfstream jet or a small ocean liner. Consider Klimt's *Adele Bloch-Bauer I*. In 2006 Ronald Lauder purchased the twentieth-century portrait for $135 million. With that same amount of money, the cosmetics magnate could have acquired a midsized computer firm (technology giant Cisco bought the hardware designer Reactivity for $135 million in 2006) or created a blockbuster movie and had money left over for a summer home in the Hamptons (the upfront budget for the movie *Pearl Harbor* was $130 million).

Art wasn't always so expensive. The boom began in the 1960s, and since then prices have taken off at irrationally exuberant levels, with the values of some well-known artists jumping more than 1,000 percent. The appreciation is far greater than other traded commodities, be it stocks or real estate or oil, and while the market has had some dips over the years, the frenzy seems to always top itself. When the Metropolitan Museum of Art bought Rembrandt's *Aristotle Contemplating the Bust of Homer* in 1961, many thought the museum had been conned. The $2.3 million price tag was more than twice the previous auction record, and *Time* magazine, which ran the painting on its cover that week, noted that, "the only fitting motto is: 'Let the buyer beware.'" But the market continued its upwards spiral. The record for the most expensive painting sold at auction has been broken ten times since then; forty-five years to the month of the Rembrandt sale, Christie's held an auction where almost every other artwork went for more than $2 million.

The engine behind the boom is partly the prices themselves. Many collectors buy big-time artists because they command big-time prices, and with an increase in money, comes an increase in prestige. The art market also provides a curious twist on the usual supply-and-demand model, because there is, in the end, an extremely limited supply. There is only one *Mona Lisa*, one *Starry Night*, one *David*. But the biggest driver might be the notion of art as an investment. In the past, people bought paintings and sculptures for beauty or status or merely to have an image of something important to them. Now people buy art for profit, purchasing paintings like a broker arbitrages Coca-Cola or Microsoft stock. Even some investment banks have gotten into the business, buying Pollocks low and selling them high. "We look at million-dollar deals every week and often buy $1 million to $2 million of art a week," Rhea

Papanicolaou of the London Fine Art Fund told me. Her fund showed an average of 47 percent return on sales, she said. "If you have an excellent team of experts, are sitting on a lot of cash, and are prepared to hold art over a ten-year period, you can make substantial profits."

The estimated worth of the stolen Gardner paintings have shown the same meteoric rise as the rest of the market. When Gardner purchased the Vermeer in 1892, she paid 29,000 French francs, or about $6,000. A few years later, Gardner's friend Ralph Curtis wrote her from the Hague, "[Hofstede de Groote] says your *Concert* is now worth *easily* between hundred and fifty and two hundred thousand. Tell [your husband]—he can't make investments like that in State Street!" The joke remained true for much of the next century—and there seems no doubt that the thieves knew that the Gardner works were highly valuable commodities. Six months before the theft, Christie's sold Manet's *The Rue Mosnier with Flags* for $26.4 million. The price more than doubled the record for a work by the artist, and the sale made headlines across the country. The auction record for a Rembrandt painting was set just a year before the robbery when *Portrait of a Bearded Man in a Red Coat* sold for about $10 million. And after the heist, some blamed the museum break-in squarely on the market itself. "The [Gardner] theft is the blue-collar side of the glittering system whereby art, through the '80s, was promoted into crass totems of excess capital," wrote critic Robert Hughes. "If one wanted a perfect example of how the crazed art market has come to work against American museums and their public, what happened in Boston last week would be it."

Whatever the case, the art market continues to skyrocket—and the notional value of the stolen Gardner art climbs along with it. When the FBI first announced the caper, they estimated the loss at $200 million; eight years later, the *Boston Herald* put the price at over $400 million, with the Vermeer at $238 million, *The Storm* at $140 million, and the rest of the works in the many thousands. In 2000 FBI agent Thomas Cassano gave a talk about the Gardner theft at the International Foundation for Art Research in New York City, and when he priced the total value of the loss at $500 million, the audience began hooting and cheering, "More! More!" Today, a few dealers say the stolen Gardner paintings could be worth as much as $600 million. "In this crazy art market, all you need is one big spender. If those paintings got returned, all you would need is a Bill Gates or a Geffen to suddenly get involved, and you could see the Vermeer alone going for as much $300 million," art dealer Alex Boyle told me.

When crooks hear the prices commanded by top paintings and sculptures—and realize how poorly secured they are—art theft becomes a given. A few years after a Leonardo da Vinci codex sold for a record-breaking $31 million, two men strolled into the Drumlanrig Castle in Scotland. They looked like regular tourists. They wore sensible shoes, thick coats, and baseball hats. Then, about halfway through the tour, one of the men threatened a docent with a knife, while the other pulled da Vinci's painting *Madonna with the Yarnwinder* from the wall. The men leaped out of a kitchen window and into a waiting VW Golf sedan. The heist took less than ten minutes—and the thieves disappeared with a four-by-six foot piece of canvas valued at more than $200 million. With such a massive return on such little effort, one has to wonder— why do crooks steal anything else?

I ONCE ASKED SMITH if he had a favorite artwork.

"Oh, I don't know," he said. "Probably the U-boat at the Chicago Museum of Science and Industry."

"You're kidding." The exhibit was a massive German submarine, the only Nazi U-boat ever captured by American forces during World War II.

"When I fought in World War II, those U-boats tried to kill us," Smith explained. "They were lethal, and I found walking through that exhibit just fascinating. It was a way for me to connect to that history of mine."

Smith paused for a moment, and I was sure some sort of joke was coming. "And I guess I know that no one was going to try and steal it either," he deadpanned.

The U-boat weighs 350 tons and is about the length of a city block, but if someone actually managed to nab the submarine, it might be one of the easier items to recover. When thieves steal a minor item—a small, terracotta statue or an Audrey Beardsley sketch—it can be slipped back into the legitimate trade. But when crooks swipe a world-famous Vermeer or a lionized military artifact, they typically find themselves in a bind. While it might have been an effortless heist, the thieves can't unload the artwork at an auction or sell it to a fence or even ease it into the blackest of black markets. The work is too well known, too recognizable.

Experts call it the curse of the stolen masterpiece, and the art theft Catch-22 can stymie the most experienced criminals. In 2003 a gang broke into the Whitworth Art Gallery in England and pocketed a half-dozen prints by Van Gogh, Picasso, and Gauguin. The robbery was deftly executed. The thieves evaded alarms, closed-captioned cameras, and a set of guards. But a few days after the heist, the police landed a tip that the art was stashed behind a public toilet. While the criminals left a note claiming that they wanted to "highlight a breach in security," they appeared to care little for the prints. The artworks had been stuffed into a cardboard tube, the Van Gogh had a rip, rainwater had eaten away at the Picasso. Police now believe that the thieves ditched the items. "The reality is that they were good crooks, but not professional art thieves who work out what to do with the artwork before they steal it," said Dick Ellis, former head of Scotland Yard's Arts and Antiques Squad.

There are markets for stolen masterpieces, to be sure. Thieves might use a looted painting as a collateral for a bank loan or a financial deposit. This is particularly popular in Switzerland and Japan where lending officers are private and generous, and the laws concerning "good faith purchase" are lax. Professional art thieves might wait a few years and then attempt to ransom the looted paintings back to the owner. Museums will pay for particularly valuable stolen works, usually about 10 percent of their value. A middleman—a defense lawyer or underworld front man—will typically arrange the deal, delivering the paintings to an empty hotel room or airport lounge where the works are "found" by police. Increasingly, criminals have been turning looted masterpieces into a type of underworld currency, trading the stolen canvases for guns or drugs. A few years ago, investigators recovered a Metsu pilfered from a mansion in Ireland that was being used as a down payment for a cocaine deal in Istanbul, and after Titian's *Rest on the Flight into Egypt* was swiped from an English country estate, the painting passed through the hands of five different gangsters, each time used as a bargaining credit. But the collateralization of a stolen painting typically makes it easier for detectives to recover a canvas because the work will move from criminal to criminal like a poker chip at a card game, and at some point, someone will try to cash in.

THERE'S ONE PLACE, though, that the stolen Van Goghs and Matisses don't go, and that's to a shadowy, art-hungry billionaire. It's a familiar trope. Somewhere in the Caribbean, in the basement of a columned mansion, a tuxedoed gentleman pulls back a set of velvet curtains and admires a stolen Monet. He ordered a cat burglar to swipe the painting for him, and now, holding a snifter of brandy, staring at his illegal masterpiece, he says softly: "All mine. It's all mine."

Smith called it the Dr. No theory—after the criminal genius of the James Bond film—and the scenario comes up after almost every major art theft. The day after the Gardner heist, the *Boston Globe* wrote that, "the art treasures seized from the Isabella Stewart Gardner Museum yesterday were probably contracted for in advance by a black-market collector outside the country." Other newspapers covering the heist echoed the storyline, including the *New York Times* and the *Boston Herald*. Even Anne Hawley suggested that the robbers might have followed a "hit list" given to them by a collector. The mastermind "could only probably be a person who is determined to keep them private for the rest of their life," she said.

It's not surprising that the idea of a Dr. No has so much traction. Anyone who has spent any time at an auction house knows that some art lovers will do almost anything to land a coveted painting or sculpture. Mrs. Gardner once joked about murdering someone over a Giorgione; Andrew Carnegie referred to his art collection as his mania; the 105-year-old investment banker Roy Neuberger continues to collect art to this day. But when I asked Smith about a Dr. No, he gave a soft, admonishing chuckle. He didn't think much of the theory because he had never seen a gossamer of proof. In his decades of experience, he never found a secret stash of stolen paintings in a billionaire's mansion or caught an art thief who actually worked on behalf of one. Nor had any other art investigator or law enforcement official that he was aware of. While collectors will occasionally purchase works with weak provenance—and maybe a crook might put a stolen Hopper on his wall to impress his friends—billionaire art-lovers just don't snap up looted paintings or broker art heists. It's not worth the risk.

Criminals, though, continue to dream of a real-life Dr. No. A suspect in the heist of a Picasso from a Brazilian museum recently told authorities that he planned to sell the work to a wealthy art collector in Saudi Arabia. The mystery buyer never materialized—and law enforcement soon arrested the thief. Smith believed that the theory misled the

The finial stolen from the top of the Napoleonic battle flag.

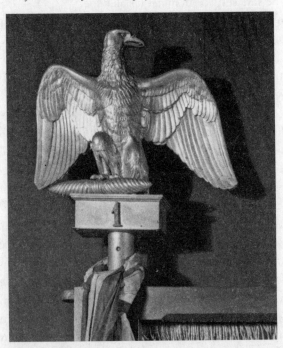

public too, because it made art heists seem dreamy and romantic, when in truth the thieves were cruel and unscrupulous. "You have to remember, the people who steal art are not nice," Smith told me. "They're crooks, and they steal things that don't belong to them."

A FEW WEEKS after the robbery of the Gardner, Smith traveled to Boston to visit the museum. He wanted to get a feel for the caper, and together with the museum's security director, he followed the path of the intruders through the building. Smith examined how the thieves entered and exited the side entrance; he studied the watch desk where the guards were handcuffed and bound with duct tape. Smith asked himself the same questions that he always asked himself at the scene of an art crime. Were the thieves professionals? Did they have an inside angle?

At first glance, it seemed to Smith that the thieves were little more than ham-handed amateurs. After taking control of a museum filled with priceless masterpieces, the men spent a quarter of an hour in the Short Gallery, pocketing five unpolished Degas sketches. The works are haphazard doodles; the two versions of the *Program for an Artistic Soiree* depict nothing more than a few barely imagined faces and legs. And it didn't seem that the thieves swiped the works out of a powerful interest in Degas either: Because if the museum crooks felt such a passion for the French Impressionist painter, why didn't they pilfer the stunning *Portrait of Joséphine Gaujelin* in the Yellow Room? The men were only about fifty feet from the canvas when they stole the Manet from the Blue Room.

The thieves also swiped a small Chinese beaker, or ku. The artifact dates back to the Shang Dynasty and was meant to hold wine during religious ceremonies. But if the intruders were looking for breathtaking Chinese artifacts, why didn't they also pocket the rare tomb figures that sat right in front of the Govaert Flinck? They must have literally touched the small, lustrous animal-like figures when they lifted the Dutch painting from its setting. The most confounding larceny, however, was the finial. While the intruders were a short distance away from one of the most valuable works in the country, Titian's *Europa*, and no more than twenty feet from a Botticelli and two Raphaels, they clambered on top of a cabinet and ripped a bronze trinket from the top of a French Army flag. Similar items sell on eBay for as low as $10.

The men were not expert art thieves. Smith was sure of that. A high school art student would know that slashing a four-hundred-year-old painting from its frame could destroy the work. An Old Master painting is as dry and brittle as a potato chip, and if it's removed from its setting, the canvas can bend and buckle and crack, the paint peeling off in thick flakes like dried glue. The thieves did not seem to research their targets either, and most investigators believe that the intruders thought that the Flinck was actually a Rembrandt. When Isabella Stewart Gardner purchased the landscape in 1900, she also believed the work was a Rembrandt. So did Berenson, who wrote, that it was "beyond question the finest of [Rembrandt's] landscapes." But Govaert Flinck, one of Rembrandt's apprentices, created the painting. A Harvard University grad student Cynthia Schneider made the discovery a few years before the heist, uncovering evidence that Rembrandt's signature had been forged by a nineteenth-century art dealer. But at the time of the robbery, the change in attribution had not been widely discussed, and some visitor guides still identified the landscape as by the Dutch Old Master.

The Gardner crooks must have believed that *A Lady and Gentleman in Black* was a Rembrandt too. But it turns out that the painting also may have been created by someone in his workshop. The Rembrandt Research Project de-attributed the work in 1987, noting that some of the details looked flat and lifeless, essentially un-Rembrandtian. Other experts—then and now—argue that Rembrandt did in fact create the painting. They point out that Rembrandt was twenty-six at the time, and there was no evidence that he had a workshop at such an early age, certainly not one capable of producing a painting with such psychological depth. Today, the Gardner itself takes a position somewhere in the middle; they concede that Rembrandt's students played a large role in creating the work. "If I had to answer, I would say it's by his workshop, and maybe Rembrandt did some of the arrangement," head curator Alan Chong told me.

While the intruders were not professional art thieves, they showed larcenous expertise. They didn't brandish handguns or scream at the guards or appear edgy like a first-timer might. Instead, they subdued the night watchmen with a bold confidence, waiting patiently until both men were in front of the control desk before pushing them against the wall and expertly snapping handcuffs over their wrists. The thieves also appear to have made detailed preparations for the heist. They wore fake mustaches, dressed themselves in authentic-looking police uniforms, and landed inside information about the museum's security system. "Thieves are generally faster than greyhounds, but it would appear that these thieves knew, even before they entered the museum, that they had plenty of time and apparently they did not hurry," Smith once noted in a letter. This "would lead me to feel that their confidence was due to intimate knowledge of all systems and procedures."

The intruders also seem to have tested the museum's defenses like criminal professionals would. A few weeks before the heist, a guard was sitting at the control desk, watching the video monitor, when he saw a group of men roughing up a young man outside of the side entrance of the museum. The young man pounded on the door and screamed for help. "*Let me in!*" the young man pleaded. The guard called the police, but before they arrived, the group—including the young man—piled into a car and sped off. Most investigators now believe that the incident was a practice run. "If we're honest, we don't really know," Smith explained. "But the actual thieves to me sound like down-to-earth bur- glars."

Much later, when I had finally dug deep into the case, it would be these clues that would help me unravel one of the most important mys- teries of the Gardner heist.

6. LANDSCAPE WITH AN OBELISK

Something That Big

SMITH TOURED ME through the rest of the Jewish Museum. Despite the theft of the Chagall, he believed that the museum was one of the most well protected art institutions in the country, and he wanted to show me how a gallery could expertly defend itself against theft. At the front entrance, he explained that every visitor needed to pass through a metal detector and that the guards used X-ray machines to search for guns and explosives as well as other weapons that could be used to damage a canvas, such as a sharpened stick or a vial of acid. Inside the galleries, security guards stationed themselves at the entrance of every room, and cameras hung prominently from the ceiling, scanning for signs of trouble. "People need to know that they're constantly being watched," Smith told me. "That's very important."

Downstairs, Smith led me to the museum's control room. It was at the end of a drab alley, behind a thick steel door, far away from the sight of any visitors. Two security officers sat inside the small space, studying the feeds from the video cameras and motion detectors. If the watchmen saw anything suspicious, they could communicate with the guards inside the galleries via two-way radios or ring a panic button that would call in the police. Even the control room itself was protected. To prevent a gunman from hijacking the museum, plates of bulletproof glass enclosed the space and the door could be opened only from the inside. "This place is top of the line," Smith said proudly.

The Jewish Museum's art was not absolutely secure—the theft of the Chagall had occurred just three years before. But a museum could never fully protect itself from a robbery, it couldn't stash its artworks in an underground vault or put up barbed wire like a jail. Museums were, after all, museums. The issue, Smith explained, was that there was a conflict at the core of any effort to display art. On one side, there were the curators and museum supporters, people who want to offer an intimate, nose-to-the-canvas experience. On the other side were the security and screening personnel, people like Smith, tough-minded realists who wanted to put paintings and sculptures behind three-inch glass shields and hair-trigger alarms.

For the most part, the curators win out as accessible art exhibitions garner positive reviews, while meticulous security measures bring complaints. After a thief stole Edvard Munch's masterpiece *The Scream* and left behind a note that said "Thank you for the poor security," the Munch Museum in Oslo turned their galleries into an artworld Fort Knox, with armed guards, a labyrinth lobby, and massive steel doors that snapped shut at a moment's notice. The press dubbed the building Fortress Munch, and visitors grumbled that the experience was cold and austere, that they could no longer appreciate the brushstrokes of the Norwegian painter's masterpieces because of the bulletproof glass that shielded the canvases.

But few institutions are as well protected as the Jewish or Munch museums—and most don't have half as much security. An institution's alarm system will not send a direct signal to the police or there will not be a breaker alarm on the windows or the guards will be poorly trained. Sometimes the institutions will lack all of the above. In 2003, a man slipped into the Kunsthistorisches Museum in Vienna by clambering up some scaffolding and smashing open a second-floor window. The thief had gone out drinking that evening, and investigators later described the heist as a boozy, spur-of-the-moment robbery. Inside the museum, the thief cracked open a display case and nabbed a rare Cellini masterpiece worth more than $5 million, and while a motion detector went off, none of the three security guards working that night bothered to check the room. The heist was discovered the following morning by a cleaning lady.

Some museums have such little protection that they get robbed time and again. Early one morning in 2002, a gang of criminals rammed a Mitsubishi off-roader through a ground-floor window of the Russborough House. Owned by diamond heir Alfred Beit, the Palladian mansion stretched the length of two football fields in County Wicklow, Ireland and contained one of the largest private art collections in Europe. The intruders ran inside, snatched five paintings including two world-famous Rubens, and disappeared in a getaway car. While the heist was over in less than two minutes, the thieves didn't need to rush. The security system consisted of an alarm that rang in the local police station more than two miles away and an elderly caretaker who was in another wing of the house. And although it was the fourth heist of the mansion in three decades, the Russborough artworks are not considered the most frequently stolen. That dubious award goes to Rembrandt's *Portrait of Jacob de Gheyn III*. The painting has been nabbed four times from the Dulwich Picture Gallery in London and earned the appellation the "takeaway Rembrandt."

Museums neglect security for all sorts of reasons. Lack of foresight, lack of imagination, lack of vigor, and even the world's most prestigious museums suffer from a lack of resources. Over the past few decades, governments have reduced or eliminated subsidies. Private institutions have come to rely entirely on the fickle ways of fund-raising. Budget problems have become so severe that many institutions have limited services or darkened galleries. In 2003 the most popular museum in Britain, the Tate Modern, displayed a notice in the bathroom thanking a donor for paying for the toilet paper. The sign, to be clear, wasn't a wry comment on modern art—an anonymous benefactor had stepped forward to help buy some extra two-ply. In 2006 the Milwaukee Public Museum nearly went bankrupt, buried under more than $25 million in debt. In 2007 the Denver Museum of Art reported a deficit of more than $4 million and had to fire more than two hundred employees.

At the same time, the cost of security is going up. A full roster of guards can eat up half of a museum's operating budget and that doesn't include infrastructure costs such as video cameras, motion detectors, and electronic keys. A small institution like the Jewish Museum will spend more than $1 million a year on security services. Since 2001 the Smithsonian has increased its security budget by more than $30 million, and the museum now shells out almost $70 million a year for its team of five hundred guards. But even that money might not be enough. A recent government report found that the Smithsonian did not have enough guards to respond to alarms or cover entrances, and in November 2006 someone managed to swipe some mammalian fossils from one of the galleries.

Guards are often a weak point. Museums don't provide much in terms of training—usually just a week-long introductory session—and the salaries are painfully low. Most institutions pay just a dollar or two more than a burger-flipper at McDonald's. Guards also give the position short shrift, and the FBI estimates that more than 80 percent of all museum heists have an inside angle. A guard might provide a thief with a detailed description of the alarm system, or the night watchman will pocket a woodcut while working late one evening. In August 2001 a group of thugs sneaked into the home of Spanish building magnate Esther Koplowitz and swiped nineteen paintings worth more than $65 million, including Goya's masterwork *The Swing*. It was the largest art theft in the history of Spain—and it turned out that the guard let the intruders into the home in exchange for some cash and a few nights with a prostitute.

Still, museums could do more with what they have, and when Smith ran security checks as part of his underwriting efforts, he often recommended reforms. Some were as straightforward as regularly checking the walls to make sure no one had replaced an original de Kooning or O'Keeffe with a copy. Other improvements were expensive and high-tech. Smith advocated securing valuable paintings with hidden, wireless alarms that could track the work if it was taken from the building. But Smith often found that the biggest problem was not the technology or the guards or even the alarms, but the fact that galleries didn't really believe they would ever get robbed. "Museums often think that they're protected by that art mystique," he told me, "but it's often the reverse that's true. Thieves steal art because it's easy."

I CAME ACROSS widely different accounts of the security of the Gardner at the time of the heist. Some told me that the institution barely had any protection against theft, that the museum was as secure as a rural hunting cabin. Others claimed that the Gardner's security system was solid, state-of-the-art, that the thieves had figured out the institution's only weak point, and so I contacted Jim Kern. He had been a guard at the museum for years, and on the night of the theft, he had worked the second shift, signing out for the evening just a few hours before the thieves slipped inside the building.

Kern lived in Chicago, and early one evening I rang the bell of his small row house. I waited for a moment at the door until I heard him bounding down the stairs, yelling "*UB*" like we were old college friends. In his mid-thirties, tall and broad shouldered, he wore ripped jeans and a shirt that hung open over a white tank top. His blond hair was razored short, a pair of mischievous eyes stared out from behind a pair of rimless glasses. "You should know that this house is a total mess," he said, inviting me into a foyer piled high with winter coats, bicycle wheels, and old soda bottles. "I bought this place recently and my full-time job right now is fixing it up."

I followed Kern up a set of stairs and into what he called the living room. It looked more like a construction site. There was no drywall, just exposed wood studs, and in the middle of the floor was a large, sloping heap of construction materials, buckets of paint, boxes of screws, two-by-fours, a porcelain toilet. A small paint-speckled transistor radio was perched on top of a crate, squawking out a basketball game. "So you want to see the paintings?"

"The Gardner paintings?"

Kern nodded, looking over the top of his glasses like a third-grade teacher staring down the class prankster. "I'm serious, man," he said.

Kern opened up a door to a back room, stacked with more building materials along with mounds of clothes, piles of magazines, a computer, a mattress, and the complete twenty-volume set of the encyclopedia of the Ukraine. Along the far wall, next to the corner, was a built-in bookcase, empty except for a Mr. T. bobblehead doll. Kern reached into the shelf and shifted the bobblehead to the side. The whole bookcase swung toward us.

"It's a fake," he explained. "I built it myself. Hinges, shelves, everything. Nice, huh? And, of course, a good place to hide the paintings."

Kern stepped into the small walk-in closet, mumbling "Gardner paintings, Gardner paintings" as if he had accidentally misplaced them earlier that afternoon. Then he reached up on a shelf, felt around for a moment, and brought down a small canvas. It was a Modernist work, a swirl of dark yellows and browns, and looked like a college art student had painted it. "You think . . ."

Kern had ordered Asian take-out for both of us, and I ate a spicy mango salad on a turned-over plastic bucket, as Kern told me about his experience working at the Gardner. He was nineteen years old and had just graduated from high school. He was playing drums in a heavy metal band and lived in Roxbury, not far from the museum. Like the other guards, he earned $6.85 an hour, a little more than two dollars over minimum wage. "Back then, I thought that it was great money," he said. "The museum didn't ask for much. They wanted someone who was not an idiot, who would be friendly, and do what was asked of them, which was to go to work on time and take the job seriously."

Kern usually worked the third shift, which went from midnight until 8 a.m. the next morning. "You walked around. You looked for leaks. That was the thing that I was most worried about, that there would be a leak that would damage something," he explained. "If something out of the ordinary was going on, you were supposed to notice. But nothing out of the ordinary ever happened."

"Did you have any previous experience? I mean as a guard?"

Kern gave a dramatic frown, as if he thought my question was the stupidest thing that anyone had ever asked him.

"But didn't you worry about a robbery?"

"Never thought about it. That wasn't the museum's concern. No one ever thought that would happen. I mean no one."

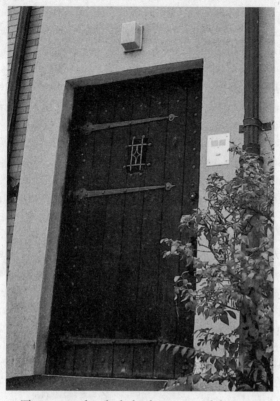

The entrance by which the thieves entered the museum.

"What about letting people inside?" I asked. "Did you have instructions about that sort of thing?"

"Nothing," Kern said, "and people occasionally came in. If a friend came to visit you at 11:30 at night, you wouldn't make them wait outside. They came inside. So did the pizza deliveryman. We knew him. I personally went there at 3 in the morning once just to play cribbage with another guard."

"And what about these rumors about people smoking pot and drinking on the job?"

"It happened," Kern said. "I mean there was nothing in the job description that prevented you from doing your job high."

"Didn't that strike you as unusual?" I asked. "I mean there were multi-million-dollar paintings in there. Shouldn't everyone have taken security seriously? Made sure to protect the works?"

Kern looked at me. "From hindsight, of course, the security seemed crude. We know now that the guards were vulnerable. But at the time, it seemed adequate. It was a small museum with limited resources. What did you expect?"

I did expect the security to be tighter—at the time thieves were raiding Boston area museums and galleries with vicious regularity. One afternoon in February 1989, two men strolled into the first-floor gallery of the Boston Museum of Fine Arts—right across the street from the Gardner—and lifted a fourteenth-century Chinese Yuan Dynasty vase out of a vitrine. Later that spring, a man stuck a pistol into the ribs of the store manager of the Arvest Galleries on Newbury Street and stole ten paintings worth tens of thousands of dollars. In the year leading up to the heist, criminals also robbed the Block Gallery, a museum in Yarmouth, and at least a half-dozen private homes. Thieves snatched artworks with such violent consistency that the *Globe* ran a 6,000-word article in the winter of 1989 warning readers of the trend. HOT ART: WITH PICASSOS GOING FOR $38 MILLION, ART THEFT HAS BECOME A BOOMING BILLION-DOLLAR ILLEGAL BUSINESS, SECOND ONLY TO NARCOTICS, read the headline.

The Gardner had also been robbed before. In 1970 a man threw a bag of lightbulbs onto the floor of the Dutch Room, and in the ensuing confusion, he pocketed the tiny Rembrandt self-portrait hanging next to the door. The thief was never caught, but the etching was eventually returned by an art dealer who said that he had recovered it from an underworld figure. In 1982 investigators believed that they uncovered a plot by mob associate Ralph Rossetti to steal a Matisse and a half-dozen other paintings from the Gardner. According to law enforcement, Rossetti and an associate planned to throw a grenade into the courtyard of the museum and then swipe the paintings as visitors ran for the door. The attack never occurred because police arrested Rossetti in connection with an unrelated art theft, the heist of twenty-three paintings from a Newton, Massachusetts home.

So why hadn't the museum learned from all these capers? I called the former director of security, Lyle Grindle. A stocky man with the wide shoulders of a lumberjack, Grindle had worked for the museum for more then twenty years, and when we met for coffee one morning, he confirmed the basics of Kern's account in his no-nonsense Maine accent. "Back then security was not taken seriously. We were not as protected or as secure as we could have been. There just wasn't a sense that we had to protect the museum from theft. I mean no one thought that something that big could even occur."

The Gardner was not any more vulnerable than other art institutions in the area. The museum hired Grindle in 1981 to improve security, and he brought the institution's defenses up to basic industry standards. He installed closed-circuit cameras at the entrances, placed motion detectors in all of the galleries, and built up the team of security officers from twenty-five to more than forty. The board gave him the money to do this, Grindle said, because of the threat of the 1982 raid, and when independent security consultant Steven Keller reviewed the museum's defenses in the summer of 1988, he did not list any major issues in his final report. "They had a pretty good operation for that time and place," Keller told me. "There was nothing in the security of that museum that was particularly bad."

Still, the Gardner lacked some key defenses, and when Smith toured the museum shortly after the heist, he noted that the watch room wasn't enclosed, the side entrance didn't have a protective, second door, the phone lines didn't appear to be secured. Keller had suggested similar improvements in his 1988 review, and while some of the reforms were included in a renovation plan, the initiative had not been implemented due to lack of funds. Looking back now, Grindle wishes that he had lobbied harder for those security upgrades. "I don't know if the thieves would have been able to get the guard out of the room if there had been a glass wall there, protecting the guard in the watch desk," he said.

But ultimately the museum's biggest vulnerability was the guards, and I asked Grindle: Why did he hire people as quirky and irreverent as Kern? Why so many oddball musicians? And why did he ever sign on Ray Abell, the guard who worked the night of the theft? By many accounts, Abell was an oddball character. He would come into work looking like a Mötley Crüe groupie, wearing flashy hats, loud T-shirts, his curly hair hanging down his back in a long pony tail. Grindle tossed his hands and admitted that the theft would not have occurred if Abell had followed policy. "We had instructed the guards not to let anyone in. There was a rule book that said that," he told me. "But I had to fight to get a salary for the guards that was $4 an hour. That was in 1981. And even then, you just couldn't find quality people who would work for a few dollars above minimum wage. I mean to get someone to walk around a spooky building all night long was tough."

Grindle told me that he pushed for higher guard salaries so that he could be more selective, but the board of trustees, Grindle said, denied the request. "The trustees kept telling me, 'we don't have the money', and I could see that times were tight, so I let it go." While Grindle might have done more to mitigate the role of the guards—he could have installed dead man's switches, an inexpensive device that guards have to ring to show that they're at their stations—it is clear that the museum was in severe financial trouble. When Isabella Stewart Gardner died, she left the institution with $3.6 million, and for decades the money was more than sufficient and the board would often distribute budget surpluses to local charities.

But by 1984, rising management costs required greater revenues than the endowment provided, and the museum began to run in the red. The financials grew worse over the following years, and by 1988, the endowment yielded only $1.3 million toward the $2.8 million in operating costs. In theory, other sources of cash—fund-raising, grants—could have made up the difference. But they didn't come close and in 1988, there was a deficit of more than $140,000. The financial situation became so bleak that trustees put off basic building maintenance—and the museum began to take on the appearance of an abandoned army garrison. "The physical condition of the Gardner Museum is frail," wrote Thomas Hoving, former director of the Metropolitan Museum of Art, in July 1990. "The skylight is leaking in the court; the walls are stained; the lighting is atrocious; some works of art are sitting in direct sunlight; there is no air conditioning."

The problem was that the trustees seemed to believe that Gardner's endowment would carry the museum forever, that they didn't need to pay close attention to the institution's financials. "The board members back then tended to be somewhat innocent," said Arnold Hiatt, who joined the board in 1988 and now serves as a lifetime trustee. "They were all really wonderful gentlemen, and I mean exactly that, gentlemen. They hadn't worked in corporations or had any business skills." By the mid-1980s the trustees had recognized the severity of the situation and fired director Rollin "Bump" Hadley and expanded the board to bring on people with business skills, like Hiatt, who was the CEO of the Stride Rite Corporation. The board also developed a detailed renovation plan, organized a massive membership drive, and hired Anne Hawley as the new director. A strong fund-raiser, Hawley had headed the Massachusetts Council on the Arts and Humanities and immediately made a slew of decisive changes. She cut programs, revamped staff, requested a full security review, but it was too little, too late. Before I left Kern's Chicago row house, I asked him if he remembered anything unusual about the night of the theft.

"Nothing. I went to work and at 11:30, I left," he said, "and when I came into work the next day, the museum had been robbed."

"Nothing strange?"

Kern laughed.

"Nothing at all?

"Zero."

7. KU

Unfinished Business

ON MARCH 18, 1990, at around 6:45 a.m., Edgar Queens-bury arrived at the side entrance of the Gardner museum. It was a cool and cloudy Sunday morning, the streets still wet with the rain that had fallen the night before. The sun had risen over the Fenway an hour earlier and most of the city remained in bed, hugging their pillows, sleeping off their Saint Patrick's Day hangovers. Queensbury was the museum's maintenance man, and he buzzed the call box, waiting to be let inside. There was no answer. He rang again. Kelly Sanmarino, the daytime guard, showed up just after Queensbury, and they began tapping on the windows trying to rouse the guards inside. Had something gone wrong? Where were the night-shift guards? Sanmarino hurried across the street to a Northeastern University dormitory, where she found a phone and called her supervisor, Fred O'Shea. He arrived some ten minutes later and opened the side door with a master key. The three slowly walked inside. It was quiet. The halls were dark. No one was at the watch desk.

O'Shea called 911, and the news sputtered over the police radio. "B and E in progress, 280 the Fenway." At that moment, Boston Police detective Paul Crossen was pulling off the Southeast Expressway. He turned around and sped toward the museum, along with a half-dozen other squad cars. Crossen arrived at the Gardner within minutes,

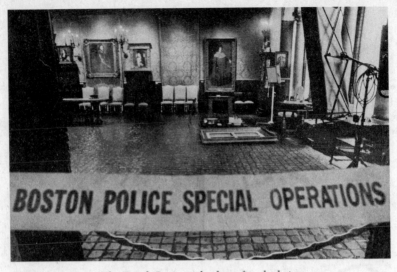

The Dutch Room in the days after the heist.

secured the main doors, and then took a team of officers up to the fourth floor to search the scene. He still wasn't sure what had happened. Were the intruders still inside? Could there be a bomb?

Room by room, Crossen and his team moved through the galleries. Their guns drawn, they rifled through closets, looked behind large pieces of furniture. Two police dogs accompanied the search group, and they scampered through the galleries, their claws scratching loudly on the wooden floors. More than twenty minutes passed before the police reached the basement. One detective found security guard Ralph Helman near the stairs. Another discovered Ray Abell under the boiler pipe. Both guards were still bound with duct tape.

News of the heist went out to dozens of museum and law enforcement personnel. Anne Hawley got the call from Lyle Grindle just after 8 a.m. When the beeper of FBI agent Edward Quinn went off, he was sitting in church, seven minutes into Sunday mass. Karen Haas, Gardner's acting curator, was already on her way to the museum that morning. She was hoping to have a quiet Sunday at the office. By midmorning, there were more than two dozen people on the scene, FBI agents, city police, state troopers, EMTs, bomb experts, and a fully staffed ambulance.

The museum's galleries were a sprawling mess, the floors covered with shards of glass, cracked frames, shreds of canvas. The FBI crime scene specialists snapped photographs and dusted for fingerprints and collected the only thing that remained of the Rembrandts—a few paint chips. All the evidence would eventually be bagged, tagged, and flown to the FBI crime lab in Washington. Karen Haas spent most of the day hunting the galleries, trying to figure out which of the thousands of treasures had been pilfered, and even then she wouldn't find everything. It wasn't until Tuesday afternoon that the museum announced that the intruders had swiped the finial from the top of the Napoleonic battle flag.

Over the course of the day, people congregated in front of the museum's black iron gates. Some saw the news on the television and wanted to see if there was anything they could do to help. Others hoped to spend a Sunday afternoon wandering the galleries and arrived only to find a notice taped to the front entrance: "Closed today." Whenever Princeton University graduate student Debora Schwartz came to Boston, she visited the Gardner, and when she heard about the break-in that morning, she pulled her copy of the museum's catalog from her knapsack and began flipping through its pages, searching for pictures of what had been stolen. "*The Concert* is one of the most beautiful paintings I have ever seen in my life," she explained. "I feel like someone has kicked me in the gut."

As reports of a massive museum robbery screamed over the newswires, reporters from all over the world began ringing the Gardner—Japanese television, German radio, Norwegian newspapers. One theft press conference had so many attendees that journalists stood in the street to hear the latest news. Almost all the resulting articles noted that the museum did not have insurance. It made the loss seem somehow even more tragic. A spokesperson told reporters that the museum could not afford insurance, that a policy would have cost $3 million, a price tag well beyond the institution's $2.8 million budget. The museum also pointed out that Gardner's will forbade new purchases, and so even if the museum had had insurance, they would not have been able to buy replacement artworks. It turned out, though, that the Gardner could have landed a policy. Art institutions rarely underwrite their entire collection. Even the most skilled burglar would find it impossible to cart away an entire building's worth of art, and depending on policy details, a museum like the Gardner could have found $10 million in theft coverage for $10,000 to $50,000 a year.

Whatever the case, the lack of insurance left the museum without key recovery tools. They didn't have an insurance adjuster, someone like Harold Smith, who could help investigate the case. More importantly, they didn't have the deep pockets of an underwriter who could immediately offer a large reward for the stolen masterpieces. In the hours following the heist, board member Arnold Hiatt frantically solicited the top auction houses, Sotheby's and Christie's, for their help in setting up a bounty for the paintings, and within three days of the robbery, Anne Hawley stood in front of Sargent's *El Jaleo* and announced a $1 million reward for any information leading to the safe return of the stolen treasures. The money would be paid, "no questions asked."

WHEN FBI AGENT DAN FALZON'S PAGER BUZZED with the news of the Gardner heist, he was in his Beacon Hill studio. He was twenty-six, single, and so dedicated to the job that he lived a half mile from the office in order to get into work each morning before seven. Falzon had grown up in San Francisco, where his father, Frank Falzon, was one of the city's best-known police officers, the detective who bagged infamous serial killer Richard Ramirez. After college, Falzon followed his father into the San Francisco police department and landed a job as a beat cop. But Falzon dreamed of working big cases—he had helped Falzon Senior on the Ramirez investigation—and so he took a pay cut and joined the FBI. Boston was his first assignment. He earned $30,000 a year.

When Falzon arrived at the Gardner that morning, he knew almost nothing about the museum or art or Isabella Stewart Gardner. On the rare weekends that he wasn't working, he spent time at football games, not with Vermeers. But Falzon had successfully cracked a major art theft case before. In his first big assignment for the bureau, he recovered two Old Master canvases and collared art thief Myles Connor in an elaborate sting, and so early on that wet Sunday morning, the FBI gave him the Gardner caper. "I took the case very personally. After walking through the museum, it's hard not to," Falzon told me, "and it soon took over my life."

Falzon and his team of nearly thirty FBI agents chased down thousands of leads in the days after the theft. They talked to hundreds of suspects. They spoke to dozens of witnesses. They put up roadblocks outside of the museum to see if they could find any bystanders. They interviewed all of the Gardner's staff. They reviewed old employment records. They searched for anyone who might have had a connection to the thieves, electricians, carpenters, paint restorers, ticket takers. They flew to Canada, they flew to Mexico. They made several trips to Europe. They once tracked down a catering company that had delivered canapés for a party. "I didn't know a clock," Falzon told me. "I went to work, and I came home and ate and worked out and went back.

FBI sketches of the two Gardner suspects with and without fake mustaches.

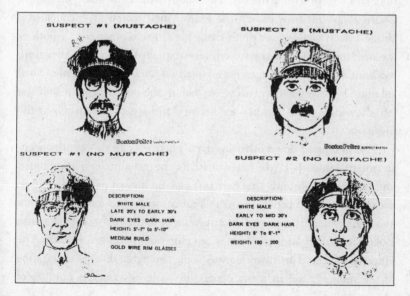

I lived that case. And it wasn't like I was dragging my ass. I wanted the case. I was young and lean, and I thought we had the will to win it, and, really, there were so many days that I thought, tomorrow will be the day that I find that critical piece of information, tomorrow we will solve this thing."

At first Falzon was almost certain that the guards were involved. While night watchman Ray Abell told police that he saw the intruders pull up alongside the museum's side entrance at around 1 a.m., a witness outside the museum said that the thieves had been sitting in a car for more than twenty minutes. The intruders were also curiously considerate to the guards, and when they trussed Abell to a steam pipe in the basement, the thieves placed his cowboy hat and wallet beside him, ready for him to retrieve the next day. But the most disquieting fact was that Abell was the last guard to do a complete set of rounds and go past the Blue Room, and a review of the motion detector data showed that the thieves never stepped into that particular gallery. Had he perhaps stolen that painting?

Falzon interviewed both guards repeatedly, making them walk through the heist again and again. He investigated their backgrounds, their links to potential thieves. He required them to take polygraphs. Guard Ralph Helman passed the exam; Abell scored an inconclusive. While Falzon could never quite shake his suspicion that one or both of the men might have been involved, he eventually decided that they were too bumbling, too foolish, to have pulled off such a major crime. Abell submitted his resignation two weeks before the heist; Helman quit the job a few days later. Neither are believed to have ever returned to the museum.

Falzon chased down other insiders. There was an ex-Gardner security guard named Jeff, who had worked for the museum for a few months and resigned so abruptly that he didn't pick up his last paycheck. Falzon eventually tracked the ex-guard to France, where he interviewed him and determined that he had no involvement in the robbery. Falzon also looked into the Gardner's former director Rollin "Bump" Hadley. The Harvard-educated art historian was going through a divorce at the time of the robbery, and in court papers, his wife described a number of questionable behaviors, like closing joint checking accounts and selling off rare books without telling her. But Falzon never found anything that directly connected Hadley to the thieves.

For a long time, Falzon believed that the intruders may have stolen the Gardner paintings hoping for a ransom. The theory would explain why the intruders pocketed smaller items like the finial and the Chinese ku—the pint-sized artifacts would be an easy way to show proof of possession. But the idea, like so many others, seemed to fade as the months passed by and no one heard from the thieves. Then, months into the case, Falzon received a tip about Gerry Kaplan, an ex-con with mob connections. Kaplan had flown from San Diego to Boston three days before the heist and left the day after. He had owned an antiques store for years ("I specialized in erotic art," he told me) and had been involved in other art thefts, once writing a bad check to buy a canvas from an unsuspecting dealer. But Kaplan denied any involvement. He claimed that he had flown into Boston that week to visit an old girl-friend and had an alibi for the night of the heist, and after an FBI wire-tap and two polygraph exams, he appeared to be all but removed from the suspect list.

Many of the leads flooding into Falzon's office confused copies of the stolen art for the real thing. On one occasion, a man was walking his dog in Charlestown and saw what appeared to be *The Concert* hanging on a neighbor's wall. He called the FBI, and the next day, an agent visited the house along with a museum curator. While the group was standing outside the home, staring into the window, the owner came out the front door. "Can I help you folks out?" she asked. After the agent told her about the tip, she let them inside—the painting was nothing more than a high-quality print. In 1992, two women teaching English in Japan were invited into the house of one of their students, an eccentric Japanese art collector, who claimed to own *The Storm*. When the women returned to the States, they told the FBI about the canvas. It took six months of diplomatic wrangling, but eventually Fal-zon and a Gardner curator flew to Japan on the first American search warrant ever issued in that country. They entered the man's house with a half-dozen Japanese agents, but within a moment of eyeballing the painting, even Falzon could tell that it was a crude draw-by-numbers imitation.

Not everyone was happy with the investigation, and some thought that the case did not seem to be a priority for the bureau. Hawley saw the signs on the first day when she heard that Falzon would be the lead case agent. "He was new and very green," she told me, "and I still wonder why the FBI didn't have the capacity to assign a senior-level person. Why didn't the case get immediate and high-level attention?" And at times Falzon did struggle to get all the help that he needed. When he tried to consult with Mireille Ballestrazzi, chief of the French government's art theft squad, an overseas legal attaché complained that he had not gone through proper channels, and when Falzon asked state and local police for assistance, he was also rebuffed. "If I had done anything differently, I would have attempted to initiate a task force between federal, state, and local officials, because we really did not have enough help from either state or local law enforcement," Falzon told me. "It was kind of like, 'OK, FBI, this is your ball. You run with it.' In a theft of that magnitude, you really need to work it from every angle."

Still, Falzon continued to work the case, and then, after almost four years, he thought he had finally landed his big lead. One afternoon, a plain, white envelope arrived at the museum, and inside was a typed letter that said that the writer could facilitate the return of the paintings if he received $2.6 million and full immunity. The letter writer seemed to show detailed knowledge of the art and suggested a way for the museum to respond to his proposal. If the Gardner was open to a deal, it should send a signal by arranging to have the *Boston Globe* publish the numeral "1" in the U.S.-foreign dollar exchange listing for the Italian lira. The newspaper printed the numeral, and the following week the letter writer sent a second note. While he praised the museum for being open to an exchange, he worried about the extensive law enforcement response. He asked if the museum wanted to get the paintings or arrest a low-level intermediary. "YOU CANNOT HAVE BOTH," he wrote. But the writer never sent another letter. Gardner officials now suspect that it was just another hoax.

MOST CRIMINAL INVESTIGATIONS grind to a halt because of a lack of leads. That never happened with the Gardner case. Because of the size of the reward, the hype surrounding the theft, new tips continued to trickle into the FBI every day. But the investigation lacked something important, and that was strong physical evidence. After FBI agents searched the museum, dusted for fingerprints, interviewed all the witnesses, investigators still knew almost nothing about the thieves. The intruders didn't leave behind any footprints or cigarette butts, and while the forensic team managed to pull about a dozen latent fingerprints from the frames, they were never confident that the impressions were those of the thieves since so many different people had handled the paintings before the heist. "I have never heard of another case on the magnitude of the Gardner where you didn't have a single concrete piece of evidence. Really, even still to his day, I don't even know if the thieves wore gloves or not. I mean that's a major thing not to know," Falzon told me. "And without physical sources, anyone in the whole world can be a suspect. You, me, someone walking down the street."

With so few parameters, investigators often found it hard to focus their efforts, and Lyle Grindle recalls the FBI asking him to escort psychics through the museum. Most of the paranormals could be dismissed outright, like the man who said that the art was in a pueblo somewhere in South America or the woman who claimed that the paintings had been plastered behind the brick walls of the museum. But sometimes Grindle would actually run down the tips. When a woman told him that she had seen a vision of Isabella Stewart Gardner who told her that the paintings were in the ceiling of the conservation lab, he got out a ladder and checked it out. "We were at a point, I guess, where we would try anything," he told me.

The lack of physical evidence also made it hard to definitively rule out suspects, and Falzon could never shake his belief that Brian McDevitt may have had a role in the heist. A Boston native, McDevitt was a skilled thief and conman. While working at the Jerry Brown campaign headquarters in Boston, he swiped the personal papers of various VIPs, including those of Congressman Edward Markey, and used the documents to steal more than $160,000 in cash and bonds from area safe deposit boxes. Then, in 1981, McDevitt tried to rob the Hyde Collection in Glens Falls, New York. He bungled the heist: After he and an accomplice kidnapped a FedEx driver, they got stuck in traffic and arrived at the gallery after it closed for the evening. But the case drew the attention of investigators because of the parallels between the Hyde attempt and the Gardner robbery. As part of the Hyde caper, McDevitt dressed up as a FedEx employee in order to gain access to the museum. The Gardner thieves had passed themselves off as cops. In the Hyde theft, McDevitt had carried handcuffs and duct tape in order to tie up the guards. So did the Gardner thieves. McDevitt had told police that he planned to swipe a Rembrandt from the Hyde; three Rembrandts were pocketed from the Gardner.

The FBI interviewed McDevitt for the first time in late 1990. He was living in Los Angeles and trying to pass himself off as a famous author who was writing a screenplay about art theft. But McDevitt denied any involvement. He said that he didn't look like the Gardner thieves, that he had a red beard at the time of the heist, and when the FBI ran his fingerprints, they didn't match those recovered at the scene. Still, McDevitt refused to take a polygraph, and just as Falzon began to press him on the robbery, one of his former associates died of a drug overdose. Was someone murdered over the case? McDevitt died in 2004, and while Falzon's gut told him that the thief was a long shot, the agent could never be sure.

The FBI transferred Falzon to San Francisco in the summer of 1996, but the Gardner case proved difficult to let go. For years after the move he would call the Boston office almost every day to learn about new developments. He would often run down fresh tips and leads. Today, at forty-seven, Falzon has a wife and three daughters. He lives about an hour north of San Francisco and spends most of his days thinking about how to defend the country against terrorism. He told me that the Gardner investigation was now behind him—or almost all behind him. While we were talking on the phone one morning, Falzon told me that he was looking up at a copy of *The Concert*. His colleagues from the Boston field office had given him a print of the painting, and he always kept it over his desk. "I recently relocated my office from the twelfth floor to the thirteenth floor of our building and the painting came with me," Falzon told me. "Where I go, the painting goes and serves as a reminder of unfinished business."

THE FBI'S BEST OPPORTUNITY to recover the Gardner paintings may have been early on the morning of February 7, 1999. It was just after 6:30 a.m., and the streets of Boston were black and cold. As the sun slowly broke through the clouds, a red Honda Accord circled a Dorchester mob hangout called TRC Auto and Electric. David Turner sat in the passenger seat, Stephen Rossetti drove, and for a number of long minutes, the two men anxiously lapped the repair shop, peering out into the twilight, gazing at the old brick building and its surrounding streets of aging warehouses and shot-and-a-Bud taverns.

Turner and Rossetti were looking for their gangland captain, Carmello Merlino. He was supposed to meet them at TRC that morning, and if all went well, they hoped to rob a Loomis Fargo armored car depot of more than $50 million, staging one of the biggest bank heists in the nation's history. But Merlino was not at the auto shop. Nor was his nephew Billy. Unbeknown to Turner and Rossetti, the FBI had already arrested the two men—and a pair of agents sat in a small surveillance plane some 3,500 feet above the Honda, watching the car cruise up and down Dorchester Avenue.

Turner and Rossetti had already made one trip to TRC that morning, and when they couldn't find their associates, they drove back to Quincy, where Turner removed two black duffel bags from the trunk and placed them in his bronze Chevy Tahoe. The bags contained enough attack gear for an army assault squad, including bulletproof vests, a police scanner, face masks, five semiautomatic handguns, a Ruger mini-14 rifle—basically a scaled-down M-14—and an armed fragmentation grenade. The handheld bomb had an estimated causality radius of about fifty feet; possession of the grenade by a felon is an automatic thirty-year jail sentence.

Turner and Rossetti made one final lap around TRC, and as they drove over to Morrissey Boulevard, two GMC Suburbans roared out of a side street and rammed the Honda. A team of FBI agents pulled Turner from the car and hustled him into a downtown federal building. They locked him in an interview room and immediately began asking him about the Gardner heist. "The FBI told me that they had information from several sources that I was an actual participant in the robbery," Turner recalled. "What was said was 'Give us the paintings right now, and you can go home.'"

Years later, once Turner was in prison, his attempt on the Loomis depot foiled, I would still hear the echoes of that Sunday morning, that Turner was in fact one of the thieves that robbed the museum nearly twenty years ago.

DAVID TURNER WAS NOT BORN into a life of crime. He grew up in Braintree, a leafy, middle-class suburb a few miles south of Boston. His mother worked at a local nursing home, his father was a mechanic. Handsome, with a wide face and sloping eyes, Turner was one of the golden boys of Sagamore Street. He shoveled snow from the driveway of a housebound widow and taught neighborhood kids how to ride bicycles. He starred on the football and baseball teams, eventually landing sports scholarships to two area colleges. He loved to ski and listen to Neil Young and drive his blue 1965 Thunderbird around South Boston. He dated some of the prettiest girls at Braintree High. His friends called him "Hollywood."

Turner's life wasn't without its troubles. Early one morning in the winter of 1981, he woke up to find his father sprawled out on the kitchen floor, dead of a heart attack, and for months afterwards, he was quiet and distant and would often follow around the fathers of other children who lived on the block. In his high school yearbook, he quoted Billy Joel, "only the good die young," and even today the memory of his father's death is hazy. He can't recall the exact details. Was he twelve or thirteen when he found his father stretched out on the kitchen floor? He's not sure.

After high school, Turner joined the Marines, but he took an early discharge because of a bad back and soon returned to his mother's

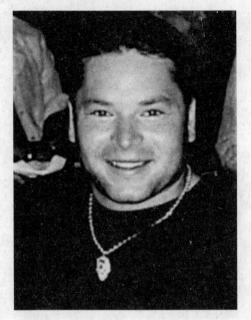

A snapshot of golden boy gangster David Turner.

house in Braintree. Hanging out at home, Turner took classes at the local community college and started spending time with a South Boston mobster named Carmello Merlino. A large man with dark eyes and a squashed boxer's nose, Merlino was a gangster's gangster. His criminal record went back decades—he earned his first arrest for armed robbery at the age of nineteen. Over the years, he had traded in illegal guns, lived on the lam, and heisted nearly half million dollars from a Brinks armored car. Even in his late sixties, receiving Social Security checks and taking insulin shots, he ran a million-dollar cocaine distribution ring.

Turner looked up to Merlino. He called him by his underworld nickname, "Mello," and would often visit the mobster's auto body shop on Dorchester Avenue to talk about cars and women and old Mafia scores. According to investigators, Turner soon began working for Merlino, picking up cocaine in carburetor boxes and hawking the drugs from rooms at the local Howard Johnson's. Turner did well at the job, say police, and before long, Merlino was sending him out on other illicit

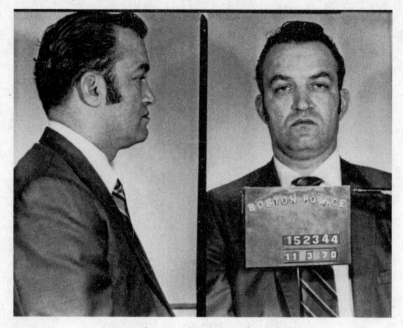

A mug shot of mobster Carmello Merlino.

errands—swiping cash from bookies, meting out thrashings to dead-beats. Turner soon started his own criminal enterprise, and Merlino's body shop grew into an underworld flea market for looted goods. "If there was something you wanted stolen, that was the place. You could go there and just put in an order, and they would have crews running all sorts of places, South Shore Malls, downtown, everywhere," retired state police officer Eddie Whelan told me.

Turner was a smart and careful criminal. He didn't go on all-weekend spending binges or buy glitzy homes. His crime scenes were clean, with-out a scrap of incriminating evidence, not a glove or a bullet casing. He always wiped down his tools to remove any last fingerprint. On a singles website, he once described himself as someone who enjoys "just having a good conversation or spending a quiet evening with those who are close to me." But Turner could be bold and ruthless, a pitiless gangster. When he discovered that Lenny DiMuzio had stolen money from him, he sprayed DiMuzio's body with bullets and then left his corpse to rot in the back of a Chevy Impala under an East Boston bridge, say investigators. Police also believe that Turner killed Steven Noon. The social worker offered Turner a ride home one summer evening, and a friend of Noon saw Turner get into his van. The next day, Noon's body was found on the side of Route 3, his face beaten so badly that it looked like a crushed orange. The van was parked a few miles from Turner's home.

The most chilling murder, though, was the death of Charlie Pappas. He was one of Turner's closest friends. They often cruised around Braintree together in Pappas's Buick; they shared an apartment together for a while. Pappas had been the one to introduce Turner to Merlino. But when police picked up Pappas on a cocaine charge, he became state's witness, fingering Turner for the DiMuzio murder, a home invasion in Canton, and a host of other crimes. Pappas might also have told police about Turner's alleged role in the Gardner theft. "We had been talking to Pappas for a few months, and we had just reached the point where he was starting to give us real information," explained former assistant attorney general Bob Sikellis. "He had a lot of other stuff that he was going to share with us."

The Pappas murder occurred the day before Thanksgiving, just a few days before Turner's trial in the Canton home invasion case. It was about nine o'clock at night, and Pappas and his fiancée, Stacey Mercon, were returning to her parents' home. Pappas had just gotten off the phone with his mother. He told her that he would soon swing past her house for some brownies, and then, as he was following Mercon up the back stairs, two men in ski masks stepped from the darkness and started shooting. Pappas was hit several times and fell to the floor, but the men continued firing as Pappas crawled toward the kitchen, smearing a long stain of blood along the inside door. Before running into a nearby playground, the killers fired one shot directly into Pappas's mouth. The bullet seemed like it carried a message—this is what happens to people who rat on David Turner.

But there was not enough evidence to make a case against Turner in the Pappas murder, and he was never charged. Nor was he ever found guilty of killing Lenny DiMuzio, or murdering Steven Noon, or sticking up the home in Canton. Police could not gather sufficient proof—and witnesses who promised to testify against Turner would be scared off or murdered. Andrea Freedman told police that the golden boy gangster had robbed her house in Canton; that Turner had charged into her home, held a gun to her head, and then left her handcuffed to a railing for more than ten hours. But then Turner's associates began threatening Freedman, and she refused to testify against him, saying that she would rather go to jail than face Turner in court. "Turner was one of the most violent criminals I ever came across," Sikellis told me. "Yet he was extremely intelligent. You could tell from the wiretaps. He could have become anything, a doctor, a lawyer. But he became a criminal, a very dangerous, singularly violent criminal."

Turner's calculated savagery—and the arrogant ease with which he escaped justice—became part of Boston underworld lore. The *Globe* dubbed him "the Teflon gangster of the South Shore," and the governor discussed the gangster during press conferences, using Turner as an example of how the state needed tougher criminal laws and a witness protection program. But Turner never backed down. He seemed to relish the role of the smart, well-mannered wiseguy, the handsome suburban thug who was always one step ahead of the law. "He loved to taunt us," Eddie Whelan recalled. "If you ever brought him in for questioning, he would sit and make small talk for hours. He wouldn't say anything about the crime, of course, but he'd have this glint in his eye, this laugh, and you knew that he knew."

TURNER'S NAME CAME UP EARLY in the Gardner investigation. "Source information of unknown reliability has recently surfaced suggesting that aforementioned subjects PAPPAS and TURNER were involved in the Gardner Museum Robbery," read an internal FBI memo from June 1992. "According to source, who is twice removed, TURNER is claiming access to the stolen paintings." The FBI also requested that the fingerprints of Turner and Pappas be compared against those found on the empty frames. The results were negative, although that didn't mean much to investigators since they never got a clean set of prints anyway.

More evidence of Turner's potential involvement in the Gardner robbery appeared when Carmello Merlino was picked up on a drug charge in 1992, and through an intermediary, he offered to return the paintings for a reduced prison sentence. He told prosecutors that the masterpieces were "very big and international," that the deal had to be kept quiet or he would be killed. But Merlino never offered any hard evidence of the lost art, and his lawyer soon began talking about trading in a different stolen canvas, namely a Colonial-era profile of George Washington that had been pilfered from the Henry Wadsworth Longfellow Museum in Cambridge. Ultimately, the feds passed on the Longfellow canvas—and Merlino was found guilty of the drug charge. And while Merlino's offer of the Gardner paintings was soon forgotten, no one really thought that the mobster was all bluff. A few years later, a confidential informant returned the Longfellow painting in exchange for $9,000.

Turner remained a top suspect, and when FBI agent Neil Cronin took over the Gardner investigation, he zeroed in on the gangster. Cronin would tail him around South Boston and eventually developed a source within Merlino's crew, a mob associate named Richard "Fat Man" Chicofsky. Chicofsky's moniker no doubt derived from his size—besides for being short and bald, he was titanically fat. Chicofsky had known Merlino for years, and they would often meet at Merlino's repair shop to discuss underworld happenings. Cronin interviewed Chicofsky dozens of times, and the Fat Man soon told the FBI agent that Turner was one of the Gardner thieves, that the golden boy gangster would receive as much as 40 percent of the reward money if the paintings were ever returned.

Cronin couldn't do much with Chicofsky's inside information. It would never hold up in court—Chicofsky was an accused con man, a career collaborator, and he would eventually be thrown out of the FBI informant program for lying. So one evening in November 1997, Cronin drove down to Hyde Park, a concrete suburb just south of Boston and parked himself in front of Merlino's two-bedroom clapboard. The night was cold and blowy, and Cronin waited in his government car until he saw the mobster pull into the driveway. The FBI agent called out to

Merlino as he walked across the yard. "Do I have a problem?" Merlino asked repeatedly.

Cronin offered Merlino a deal. If he returned the Gardner paintings, the feds would not prosecute him or Turner or any of their associates for the museum robbery. But if Merlino and his friends waited too long, the offer would be rescinded and whoever had the art would go to jail. Merlino understood the implied threat, and he told Cronin that he did not have the paintings, but he might know who did. "Maybe I can get some money from this," he told Cronin, laughing.

For the next few months, it seemed as if Merlino might actually negotiate the return of the Gardner art. He would meet with Turner, he would meet with Chicofsky, he would meet with his lawyer Marty Leppo. While standing in his body shop examining car parts—"What the fuck is this, I know I bought it, but what is it?"—Merlino would talk about how he would collect the $5 million reward. "Lawyers, you always need a fucking lawyer." His plan—or at least what he told Chicofsky—was that he would first return Rembrandt's *Self-Portrait* to prove that he had control of the art. Then he would give back another six paintings. He planned to keep the other five as a bargaining chip, a sort of insurance, if anything went wrong. "[The museum] will pay," Merlino said. "They want those motherfuckers bad."

It was clear, though, that Merlino did not have direct access to the art, that he was attempting to secure the masterpieces from someone else. "If I had these [paintings], I'd give them to ya, and if I had them before I wouldn't of did five motherfuckin' years [in prison]," Merlino told Cronin. But Merlino didn't talk much about the person or persons who controlled the art. Sometimes it seemed like it was a close friend or relative, other times it appeared to be an associate or underworld figure. Still, Cronin prepared for the return of the masterpieces and delivered an immunity letter: "At 1:00 p.m. on Wednesday, January 14, 1998, you or a representative will deliver one painting, of your choosing, to the FBI at the Isabella Stewart Gardner Museum," the letter read. "You will be given $10,000 cash, and you will be allowed to leave."

But the art never showed up. Merlino never gave a reason. It will happen when it happens, he told Chicofsky. That might have been the end of the saga—until Merlino and Turner were arrested trying to raid the Loomis armored car depot. Cronin made sure to be there early that Sunday morning. The agent believed that Turner might flip and give up the Gardner paintings in order to get out of the armed robbery charges. But on that cold February morning, when Cronin finally had Turner in the white-walled confines of an interrogation room, the golden boy gangster denied everything. "I told the agents that I had no idea who stole the paintings or where they were being stored, and I didn't know anyone who had access to them," he said. Then he asked for his lawyer.

The Loomis case went to trial in 2001, and during the case, Turner didn't contest showing up at TRC with a platoon's worth of weapons. Nor did he deny trying to steal $50 million from the depot. Instead, Turner claimed entrapment, that the FBI had lured him into the Loomis theft in order to recover the Gardner paintings. The jury didn't believe Turner. They found him guilty on all counts, and the judge sentenced him to thirty-eight years. As the ringleader, Merlino landed forty-seven. Throughout the trial and sentencing, Turner never appeared to volunteer the Gardner paintings as a bargaining chip, and some investigators believe that it showed that he never participated in the heist, that it was another dead lead. "If he was sitting on a 'get-out-of-jail-free' card like the Gardner art, he would have used it," former state police officer Joe Flaherty told me. But others believed that Turner didn't have enough information to make a deal—or simply didn't know who actually controlled the missing art.

All that was certain was that Turner saw himself as the type of criminal who would never confess, that he would rather die in prison then become a police snitch. Investigators knew this about Turner—it was glaringly evident in the reams of wiretaps. In September 1991, a listening device picked up a phone call between Turner and Gray Morrison, a few weeks after two thieves robbed the Bull & Finch pub. During the conversation, Morrison told Turner about a book that he was reading, which argued that honor among thieves was a myth.

"No matter who you go with, no matter how strong they are, you never can tell which way they flip, man, they could be the coolest, fucking, baddest motherfucker in town," Morrison told Turner, "and all the sudden, wham, just one time flip. He said the only person to trust is yourself."

"Uh hum," Turner said.

"Like damn, what the fuck," Morrison said.

"Mm, mm."

"You keep it all to yourself"

"Man, I don't talk about nothing."

8. THREE MOUNTED JOCKEYS

Infiltrate and Infatuate

BEFORE I BEGAN my search for the lost masterpieces, I wanted to learn more about the FBI's investigation. I knew I shouldn't expect much. Smith believed that the bureau had lost almost all interest in the robbery, and it once took the art detective nearly two months to set up a conference call between the lead case agent and a Gardner informant. Still, the bureau continued to solicit tips, and so I contacted Bob Wittman, the head of the bureau's art theft team. We met in the lobby of the FBI's Philadelphia field office, and Wittman looked more like an advertising executive than your typical G-man. Heavy silver cufflinks hung from his wrists. A pair of elegant socks danced above his black shoes. His mane of silvery hair looked thick and well-groomed; his eyes were dark, sharp, and brown. I shook his hand, and he guided me through a thick steel door, past a labyrinth of carrels and conference rooms, back into the catacombs of the field office.

Then he pushed open the door of the men's lavatory. "I can just wait out here," I said.

"No, come on in. I just have to go to the bathroom," he replied, moving into the restroom.

Wittman stepped in front of the urinal and said over his shoulder: "So tell me about your project."

I began to explain how I had become involved in the case, when Wittman interrupted me, saying as he said in later interviews. "Everything you know about the case, it's all bullshit. I can tell you that right now. It's all speculation bullshit."

I stumbled for a moment. "Is there hard stuff out there?"

"I can't get into it," he said. "But I'm telling you this because I like you. You seem like a nice dude. You need to wait a little while. If you want to do a history of speculation, that's fine."

Wittman washed his hands, glanced at himself in the mirror, and guided me into his office. He showed me the view—a sweeping sight of Philadelphia's Liberty Square—and then moved to a bookshelf and pulled out a copy of the glossy *W* magazine, which featured an article about his work.

"You should read the piece. It's good," Wittman said. Then he quipped: "But I wish they'd described me as good-looking. You'll write that I look like George Clooney, right?"

I laughed. "Of course."

Wittman gestured for me to sit down on a white sofa. He eased himself into a large, winged chair. "So how much did they pay you?"

"Excuse me?" Besides my wife, no one had asked me the question before.

"How much did they pay you for the book? A million dollars?"

I frowned. "Nowhere close."

"Quarter of a million?" he said. He was now leaning forward, his elbows perched on his knees.

I shook my head.

"How about $100,000?"

"Less than that," I said, "a lot less than that," mumbling something about how I would be lucky to clear minimum wage after all my expenses.

Wittman stared at me. "If you want me to be honest with you, you have to be honest with me. Make me feel comfortable, earn my trust."

"Of course."

"You know if you're working undercover, they teach how you to mirror people. So if I'm leaning forward, you should lean forward. If I'm laughing, you should be laughing."

He paused and gave me a wide grin. I smiled wanly.

"Why do you look so uncomfortable? I'm just kidding with you," he said. "Really, I'm a nice guy."

Wittman and I talked for three hours that morning, and I never found him to be a nice guy. But I grew to sort of like him, or rather, I found him remarkable company. He was excellent at what he did. Over the course of his career, he had returned an original copy of the Bill of Rights, found three Norman Rockwell paintings stashed in a Brazilian farmhouse, and recovered a presentation sword stolen in 1932 from the U.S. Naval Academy. After gunmen used diversionary explosives and a speedboat to swipe a Rembrandt from the National Museum in Stockholm, the Swedish government brought in Wittman to pose as a buyer, and within days he bagged the four men selling the priceless canvas.

At times, I found myself seduced by Wittman's buttery charm. During our conversation, he asked detailed questions about my family, remembered my wife's name, and appeared gleefully happy when I told him that my daughter had just learned to walk. "Those first steps, they're amazing," he said. But within moments, without a touch of warning, he would turn tough and slippery. When I asked him something that he didn't want to answer, he'd bark, "Next question." If I told him something that he wanted to know more about, he'd start firing queries at me. "Who told you that?" And if I gave him the source of my information—and he didn't think much of it—Wittman would dismiss it with a wide, contemptuous wave. "They don't know shit."

Wittman believed that the best chance to recover the Gardner art would be a sting. "Sooner or later the people who have those paintings will look for a buyer and that buyer will be me," he said. And he spent the rest of that morning explaining the tough brand of persuasiveness required of undercover agents—how he needs to win the confidence of crooks while making sure no one finds out that he's a cop. To recover the Gardner art, his life will depend on his ability to make bold-faced lies while gaining a person's trust. He will act, in other words, like he acted with me—using a mix of charm and churl, of good cop and bad cop, to always keep control of a situation.

"Undercover work is not like acting," Wittman said. When an actor flubs a line, the audience might hiss or boo. If Wittman made a mistake, his audience could kill him. It's usually something small that tips off the crooks. An agent will misspeak, or a criminal will notice a hidden camera. Wittman once almost blew a sting because he brought along snapshots of a painting that he had printed from his work computer. "Are these pictures from the FBI website?" the crook asked. Wittman quickly explained that the FBI's website was the only place that he could find a decent photograph of the Old Master canvas. The thief believed him—and was arrested a few days later.

Wittman knows his art. He can talk fluently about issues of provenance and price and découpage; he understands how to use the technical tools of the trade, like shining a black light on a painting to see if it has been tampered with or gazing through a jeweler's loupe to study the authenticating details of an artist's brushstroke. But Wittman's most important skill might be that of earning someone's trust. "Going undercover is about creating rapport," he told me, leaning forward in his chair, his palms splayed open. "That's what makes a criminal trust you enough to sell you a million-dollar painting."

The subjects of Wittman's stings rarely have any idea that he's an agent, and many have a hard time getting over how well they got snookered. When Wittman worked to recover a nineteenth-century eagle-feathered Cheyenne war bonnet, he developed a close relationship with Joshua Baer, a well-respected New Mexico art dealer. Over the course of six months, the two men had long discussions about food, art, and wine. Baer invited Wittman into his home for dinner with his wife and family. Wittman offered to put up Baer's daughter if she came to Pennsylvania to look at colleges. After Wittman tagged Baer in a sting, the New Mexican art dealer felt so betrayed that he emailed Wittman. "I don't know what to say," Baer wrote. 'Well done?' 'Nice work?' We're devastated."

I asked Wittman if the ethics of undercover work ever bothered him, if he ever dwelt on the fact that he tells outright lies, that he is doing something wrong to make a right. He paused. He grinned. He waited for me to go to another question. We sat in silence for a moment. Then I asked about the Baer case. "That was difficult," he admitted. He explained that he had emailed Baer back the next day. "This was the toughest case I ever had because I truly like you and your family," he wrote. Wittman looked at me and gave a heavy shrug. This was his job. "You infiltrate and infatuate and then you betray," he told me. "That's what you need to do to get the art back."

WITTMAN IS the nation's only full-time art theft undercover agent. No other state or local agency has one, and there are persistent rumors that the bureau might even scrap Wittman and his art theft team. For years, Robert Goldman was one of Wittman's closest partners—he prosecuted the criminals swept up in Wittman's undercover operations. But in 2006 Goldman quit the Justice Department after senior officials told him that he should no longer pursue national art theft cases and focus only on local crimes. "They pulled the rug out from under me," Goldman said. (Wittman denies that the FBI has any plans to drop him or his team.)

Art theft has never been one of law enforcement's top priorities. Part of the problem is the culture. Cops want muscular crimes, something with blood and butchery and a hapless victim—and art theft can seem delicate, effeminate, somehow suspect, with the injured party not always self-evident. When police hear about the theft of a Cubist lithograph or a sixteenth-century mosaic, they will sometimes wonder, what's the harm? Who was hurt? Some old rich guy? "The value of, for example, *The Storm on the Sea of Galilee*, is incalculable and therefore priceless. But nowhere, does that reasoning come into police thinking, strategy, or performance evaluation," explained art detective Charley Hill, who served for more than two decades on Scotland Yard's Art and Antiques Squad.

The lack of investigative interest makes for some unexpected recoveries. Stolen paintings will be discovered behind a dishwasher as part of a raid on a drug dealer's home, or an oblivious rogue will bring a looted canvas to Sotheby's to see if he can get it appraised. (Most auction houses use databases like the one maintained by the Art Loss Register to ensure that they do not sell stolen art.) One spring morning in 2003, a New York City woman was on her way to work when she spotted a brightly colored canvas nestled between two garbage bags. The woman took the oil painting home and soon discovered that it was a Rufino Tamayo worth about $1 million. The painting had been stolen from a storage container in Houston some twenty years earlier—how it came to New York City, how it ended up on a street corner waiting for the dump truck, remains a mystery.

Before I left Wittman's office that afternoon, I asked him about his big Gardner lead, what made all of my work speculation bullshit. But he wouldn't comment. "If you want the truth, you need to wait. What might be better is the book that explains how it almost ended but got fucked up."

"Can you tell me when you'll get the works back?"

"If I'm honest, I'll tell you that I don't know. Maybe it will be next week, maybe next year," he said.

"Really," I asked. "Within the next year?"

"OK," he laughed. "By the time I retire."

"When's that?"

"Two years."

So were the Gardner thieves trying to sell the works? Was it an experienced fence? How would the deal go down? "It hasn't happened yet, so how could I know?" he said. "And if I tell you I'll be tipping off the people who have them, and that's all I'm interested in, really."

Wittman being Wittman and the FBI being the FBI, I was skeptical. Wittman wasn't the lead case agent on the Gardner case. That job fell to the Boston field office's Geoff Kelly, and when I spoke with Kelly, he wouldn't comment on any recent leads. And there were plenty of signs that the lost Gardner art was no longer a priority for the agency. When Warren Bamford became head of the Boston FBI field office in January 2007, he met with reporters and discussed his top concerns: counterterrorism, gang violence, and finding fugitive James "Whitey" Bulger. There was no mention of the Gardner case, and a few things made it seem as if Wittman didn't follow the heist that closely either. Some months after we met, I called the agent to check in, and during our conversation, I asked him about some of the people who've been accused of being behind the heist over the years, people like David Turner and Bobby Donati and George Reissfelder. "Nope," he said. "Don't know them."

I also knew that the bureau had set up stings for the Gardner art before, all of which had been wildly unsuccessful. Shortly after the theft, Wittman's predecessor, FBI undercover agent Tom McShane had developed a covert identity as a shady New York art dealer named Tom Russell, complete with a driver's license and credit cards. In the disguise, McShane flew to Toronto to meet with a mobster who claimed that he controlled the Gardner stash. McShane spent hours with a well-known Boston art fence who claimed that he could broker the return of the lost art for $20,000. But none of the stings went anywhere. "The guys who did the Gardner job were professional. That's why we haven't heard anything from the paintings in all these years," McShane told me. "They're probably not going to do something stupid now like go to a hotel room to meet with some art dealer or collector type."

After I left Wittman's office, I wondered: Was he bluffing? Did he have some sort of big lead? Was he really planning an undercover operation that would bring back the missing masterpieces? I wasn't sure. But what I did know—and I knew for sure—was that if someone offered the lost paintings for purchase, I would want Wittman to head up the sting. Wittman was what he joked about being, the bureau's top art theft undercover agent. But I also knew that almost two decades had passed since the night of the theft, and there hadn't been a single arrest, there hadn't been a single confirmed sighting of the lost art. Like Smith, I was tired of waiting.

WHEN SMITH BEGAN reinvestigating the Gardner case, he started slowly. He knew that the FBI had exhausted all the obvious leads, that they had interviewed all the salient suspects. The last big investigative push had been in March 1997, on the seventh anniversary of the heist, when the Gardner's board of trustees voted to pay for the reward out of its own pocket and raise the bounty from $1 million to $5 million. The news inspired a whole new round of tips and leads and angles—all of them without success. So Smith reread old newspaper articles and quizzed law enforcement sources and penned a letter to the museum to see if he could meet with their private investigator. "The loss that you suffered, which was catastrophic to say the least, has always intrigued me, because of [the] various unexplained factors," he wrote.

Eventually, Smith uncovered a promising lead—an antiques dealer named William Youngworth III. A heavyset man with dark eyes and a wide, crafty smile, Youngworth had just been released from prison and claimed to be able to broker the return of the Gardner art. There was good reason to believe him. Three years earlier, on a warm morning in July, a team of FBI agents raided Youngworth's antiques store in Randolph, Massachusetts, a few miles south of Boston. The warrant was for a sawed-off shotgun, a Mac-10 automatic rifle, and two rocket-propelled grenade launchers. But it appeared that the FBI was actually just hunting for the Gardner art. Special agent Neil Cronin oversaw the search, and FBI agents spent more than ten hours combing the one-acre property, turning over furniture, ferreting through steamer trunks, backhoeing up the front and backyards. The agents didn't find the paintings, nor did they uncover any grenade launchers, just a few antique revolvers and the butt of a marijuana joint.

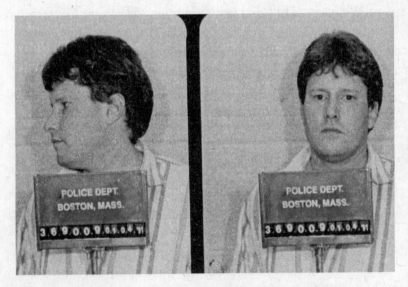

A mug shot of antiques dealer William Youngworth.

But that afternoon, while sitting in the holding cell of the Randolph police department, Youngworth tried to barter his way out of jail with the missing Gardner masterpieces. He first led police to a beeswax seal from the founding charter of the Massachusetts Bay Colony. A thief had filched the seal from the Massachusetts State House in 1984, and Youngworth had secreted the artifact in a bookshelf in his living room. Then Youngworth brought up the Gardner case. He told the detectives that he could mediate the return of the stolen paintings if they dropped the charges against him, gave him the $5 million reward, and freed art thief Myles Connor from prison. Youngworth worded his offer carefully, so that he would not be prosecuted for holding stolen property. "I am leading you to believe that I have information on the Gardner case," he said.

Few took Youngworth seriously. In the New England underworld, he was a small-timer, a grifter, and there was no way that he could have been a participant in the heist. At the time of the robbery he was riding out a two-year jail sentence for a firearms violation. But a scrappy *Boston Herald* crime reporter by the name of Tom Mashberg saw potential in the lead and asked Youngworth for proof that he might control the works. A few weeks later, a driver picked up Mashberg in a Crown Victoria and drove him to an old warehouse about an hour outside of Boston. The area was deserted. A woman came out of the shadows and peered into the car. "Billy sent us," the driver said. She nodded and let the men pass.

The driver escorted Mashberg to the fourth floor of the darkened warehouse and unlocked a storage bin. Inside were some plastic bins and a few steamer trunks. The man reached into one of the bins and gingerly removed a painting, unfurling what appeared to be Rembrandt's *The Storm on the Sea of Galilee*. Mashberg could see the frayed tears on the side of the canvas; he could see Rembrandt's fluid signature on the rudder. "That's the rest of them," the man said, shining his flashlight on a half-dozen tubes that were stashed within a canvas satchel.

Mashberg was certain that he had seen the Gardner's lost Rembrandt, and the *Boston Herald* ran a front-page story a few days later, with a screaming, three-inch headline WE'VE SEEN IT. Youngworth also arranged for Mashberg to receive twenty-five photos of the paintings as well as a small vial of paint chips. The tabloid then hired Walter C. McCrone, an art expert who had done work for Scotland Yard and the Vatican, to study the chips, and he confirmed that the oil paint came from a canvas by the Dutch Old Master. "Everything is utterly perfect for a Rembrandt paint layer. And none of the indicators that would show it to be inauthentic—modern materials or other errors forgers make—are discernible," McCrone said.

In the weeks that followed, it looked as if Youngworth would arrange for the return of the lost art. The U.S. attorney met with Youngworth to discuss an immunity deal. Youngworth's lawyer began to examine his tax liability on the reward money. LOOKIN' GOOD proclaimed one of Mashberg's headlines in the *Boston Herald*. And when the deal took longer than expected, Anne Hawley and board member Arnold Hiatt met with Youngworth for lunch at the Hotel Plaza Athenee on Manhattan's East Side. In a private room, over a lunch of rare steak, Youngworth explained that he wanted an ironclad offer of immunity, while Hiatt said that Senator Edward Kennedy might have to intervene to help speed up the discussions. "There are a number of people in high public places that want to see this happen," Hiatt told Youngworth. Before the meeting was over, Hiatt wrote Youngworth a check for $10,000. It was a down payment, the trustee told the antiques dealer, a show of good faith and further cooperation.

But there wasn't any further cooperation—and the good faith would soon evaporate, the situation devolving into a confused stalemate. The problem was that the feds didn't really believe Youngworth. They wanted hard evidence, like the finial or the ku, and before that happened, they would only offer Youngworth partial immunity. "We regularly cut deals with some real bad people. We do it all the time with murderers and drug dealers, and we would have been happy to give Youngworth a deal if he had given us some proof, but he had nothing but a newspaper article," former U.S. attorney Donald Stern told me.

Youngworth rejected the offer from the feds. He said that partial immunity was a dangerous trap, that he would get arrested the moment he told law enforcement what happened to the stolen art. Youngworth also began accusing police of harassment, of placing listening devices under his son's bed, tapping his phones, surveilling him night and day. He believed that law enforcement didn't want to be seen making deals with an ex-con, that they didn't want a convicted felon to land the reward money. "The only true thing they ever told me is that they want to get [the art] before me," Youngworth explained.

Then a jury found Youngworth guilty on the unrelated charge of receiving a stolen van, and Youngworth's wife died of a prescription drug overdose. And to put the final nail in the coffin of the negotiations, the museum publicly announced that while the paint chips were from a seventeenth-century Dutch painting, they did not come from Rembrandt's *The Storm on the Sea of Galilee* or *A Lady and Gentleman in Black*. Youngworth fired back, saying that the chips were from the Vermeer, not the Rembrandt, but by then the blood between the factions had become far too bitter. Shortly before being shipped off to prison, Youngworth told Mashberg that authorities acted in a way "to snap the olive branch extended by myself," and it seemed as if Youngworth's paintings—real or fake—would fade away as mysteriously as they appeared.

SMITH HAD A FEELING that Youngworth knew something. Maybe the antiques dealer didn't have control over the paintings, maybe he didn't know who committed the heist, but Smith believed that Youngworth had some connection to the lost art. The events seemed too elaborate for a hoax, and soon after Youngworth got out of prison, Smith reached out to him. But Youngworth was completely suspicious. He was convinced that law enforcement was still out to get him, that FBI agents were still spying on him, following his every visit to the grocery store. "I guess they think a map with an X is about to fall out of my pocket," he said.

Smith kept at it. He explained to Youngworth that he had no interest in pushing a prosecution. "We're not the police, we're not the FBI," he told Youngworth, "our main goal is the recovery of the item." Smith tried to make Youngworth comfortable by spinning jokes, like how his wife fell asleep in a taxicab on their wedding night. "It made it very romantic, you know?" And over time, the two men forged a relationship. They talked on the phone, they exchanged emails. Smith also shipped Youngworth money—a few hundred dollars here, a few hundred there—and the antiques dealer began to relate details that appeared to corroborate his story. He told Smith about an ex-Gardner employee who failed a polygraph test and may have been the inside connection. He described how some of the works had been rolled and unrolled so many times that the canvases had become badly damaged. "They were handled pretty roughly to start with," Youngworth explained.

Youngworth also told Smith about his connections to the Boston underworld. Born in Marshfield, an old harbor town about thirty miles south of Boston, Youngworth was barely eight years old when his own mother, high on booze and barbiturates, died of a heart attack on Christmas Eve. After her death, Youngworth was sent into foster care and began a life of minor crime, earning his first arrest at age seventeen for receiving stolen property. While Youngworth would eventually graduate into larceny, drugs, and robbery, his best scores were art scams, and he boasted of his skills at pushing fake Oriental rugs and hawking sham Shaker furniture. During a thirteen-year stint for armed robbery, Youngworth also became friends with some of New England's most infamous thieves, including a museum crook named Myles Connor.

At first, Smith believed Youngworth's story. "Youngworth claims he can get these paintings in a half hour," he told a reporter at the time. "If everyone connected with this case was given amnesty, it would be solved." For Smith, Youngworth's underworld connections were a key part of his account. Smith believed that Youngworth had caught a glimpse, or perhaps even acquired the Gardner paintings, through some of his criminal contacts. Maybe he uncovered a sketch in one of Connor's safe houses or an associate gave Youngworth a Rembrandt for safekeeping. Smith hoped to break the stalemate between Youngworth and the feds by serving as the go-between, the outside broker trusted by both sides, and he rang up friends in the Justice Department to see if they might be willing to reopen discussions, if they might again consider a deal with Youngworth.

But when Smith began asking Youngworth for proof—a snapshot of a canvas, more paint chips—the antiques dealer waffled. He said that he didn't trust the feds, that he was afraid of a setup. "The Boston FBI orchestrated a complete framing of me to put me in a cell to extort my cooperation on the Gardner," Youngworth told Smith. Still, Smith pushed Youngworth, and when Youngworth continued to waiver and balk, the art detective began to have his own doubts. Youngworth was, after all, a time-tested con man. He had more than ten different aliases—he was Arnold Fireman, Ronald Anderson, John McBride. He had been arraigned more than sixty times, mainly for scams of one sort or another, forgery, passing bad checks, creating fake IDs.

It seemed that Mashberg's late-night viewing of the Rembrandt might have been a hoax too. Mashberg recalled that the man who showed him the Rembrandt had said that the paintings were being stored in poster tubes. But the stolen Flinck was painted on wood and could not have been rolled up. Mashberg also said that the man had unfurled the Rembrandt canvas. But the back of *The Storm* had been sealed with wax during a restoration process and the painting was about as flexible as a greeting card. "It would have been very difficult to roll up that painting because of the wax. It made that painting very stiff," said Barbara Magnum, who had been the Gardner's chief conservator at the time of the heist.

But what really worried Smith was that Youngworth's story kept changing. At first, Youngworth said that the Japanese mafia, the *yakuza*, was behind the caper. Then he claimed that he himself was the mastermind. Then, it was a group of bank robbers. Youngworth was also evasive about the location of the paintings. Sometimes he said that the artworks had left the country, that they had been sold and scattered across the globe. Other times he would tell Smith that the paintings were in New York, that he could recover them all within thirty minutes. At one point, Smith asked Sandy Guttman to review an interview with Youngworth. Guttman had been a robbery detective for more than twenty years and worked closely with Smith on various art theft cases, including the Gardner. "No direct answers, diverting the topic, he didn't make any eye contact," Guttman told Smith after examining the videotape. "The guy was bullshitting."

Smith knew scams. During his fifty years as an art insurance adjuster, he had come across thousands of them. People would falsify claims or start a fire in order to collect the indemnity. At least once a month, Smith would get a call from someone looking for insurance on a fake painting or sculpture, hoping that the policy would help him sell the work on the legitimate market. But Smith wanted to be absolutely sure about the Youngworth angle, he wanted to make every last effort, and he gave the antiques dealer a final opportunity. If Youngworth could offer a single piece of concrete evidence, Smith would do everything that he could to land him immunity and the reward money.

Youngworth eventually sent Smith an email, writing that he would show Smith the Vermeer, but he would need $1,400 in cash and the visit would require "a couple of days of hard travel." During the trip, Smith would not be allowed to have any contact with the outside world, not a single phone call. For Smith, the offer seemed to be nothing more than a shameless hustle. Why would Youngworth want the money up front? How else could one explain the bizarre demands? Later, years after Smith had rejected the offer, I asked him about Youngworth. "He's nothing but a con man. It's been years, and he hasn't gotten the paintings back," he told me, "and, really, there's not much someone like him wouldn't do for $5 million."

YOUNGWORTH CONTINUES TO maintain that he can broker the return of the Gardner art. In March 2004 he gave a long interview to ABC News, claiming that he knew who took the masterpieces and how to get them back. "I believe I have a very accurate picture of everything that's transpired," he told ABC investigative reporter Brian Ross. As part of the story, Ross presented two Polaroids that appeared to feature the Gardner's lost Rembrandt self-portrait. Ross had received the photographs in a plain envelope with no return address, and the Polaroids showed the Rembrandt placed atop of a copy of the Boston Globe to show the date.

"The photo could be an elaborate hoax. But, if authentic, it could prove that the Rembrandt still exists," Ross explained.

I trusted Smith's conclusions about Youngworth, and when I contacted *Boston Herald* reporter Tom Mashberg, he told me the same thing Smith had. "I would urge you to be very cautious. The level of Youngworth's mendacity is astonishing," Mashberg told me. "Youngworth may have had a slim connection to the paintings at one time, but he doesn't have anything anymore." Still, I wanted to talk to Youngworth. My Gardner theft website had been up for a few months, and I was surprised at how many of the tips were unvarnished hoaxes. A retired New York City cop emailed me and said that he had a source who might know the location of the art, and if I paid him a few thousand dollars, he would share his lead. (He wanted the money as an advance; I passed on the offer.) Then a young man named François called me at 7 a.m. one morning to tell me that he had solid information that the Gardner masterpieces were fakes. (I checked with a half-dozen sources. It seemed close to impossible.) Although there were better leads tucked away in Smith's files, I wanted to learn more about the angles that hadn't panned out, the tricks, the ruses, the nothing leads.

But when I contacted Youngworth, he refused an interview. In a series of long and often confounding emails, he explained that the rights of his story had been sold to a syndicate, and it had decided that he should not speak to me. "In addition to contractual matters I still have one very dear friend who could be hurt quite badly by all this so often I am forced to lead people away from the truth," he wrote. But I could get his side of the caper, hear his account of the heist, if I contacted one of his friends. "Speak with Charlie Sabba," Youngworth wrote, "this would serve your interest well."

I called Sabba the following day and reached his voice mail. "Bonjour," the electronic voice said. "This is Charlie Sabba. Remember art is not a profession, it is a faith." It took a few more calls—and a little more faith—to reach Sabba, but when I finally got him on the phone, he acted like we were all old buddies. "Oh yeah, Billy. He's a good friend, a great friend," Sabba told me. "Fantastic guy." On the phone, Sabba told me that he was a police officer in New Jersey as well as a professional artist. He had received his Bachelor of Fine Arts from the School of Visual Arts in Manhattan and regularly exhibited his works in small New York galleries.

Sabba lived in Rahway, a tough little industrial town about twenty miles west of New York City, just beyond the massive oil refineries of north Jersey. We met up on a bright Sunday afternoon. "Hey, my man," he said by way of a greeting. Sabba had an open face and eager eyes. White oil paint stippled his hands and chest, a navy tattoo sprawled over his forearm. A thick gold chain hung around his neck. He gave me a friendly slap on the shoulder and said that he wanted to show me some of the murals that he had painted on the city's storefronts. "You gotta see them, you just gotta." Sabba drove an old Saturn, and I followed him as he motored through the streets of downtown Rahway, stopping every few blocks to stick an arm out the window to point out one of his works. A Magritte-inspired mural on the rear wall of Fernando's Pizzeria; a tribute to French expressionist Henri Toulouse-Lautrec on a vacant storefront. "Lautrec is my hero. I love that guy. I mean I really love that guy."

Sabba had started a mural on the side of the Rahway firehouse a few hours before I arrived. The painting was large—about the size of a boxcar—and highly realistic, featuring the head of an eagle set against an American flag backdrop. "You have to understand, I'm an art zealot," Sabba told me as we stood in front of the work. "Murals used to be illegal here, and so I talked to the mayor. I told him that there are cities in Europe where the whole city is covered by murals, and so he changed the ordinance, and by the end of this summer, I hope to have fifty murals in this town."

A tall fireman lumbered over. "The guy started at ten this morning," the man told me. "Pretty friggin' good for a few hours of work."

Sabba's father, Anthony, joined us too. He told me that the mural was his favorite. "The rest of Charlie's stuff is a bit weird for me." He shrugged.

We headed to Sabba's art studio—the converted garage of his small rancher. "Glass of wine?" Sabba asked. "I'm gonna have one. I gotta wind down. I'm all hyped up from all that painting this morning."

Sabba poured two glasses and rolled open the garage door. We sat in a pair of sagging couches, Sabba's three girls played in the front yard. A hard light glinted off the window of a tumbledown sedan sitting in the street. I asked Sabba if it was hard to be both a police officer and an artist. He shook his head.

"I mean I love being a cop. I love foot chases. I love chasing people through yards. I love the physical part."

"And being an artist?"

"That's my secular religion. My real calling. I love the police work, but art, it's my life, my faith. Something I just can't do without."

Sabba took a sip of wine and explained that police officers often had a hard time understanding his desire to create art. "Cops like the world to be black-and-white. If you draw a dog, they want it to look like a dog. Draw a duck, it should look like a duck. If you draw a purple duck—" Sabba shook his head and laughed, as if to say *impossible*. "Really, it's the mind that goes into police work. It's logical and rational. Cops don't want people to ever be out of their box, and artists, they love being out of the box. They never want to walk down the middle of the street."

One of Sabba's daughters scampered over to get some money for the ice-cream truck, and he slipped her a few bills. Sabba explained that he and Youngworth had become friends after he wrote an article for the local paper that slammed the Gardner museum for its lack of security. Youngworth emailed him a note of praise, and they now meet up every few months to visit New York City museums and galleries. Sabba told me that Youngworth still worked as an antiques dealer and would sometimes use his underworld sources to help return other works of stolen art. "Billy is someone who believes in the arts. He loves those Gardner paintings. He's like me. He wants to see them go back to that museum. He tried to do it, but they made him look like a liar," Sabba explained. "You see, most cops, they want bodies. They are predatory. They prey on criminals. But they don't know art. They don't even know what they're looking at when they see a masterpiece, and the Boston FBI just weren't going to deal with someone like Billy. They wanted someone in cuffs more than they wanted the art back."

But when I began asking Sabba about the details of what happened, he couldn't help me. He didn't know why—or even if—Youngworth continued to play a con. "I don't play the cop with Billy. I don't hound him. Where's this painting? What happened that night? I offer myself as a friend. When I visit with Billy, I play the artist, not the cop." When Sabba said those words, I suddenly realized why Youngworth sent me to go see him. Youngworth didn't want me to go back and dig up all the old stories about his scams and swindles. Rather, he hoped that I heard a very specific side of his story, the story of his love for art and antiques, his deep passion for things beautiful and imaginative.

It grew late. The sun dappled Sabba's face in a ruby glow. Sabba finished off his wine and said that he wanted to show me some artworks that he had created in response to the Gardner theft. At the time of the robbery, he worked as a New Jersey State prison guard, and he had re-created each of the lost masterpieces with fingerprint ink, using a pink-hued, inmate-processing card as his canvas. "The theft really bothered me when it happened," he said. "That was a disaster, a tragedy, something that should never leave the public's attention. So I tried to understand it, you know, by making it into art."

Sabba displayed the paintings on the wall of his studio, and he pulled down the one devoted to Manet's *Chez Tortoni*. "It will be your piece of the theft," he said, handing me the work.

In Sabba's version of the stolen painting, the eyes of the gentlemen were large and round and dark. He looked sadder and more contemplative than in the original. The fingerprint card asked for the arrestee's name, height, weight, and Social Security number, but the spaces were blank except for the daubed re-creation of the stolen image, which rose above the form's lines and boxes, as if it couldn't be restricted by categorization. But the work could also be read as an argument that art itself was an illicit act, a way to transgress and transform, to keep ideas alive through robbery and rip-offs. Thieves swiped the original—Sabba made a copy.

I took the work home and framed the canvas in a small wooden setting. I gave the painting its own spot above my desk. I would often stare at the picture; I developed a sort of pride in the painting—that it was

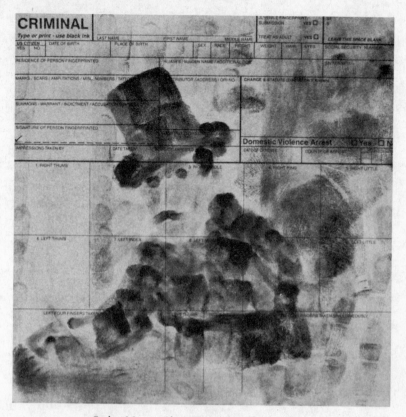

Stolen Manet, Chez Tortoni *by Charles Sabba.*

mine and mine alone. Then, late one afternoon, sitting in my chair, gazing up at the portrait, it dawned on me that owning an artwork had its own potent power—it made me feel as if I controlled some portion of its skilled creativity, that there was a direct connection between me and the art. The feeling must have been a lesser variety of the emotion that Isabella Stewart Gardner experienced when she first received Rembrandt's *The Storm on the Sea of Galilee.* "I am now as a tramp who has the Sun all to himself," she wrote to Berenson. Youngworth too must have known the feeling because it was that emotion, that passion to possess a work of art, that made art cons so successful.

A FEW WEEKS LATER, Sabba called and said that Youngworth had decided to grant me an interview, but I couldn't speak directly with the antiques dealer. Instead, I would pose my questions of Sabba, who would ask them of Youngworth, and then Sabba would provide me with his answers. Sabba said that Youngworth wanted the arrangement "to protect his deal with his syndicate." I suspected something different, that it would give Youngworth plausible deniability, that he could say that he never spoke with me. Whatever the case, I wanted to hear what Youngworth had to say even if Sabba was the one saying it, and so on a rainy afternoon, I met up with Sabba at Christie's auction house. Works by some of Sabba's favorite artists—Andy Warhol, Jean-Michel Basquiat—were heading for the hammer that afternoon, and Sabba wanted to see the auction before we made the call to Youngworth.

The auction house was lush and elegant and moneyed, with a three-story Sol LeWitt mural towering over the lobby and carpets so thick that you couldn't hear yourself walk. We padded up toward the auction room, the staccato sounds of the auctioneer like the noise of far-off gunfire.

"$100,000."

"$110,000 to the gentlemen in the back of the room."

"$120,000."

"Anyone else?"

Dealers milled in the hallway, talking, backslapping, calling their clients. "Yeah, it just sold, way past the record," one whispered into his Blackberry. "You want me to bid on the next lot?" Sabba and I pushed our way inside, and in the front of the room, standing on a small dais was the auctioneer, an attractive, boxy-jawed woman in her forties. To her right was a large electronic display screen, showing the bidding price in a dozen different currencies, including the British pound, the euro, and the South Korean won. While Sabba had no plans to bid— "I barely can afford the auction paddle" he said—he had stopped by the day before to take a look at a Basquiat painting. The work featured a large, white skull and had a crude, unfinished feel, typical of the 1980s-era Neo-expressionist artist. It sold earlier that morning for $1.6 million.

The audience was a motley bunch. Tweedy, ascot-wearing men, who looked as if they had been in the business since the days of Vermeer. Diamond-encrusted heiress types, nattering away on cell phones. Hipsters in tastefully ripped jeans and black Vans, matronly women swishing by in silky dresses, men of uncertain métier watching the room with languid stares. The crowd had one thing in common— an almost insatiable desire for art. These were, in other words, Sabba's sort of people. We watched a woman who was so nervous about landing a Rauschenberg that she chewed her way through one toothpick after another. After one dealer landed an Expressionist painting, he clenched his fists, brought them up to his chest and did a little jig, like he had just won a million dollars at a blackjack table. And everyone seemed willing to shell out piles of money. There was not a work for less than $5,000; a loose Warhol sketch of a red high-heeled shoe cost some $50,000. At one point, a white wooden collage sculpture by Louise Nevelson came up for sale, and when the bidding started, there were so many offers that I couldn't begin to count them. All over the room, people waved their paddles, indicating that they wanted to buy the work. Auction round after auction round, bid after bid, the price rocketed upwards before the work sold for almost half a million dollars. It was more than $400,000 over its estimated sale price.

We watched the sale until it was time for our call with Youngworth. Sabba and I then crossed Rockefeller Center and stepped into a wine bar. It was a small place, nearly deserted. A pale light coated the room. We sat in the back and ordered drinks, while Sabba got Youngworth on the phone. I fired off my questions one by one. How did Youngworth get access to the paintings? Could he still return them? Why did so many respected individuals, including Smith, Mashberg, and a half-dozen FBI agents consider him a con man?

With Sabba as his spokesperson, Youngworth explained that a group of armored car robbers had committed the heist on behalf of a wealthy collector. But after the Rembrandts had been cut from their frames, the man no longer wanted the paintings, and so the art was sold to Boston marijuana smuggler Joe Murray. Shortly thereafter, Murray's wife shot him in the chest, and the works slipped into the Boston underworld. As proof that he had access to the paintings, Youngworth offered details about the back of Rembrandt's *The Storm on the Sea of Galilee*, that there was an L-shaped tear in the canvas that had been repaired with a heavy black thread. As for the FBI, they didn't want the paintings to come back through Youngworth. It would make them look like fools, as if they couldn't outfox an ex-con.

"So where is the art now?"

"All over the world."

"Where?"

"The package is scattered. It got sold into a primary market. One case in point, it's an actual government."

"Which government?"

Sabba paused. "He doesn't want to answer that question. It's too specific," he said. "Let's just say they had a penchant for seascapes in a reduced format."

"Is the art in good condition?"

"*Lady and Gentleman in Black* is completely ruined. Last time he saw it, it looked like a bunch of cornflakes," Sabba told me. "He says a lot of experts didn't believe it was an authentic Rembrandt, anyway. Nevertheless, it was a great piece of art. It's a shame. It was mishandled by amateurs, Billy says."

"Could Youngworth still get the art back?"

"Sure," Sabba said, pausing again to listen to Youngworth on the phone. "But the Gardner's reward money is not enough. They would now have to pay $5 million for each of the major works, and it has to start back at the Justice Department. They need to make a public announcement that amnesty is on the table. That's the signal. That's where it starts. They have to say that getting the artwork back is the highest priority."

Youngworth's story was surprisingly persuasive. He offered convincing details about the backs of the canvases; he had a detailed knowledge of the history of the paintings. His account of the heist seemed plausible too, and other investigators had also tagged drug dealer Joe Murray as the person who took control of the loot. Sabba was also convinced, and after he got off the phone with Youngworth, he banged his wine glass on the table. "The FBI knew that he was telling the truth," he said. "That art could be back up on the walls by now."

But as the thrill of hearing Youngworth's story faded, I began to share with Sabba some of my research on the antiques dealer. I had spoken with Mark Gentile, who had shared a prison cell with Youngworth and married Youngworth's sister Mary. "Billy's the best con man that I've ever met in my life," Gentile told me, "but he doesn't know shit about the Gardner paintings. It's all a bunch of lies. Total and complete lies." Gentile told me that Youngworth once asked him to forge a copy of the stolen Rembrandt self-portrait. Gentile created the fake by photocopying the etching onto a piece of heavy cotton paper and then dipping the sheet in a bath of lemon juice and water to make it look old and worn. According to Gentile, Youngworth sent a photograph of the forgery to ABC News and then sold the work to a Rhode Island businessman. (Youngworth doesn't have many kind words for Gentile either—he once sued him for murder, conspiracy, and fraud. The case was dismissed before going to trial.)

"If you're from Boston, it's hard to grow up and not be beaten down some," Sabba said. "The big joke is that every family in Boston has a priest and a gangster, that one's a saint and one's a sinner and who do you think will return the paintings? The saint or the sinner?"

While Youngworth claimed that he had gone straight, police continued to pinch him regularly, and I told Sabba about his recent criminal record. The antiques dealer had been arrested in 2002 for stealing two iron flower planters from a woman's front porch. In 2003 he was found guilty of possessing a dangerous weapon. Later, I found out that even Youngworth's secret details about the backs of the paintings weren't accurate.

"If that's true, that wouldn't be good," Sabba laughed. "But I trust the guy."

While I felt stupid and petty for badmouthing Youngworth, what happened that afternoon fit with a picture of events that had formed in my mind since the moment that I first started reading about the incident. The Youngworth lead was not the momentous clash between criminal and law enforcement that Youngworth and Sabba made it out to be. Instead, it seemed that people felt so strongly about the lost paintings that they would disregard stark realities, that the desire to recover the works made well-meaning art lovers, people like Arnold Hiatt, Harold Smith, and now Charlie Sabba, overlook the raw facts of the situation. I got up and told Sabba that I had a train to catch—I didn't want to become one of those people.

9. SELF-PORTRAIT

I Was the One

MYLES CONNOR spent the night of the Gardner robbery sleeping in a Chicago prison cell, awaiting sentencing on stolen property charges, the final coda of a crime spree that had lasted more than three decades. An elfin man with frosty blue eyes and a mop of brilliantly red hair, he was one of the country's most infamous art thieves. He had pocketed Dutch Old Master paintings, swiped ancient Japanese dragon statuettes, pilfered Colonial-era grandfather clocks. Once, while out on bail, he filched a Rembrandt from a Boston museum and arranged for the return of the painting a year later in order to lessen his prison sentence in a different art crime. A member of Mensa, an ex-rock 'n' roller who once headlined for the Beach Boys, Connor was smart and merciless and shrewd, the sort of criminal who had earned a black belt in karate by the time he was eighteen and always made sure to pronounce it *kah-dah-tay.*

The day after the Gardner heist, or perhaps the day after that, a federal agent appeared in front of Connor's cell. He wanted to speak to the art thief. Connor had arranged heists from prison before, and the agent grilled him about the Gardner robbery. He asked Connor about his crew back in Boston, what he knew about the museum, anything that he might have heard about the missing paintings. Then the agent took

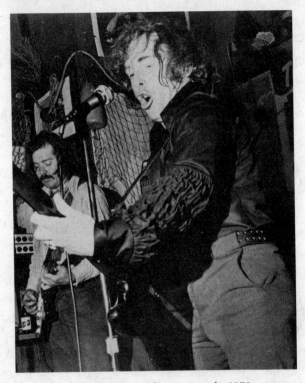

Myles Connor at a rock concert in the 1970s.

Connor's fingerprints. The art thief had once escaped from a Maine prison by making a pistol from a bar of soap, and in the summer of 1989, less than a year before the Gardner robbery, Connor sawed a five-inch hole in the ceiling of his Illinois holding cell and would have most likely broken out of the jail if he hadn't been betrayed by a fellow inmate. On that March day in 1990, the agent wanted to be sure that one of the country's most notorious art thieves had not escaped in order to commit one of the country's most notorious art thefts.

Since that day nearly twenty years ago, investigators have not stopped looking at Connor for the Gardner heist. Federal agents have interviewed his friends, searched through his possessions, questioned old girlfriends, raided his safe houses, and once began negotiations with his lawyer for the return of the lost masterpieces. Although nothing solid, not a single bona fide clue, has come from all of the investigative effort, no one has ever removed Connor from the list of suspects either. The art thief knew too much about art—and how to steal it—for anyone to say with certainty that he did not have any part in the robbery. "He was one of the first people we looked at, and that's been going on ever since," FBI agent Dan Falzon once explained.

Smith believed that until the Gardner art was recovered, every lead needed to be exhausted, and if not exhausted, they needed to be checked and re-checked. It didn't matter if you had theories or hunches or if you knew who was involved, the only measure of success was the art itself, and so soon after I started on the case, I began looking into the Connor angle.

CONNOR'S LIFE STORY sounds like Elmore Leonard might have written it. Son of a cop, brother of a priest, he grew up outside of Boston in the white-picket-fence suburb of Milton. His mother, Lucy Conant Johnson, was a direct descendent of William Brewster, a Pilgrim preacher who came over on the *Mayflower*. It's a pedigreed lineage that makes Connor a distant relative of Nelson Rockefeller, Norman Rockwell, and Katharine Hepburn. As a child, Connor showed academic promise. He aced his SATs and was slated to become an accountant or a dentist. But he also had a deep interest in dangerous things. He bought samurai swords, practiced karate, and collected an ark's worth of vicious animals—a viper, a boa, tarantulas, a jaguar, a pet alligator named Albert. He later claimed that if he hadn't become a criminal, he would have gone to college and become a herpetologist so that he could study deadly reptiles.

Connor learned the guitar, and by the time he was seventeen he was playing professionally with his five-piece band "Myles and the Wild Ones." They jammed clubs and bars and sock hops all over New England; he later shared billing with Chuck Berry and Roy Orbison. On stage, Connor did his best to cultivate a Marlon Brando, rock-'n'-roll rebel persona. Decked out in leather jackets and five-pound belt buckles, Connor would arrive at gigs shirtless, driving a Harley Davidson, sometimes steering the bike right onto the stage. During one gig in Milton, Connor showed up in a black cape and a sword cane and stoked the audience into near mayhem. When Connor's police officer father came on stage to end the concert, Connor yelled into the mic, "Aw, Dad, let 'em riot."

Connor's stage persona soon turned into something much more malicious. He would get into savage bar brawls. He began traveling in the same circles as mob bosses and organized crimes figures. "He needs psychiatric help," his mother told reporters. Connor claimed that he committed his first museum heist out of spite. The year was 1965, he was twenty-two, and the Forbes House Museum in Milton falsely accused his father of stealing some eighteenth-century pistols. Connor hoped to exact a wry sort of revenge, and after sneaking into the building late one evening, he swiped an enormous pile of loot—paintings, sculptures, vases, platters, silverware, and two Asian urns the size of dishwashers. The haul was so large that Connor's friends dumped some of the artifacts on the museum's front lawn a few days later. No one wanted to store so much stolen property.

Connor's passion for art ran deep. His mother was a landscape painter, his father collected antique guns. Connor's great-great-great grandfather was William Cole, a well-known art connoisseur and the cousin of Thomas Cole, the founder of the Hudson River School of painting. Connor loved the experience of plundering the Forbes. "There's nothing like the rush of being in a museum at two in the morning, knowing that you have run of the place," he told me. "It was like being in Aladdin's cave, a kid in the candy store."

Connor began stealing from museums regularly. He snatched a large collection of Asian artifacts from the Children's Museum in Roxbury. He hit up the Peabody-Essex Museum in Salem. The police investigated him for plotting to swipe a Rembrandt from Harvard's Fogg Museum, and when the cops raided his safe houses, it would often take several police vans to cart away all his loot. One search of Connor's apartment in Revere uncovered seven antique swords, a suit of armor, a teakwood chest, three Persian lamb coats, six oriental rugs, along with three handguns, a set of silencers, a tear-gas pen, and a box marked: "Hot, do not touch, you can be dead in five minutes," which had a five-foot-long, hooded cobra inside.

The police caught Connor for the first time in Sullivan, Maine. He was coming out of an empty mansion with an armful of Tiffany lamps when a local sheriff's deputy pulled up in a cruiser. Connor tossed the officer into a ravine and roared off in his Cadillac. Maine State police caught Connor a short while later, trying to head to Canada. The art thief did a year in prison, and within months of getting out, he was indicted for the Forbes robbery. He went back on the lam, hiding out in Boston's Back Bay neighborhood, one of the city's most exclusive areas. He hoped that it would be the last place that authorities would look for him. But eventually the police staked him out, and one evening as the art thief walked along Beacon Street, three plainclothes officers surrounded him.

"Drop your weapon," one of the cops ordered.

"Drop *your* weapons," he yelled back.

Connor fired his .38 and hit one officer in the groin. The police returned the shots, peppering Connor's torso with slugs. As blood dripped from his body, Connor ran into an apartment building, scampered up a fire escape, and made it to the rooftop of a nearby brownstone. The police found Connor an hour later. They exchanged another round of gunshots—the officers punching Connor with more bullets—and the police eventually bagged the art thief half alive, surrounded by broken glass, his pockets filled with ammunition. Connor had been hit several times and was in the hospital for more than a year recovering from the wounds. "How's the cop I shot?" he managed to ask, before he was brought down from the roof on a stretcher.

When Connor came out of jail, he started on a crime spree that made his earlier thefts seem like the work of a hapless amateur—and ended only months before the Gardner heist, certifying his spot as a top suspect in the museum robbery. He employed a variety of criminal strategies: daytime raids, late-night larcenies, elaborate disguises. He heisted almost every major museum on the East Coast, the Metropolitan Museum of Art in New York, the Smithsonian in Washington. He robbed banks, warehouses, and other criminals. He boasted that he had figured out a fail-proof way to clean out an armored car—show up with a rocket-propelled grenade launcher on the back of a pickup.

Police pinched Connor a few times, but the charges never stuck. Authorities arrested him for murdering a police officer; a jury found him not guilty. Police charged Connor with robbing a Milton bank; he was acquitted in the subsequent trial. Prosecutors also fingered Connor for helping to murder two teenage women. Again, he got off. Then, finally, it seemed like law enforcement had nailed Connor for good. It was 1974, and the FBI collared the art thief as he tried to hawk a set of Wyeth paintings stolen from the Woolworth estate in Maine. But Connor masterminded the theft of a portrait from Boston's Museum of Fine Arts in order to reduce the charges. It was a cold Monday afternoon when Connor and an associate stepped into the side lobby of the museum and walked up the marble steps to the second floor. Rembrandt's *Portrait of a Girl Wearing a Gold-Trimmed Cloak* hung in a gallery not far from the backstairs. The painting was an early work, dating back to 1632, a portrait of a young, creamy-faced woman. The canvas wasn't very big, about the size of a sheet of legal paper, and Connor quickly snatched it from its metal hook.

"What are you trying to do?" a guard shouted.

Connor's associate pulled out a 9-mm pistol and pointed it at the man's belly. "Shut up, or I'll kill you."

Connor clutched the painting to his chest and dashed down the stairs. His associate ran after him. In the foyer, one of the guards tried to grab Connor, but Connor's partner thumped him across the face with his pistol, and the man crumpled to the ground. Connor sprinted out the door. His associate fired a few shots at the foot of the stairs to scare off any other guards. "It was a snatch and grab," Connor told me later. "We had a girl in the lobby with a stroller who served as a blocker, and there was another car outside of the museum in case there was a police car. He would crash into the cops if they chased us and would pretend it was an accident. It was a well-planned operation."

At the time experts valued the looted Rembrandt portrait at as much as $5 million. It was believed to be one of the most expensive paintings ever stolen in the United States. Connor stored the work for a year at a friend's house—"People always dream of owning a Rembrandt," he told me—and then reached out to law enforcement and negotiated the return of the canvas in exchange for a reduced sentence. News of the deal made many, including Harold Smith, grudgingly admit that Connor was one of the country's most brilliant art thieves. Who else could have swiped an Old Master canvas and orchestrated its return, all while out on bail for an unrelated heist?

But Connor's larcenous orgy eventually came to a humbling end. In 1988 he moved to Kentucky and began doing business with a shady New York art fence named Joe. Connor first sold Joe a few looted Old Master paintings. Then Connor promised Joe that he could set him up with a regular pipeline of drugs, and as a down payment he gave him a kilo of cocaine. Moments later, a SWAT team burst in—Joe was an undercover FBI agent. At the sentencing hearing the following year, Connor asked for leniency. "The world is a stage, and each must play his part," he told the judge. "I did what I did do. And you can believe me that I'm sorry for it." But the judge too played a part—he gave Connor a twenty-year sentence, which was later reduced to eleven years. "You've done nothing but hurt, and take, steal, barter, deal in stolen property," the judge told Connor. "Unfortunately, you're rotten to the core."

SMITH CONTACTED CONNOR soon after he was released from prison in 2000. Smith had long suspected that Connor might have had some sort of role in the Gardner heist. When Youngworth first offered to broker the return of the art in the summer of 1997, Connor gave support to the antiques dealer, telling people that he was behind Youngworth's proposal, that Youngworth was his partner. While Connor denied having any part in the actual robbery, he bragged that he had a "cipher that will lead people" to the paintings and that he would retire on the Gardner reward money "to a life of opulent solitude." The feds appeared to believe Connor, and before they began their negotiations with Youngworth, they moved Connor to a detention center in Rhode Island so that he could participate in all-day talks over the lost art.

But Connor and Youngworth soon had a rancorous falling-out. When Connor earned illegal profits from his museum thefts and bank robberies, he would often invest the money in art and antiques. He was particularly fond of samurai swords, but he also snapped up Ming vases and Malaysian wood sculptures, eventually amassing a collection worth more than $5 million. Before going to prison, Connor secreted his artworks into a forty-foot trailer, and it was supposed to sit, untouched, in a lot behind Youngworth's antiques store. But Connor's friends told him that Youngworth had been slipping into the trailer and selling Connor's treasures to supply a burning heroin addiction. The news enraged Connor. He promised to sue Youngworth and swore that once he got out of jail, he would make arrangements for Youngworth to repay him for the theft of his art collection. Connor also told investigators that the Gardner art had been secreted away and that Youngworth was no longer in a position to return the missing masterpieces. Connor never came forward, though, and explained his own role in the caper—and that's what interested Smith.

Smith met with Connor at the home of Al Dotoli, Connor's old music manager. Dotoli lived in Quincy, just south of Boston, a few blocks from the Neponset Bridge. It was a warm spring morning. A gauzy sunshine draped the front yard. Wearing a golf shirt and khakis, Connor came out of the house and looked Smith up and down, his eyes lingering on the detective's scarred face.

"How old are you?" Connor asked Smith.

"Twenty-nine," Smith said, staring back at him, meeting him eye to eye.

Smith laughed and touched Connor's hand. "Seventy-five," he said.

Smith had a distinctive interviewing style. He wasn't aggressive. He wouldn't try to intimidate witnesses. Instead, he took his time and asked question after detailed question. He wanted to know all the particulars, every last specific, and sometimes his interviews would last for days. But after sitting down with Connor for a few minutes, Smith realized that their conversation might not take very long at all. Two years before, Connor had suffered a massive heart attack and spent two weeks in a deep coma. When Connor regained consciousness, his speech was slow ·and slurred. He could barely walk. For months, he didn't know his own name.

By the time Smith met Connor in 2000, the art thief had regained some of his long-term memory, and Smith soon got Connor to confess to having cased the Gardner in the late 1980s. As Connor recalled it, he would climb up a tree across the street from the museum and watch the guards as they did their rounds, taking notes on security procedures and safeguards. The score seemed simple, easy, and very lucrative, and Connor soon enlisted an associate, Bobby Donati. Together, the two would walk the museum like teenagers at a mall, moving from gallery to gallery, discussing whether or not they wanted to lift specific items. While Connor wanted to swipe Titian's *Europa*, Donati yearned for the Napoleonic finial. The men debated various ways of breaking into the museum, finally deciding on dressing up as police officers, a gambit that they had used successfully in a number of other heists.

Connor went to prison before they could commit the robbery, and Donati soon teamed up with an ex-con named David Houghton. An antiques dealer who occasionally fenced stolen property, Houghton supposedly hired the thieves and stashed the loot, and Connor recalled Houghton visiting him in a California prison and telling him that he and Donati committed the heist, that they stole the Chinese ku as a gift for him. Houghton also promised Connor that they would use some of the stolen art to bargain him out of jail. "[Houghton's visit] was the last contact that I had in any way with the Gardner," Connor told Smith.

Smith nodded. The account seemed believable. Rather than a Hollywood version of art theft, the canvases appeared to have followed a more typical route, pilfered by low-level thugs and stashed away for safekeeping. Smith also knew that Donati was someone who could have pulled off something as big as the Gardner. The mob associate had a rap sheet that stretched back to 1958, with convictions for theft and armed robbery, and he and Connor had worked together on a number of other museum heists, including the Woolworth robbery.

"These robbers, two of them are dead now?" Smith asked. "They die of natural causes?"

"Not really," Connor said, slowly. A massive man, weighing over 350 pounds, Houghton had coronary artery disease and died of a heart attack one evening in 1992. As for Donati, he was savagely murdered in the summer of 1991, clubbed over the head and stabbed twenty-eight times. The police found his body in the trunk of his two-door Cadillac about a half-mile from his house, his throat slit open like a slaughtered chicken. Lying next to his body was a Tootsie Roll wrapper, an invitation to a wedding, and an old birthday card smeared with blood. Donati's killers were never found.

Connor could not seem to remember much more. Smith would ask him questions, and he would stammer out a reply and get lost in the fog of his empty memories, or the art thief would shrug his shoulders and say that he simply couldn't recall any more. It seemed that if Connor ever knew the whereabouts of the Gardner paintings, the memory was now as lost as the works themselves.

IN EARLY 2005, just as I began my search for the lost masterpieces, a short article appeared at the back of the *Boston Globe*. The item described how Connor had undergone deep hypnosis and could now remember the name of a middleman who arranged the theft. Connor told reporters that he would contact the man in an effort to retrieve the artwork. "I think I can use my connections and powers of persuasion to make the case that has to be made," he said. The idea that Connor could solve the Gardner heist through deep hypnosis seemed improbable, but then everything about Connor seemed improbable—the singing career, the art thefts, the prison escapes—and so I tried contacting him. But the art thief was hard to reach. Connor did not own a phone. Some of his old associates wanted money to set up an interview. So one May morning, I drove down to the Brockton courthouse to interview Marty Leppo, Connor's longtime lawyer.

I was sitting in the back of the courtroom when I first saw Leppo. Actually, I heard him first. Late to the hearing, he burst through the wooden doors of the room. "I'm so sorry your honor. Car trouble," he said, moving down the center aisle, his arms flung in the air in a theatrical show of distress. Dressed in a tailored, gray suit, Leppo was a sparkplug of a man with a bantamweight frame and a bulldog's jowls. He greeted his client with a heavy handshake and then placed his forearms on the judge's bench. I couldn't hear what he was saying, but the judge kept nodding, and within a few minutes the case was adjourned. The trial was rescheduled for the following month.

I introduced myself to Leppo as he walked out of the courtroom, recalling what he told me during our first phone conversation. "Oh, I know a little about the Gardner," he said. "I've been involved since the beginning. Once the theft happened, one of the first persons who was called in was me, because of a remark made during a break in a trial. I smirked, for no reason whatsoever, just a smirk, and so I got a call from the U.S. attorney. I also represented a number of individuals—who I had represented before—and they all became suspects. And, of course, you know there is a curse on the Gardner."

"A curse?"

"Myles Connor lost his memory. Mrs. Youngworth died of an overdose. Mashberg got cancer," Leppo said. "Neil Cronin, the FBI agent, was killed in a car accident. Merlino is dead. Joe Murray was murdered by his wife."

"And you?"

"My golf game has gone to hell."

I followed Leppo back to his law office. The firm was squeezed into a suburban strip mall, wedged between a real estate agency and a psychotherapist's practice. We stepped inside the foyer, and across from the entrance, hanging prominently on the wall, was a framed 1988 *Boston Magazine* article that hailed Leppo as one of the city's top mob lawyers. The story noted that Leppo was particularly adept at defending criminals against charges of loan-sharking and said that he had recently given a job to Harvey Brower. A disbarred lawyer, Brower had deep connections to the New England mob and once served prison time for helping a gangster escape to Mexico. A small snapshot of Leppo had been placed on the framed cover of the magazine.

Leppo had a frenetic energy, like a shark that needed to keep moving to stay alive, and before I finished reading the article, he had hurried into his office. I followed him inside a few moments later. Leppo toured me around the room, showing me pictures of his wife, three sons, and six grandchildren. Then he pointed to a framed four-leaf clover. "A girl gave that to me. She was accused of murdering two of her husbands, and I got her off."

"Really?"

"When clients come in and sit right over there and say, 'what's the fee?' I say '$150,000,' and they say, 'ugh, I can't afford that.' And I say 'well, thank you, very much. If you want to pay peanuts, go hire a monkey.'"

We eventually moved into Leppo's conference room. It was decorated with framed reproductions of the stolen masterpieces, Rembrandt's *The Storm on the Sea of Galilee,* Vermeer's *The Concert.* "Those are beautiful pieces. If they don't ever come back, what a shame, what an absolute shame," he said.

Leppo then darted out of the room and returned with a large manila folder, overflowing with court documents, background checks, inmate letters, mug shots. "If Myles still had his memory, I would venture to say that if bad people had the art, he would find it out," Leppo said. "But he and I have been working on other leads."

Leppo sat down, rifled through the paperwork for a moment, and then removed a letter. Dating back to 1997, the note was decorated with a drawing of a set of playing cards, a five of hearts, a queen, and an ace. Leppo began reading, "For a donation to Sinn Fein party, we can negotiate a fair way out for everyone and for $200,000, justice for all."

"So did you do anything with them?"

"I did a lot."

Leppo pulled out another note. "This one came in 1999," he said. "If the art is still missing, talk to Youngworth. We're still here. Sinn Fein."

He then removed from the envelope two passes for a fund-raising event in Dorchester. "How special. They sent me two tickets to meet them."

"What happened?"

"I might tell you sometime."

I eyed the pile of papers. "So what sort of leads are you and Connor working now? Do you know where the paintings are?"

Leppo straightened out some of the pages. "I'm pretty sure from my sources that the stuff went to a church in South Boston with a gay priest and then it was split up," he said. *"The Storm* is gone forever, in my opinion. Someone else had *The Concert.* The key to the whole thing might be the top of the flagpole. I was close to it a few years ago, and everyone got spooked. But really nobody knows where that stuff is, except the people who eventually ended up with it."

Leppo checked his watch, stood up, and said that he had to go to a meeting. He promised that he would do his best to organize an interview with Connor. "Remember," he quipped. "I'm not interested in the $5 million. I would make the museum pay me $50 million, and the first $30 million I would give to charity."

I did the math in my head. "That would leave with you with $20 million."

He grinned. "As we speak, those paintings get more valuable."

LEPPO CALLED ME a few weeks later. "I have the world's most famous art thief in the room," he said, "and a lead that will make your hair stand on edge. How quickly can you get up here?"

I was in Leppo's law offices within days. He greeted me at the door. "I'm real busy today. I got a kid with a cocaine charge hanging over his head. Seventeen years mandatory sentencing. You could do that standing on your head, right?" Leppo led me back to the conference room, and as he opened the door, Connor stumbled out of a chair. He had been sleeping with his feet propped up on the conference table; his head just below a poster of the Gardner's stolen Vermeer.

"You don't need me. I have heard this story a hundred times," Leppo said before leaving the room.

Connor blinked a few times. "I stayed up late last night," he explained. His hair, once a wild red mop, was now wisps of gray lying across his head in a soft comb-over. There were rings of dirt around his fingers; his khaki pants were stained with what appeared to be ketchup. And with almost no introduction, he began to tell his long, crime-filled story. The account unfolded in a mass of fantastic images—the thrill of playing guitar with Roy Orbison, the rooftop shoot-outs with police, the well-planned museum thefts, the long nights of women and money. Even in his slurred voice, Connor's story seemed ready-made for Hollywood, complete with an archenemy, a corrupt cop, whom Connor eventually outfoxed and knocked senseless in a fistfight outside a downtown police station. In his mind's eye, Connor seemed to cast himself as Jack Nicholson or Nicholas Cage in the movie of his life, with Tommy Lee Jones or Alec Baldwin playing the corrupt cop.

"I was a very successful robber," Connor said, flashing his blue eyes. "I had an outlaw's code."

Leppo opened the door to the room. "Be careful. Connor could talk a cat out of a can of salmon."

I looked at Connor. "So what's the outlaw code?"

"The code is—" Connor began.

Leppo interrupted. "He won't steal anything that isn't worth anything."

When Leppo pulled the door closed, Connor explained that he really did have a set of criminal values. He never ratted on friends. He used force only when necessary. As a thief, he robbed exclusively from institutions that had an excess of money—banks, drug dealers, armored cars, and, of course, museums. Connor didn't feel much remorse, certainly not about the art thefts. He explained that art institutions were not the protectors of culture that everyone made them out to be. "Most art in museums resides in storage facilities, and most people who bequeath their collections to a museum don't realize that the museums put most of their art into storage and sell it off to make money for bigger acquisitions," he said. "I never had any qualms about relieving them of their property."

As Connor's story slowly wound into the here and now, he blamed his current state of penury on antiques dealer William Youngworth. "My art collection was going to be my retirement fund in the form of an antiques store," he said. "But Youngworth sold off all of that for pennies on the dollar. Not at Christie's. Not at Sotheby's. Not at Elder's. Not at Skinner's. He sold my stuff at flea markets. Old Uncle Bill's flea market." Now Connor worked as a house painter and drove a banged-up old Dodge, and Leppo handed him $20 to pay for his gas for the drive home.

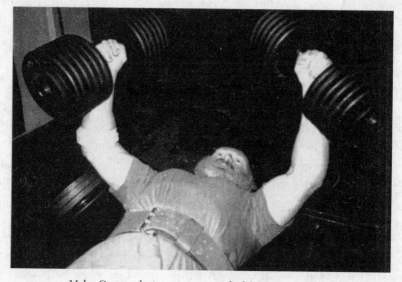

Myles Connor during a prison weight-lifting competition.

When I told Connor that Youngworth denied stealing his art collection, he leaned forward. "You know where he is?" Connor asked, pushing his palms against the table. "I would like to talk to him. I'd like to know if he still has anything. There was so much stuff that I had. I mean it makes sense that he has something squirreled away. He's not a stupid man." Connor paused and added, "I don't intend on doing anything bad to the guy."

I spent the rest of the day with Connor talking about art, theft, and the Gardner case, and later that evening, we went out for beers and ribs at a nearby Texas steakhouse. I wasn't always sure what to make of the art thief. Was he darkly wicked? Or was he some sort of an idealist, a type of modern-day Sundance Kid? At times during our talk that afternoon, he showed a roguish charm, arguing the beauty of Tlingit sculpture or expressing a belief in the universality of aesthetics. "A world without art! I can't imagine it!" Between sips of a Sam Adams, he gave a long lecture on samurai swords. "The guy who makes the blade is one artist. The guy who makes the handle is another artist. The guy who makes the sword guard is another, and he usually also makes the metal handle, called the *fuchi*, and the *menuki*, which is the middle design of the handle."

But Connor was also shamelessly villainous. He bragged about his big scores, his capacity for unrestrained violence, arrogantly dismissing concerns about the harm that he had caused his victims. "I had a gang of down-hearted, tough guys. I wasn't afraid of anybody," he said, a grin lopsiding his face. "I would take it right to people." Indeed, that afternoon, Connor told me how he had some associates nearly murder a man in an attempt to overturn a wrongful rape charge against him. Connor said that he had been unjustly convicted of sexually assaulting a young woman and that while he was in jail for the crime, he found the true culprit—a man called Halloway—and so he had some friends batter Halloway until he owned up to the crime.

"I told Halloway, 'If you don't tell me the truth, you'll be killed,'" Connor explained. "Bang, bang, bang, bang, he caught it left and right. Halloway was half killed. He was beaten unmercifully by my friends." Eventually, Halloway confessed, saying that, yes, he had assaulted the woman. Connor made him sign an affidavit, and a few weeks later, a judge exonerated Connor. "The judge said, 'I have no doubt, Mr. Halloway was the guilty party. I also have no doubt that Mr. Connor tortured and beat up Halloway,'" Connor told me, banging the table for emphasis. "So it was overturned!"

That evening, as Connor ate his plate of ribs, gnawing each bone as clean as a sun-bleached skeleton, I asked him if he would ever steal again. He was sixty-four years old and eligible for Social Security and had spent almost two decades of his life in jail. Would he risk it all again for one last caper?

Connor looked up from his plate. "You know a lot of guys come out of the can and say, 'that was the last time, I'm done.' I've never had that attitude. That's defeat, and you know, I'm not defeated until I'm in the ground."

He took a long slurp of beer. "So am I beyond a score for a tremendous reward? No." Then he smiled. "But it would have to be a big hit, because if they catch me again, they'll put me away for life."

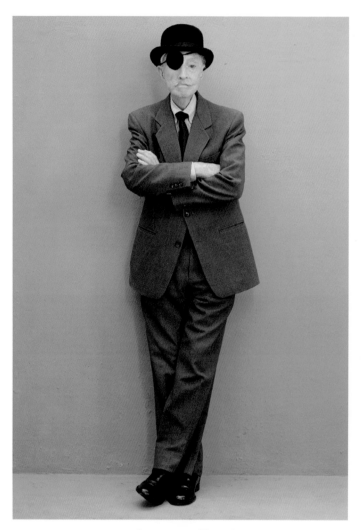

Art detective Harold Smith.
(Timothy Greenfield-Sanders)

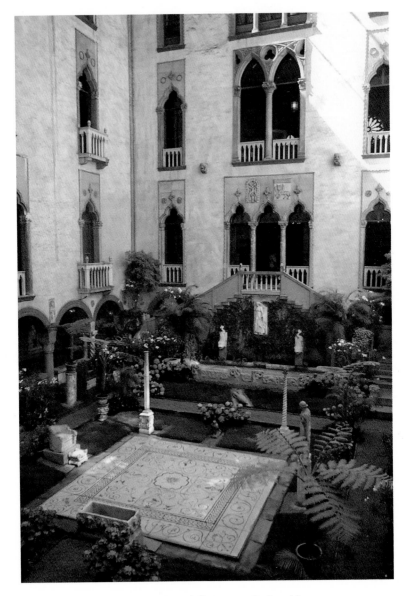

The courtyard of the Isabella Stewart Gardner Museum.

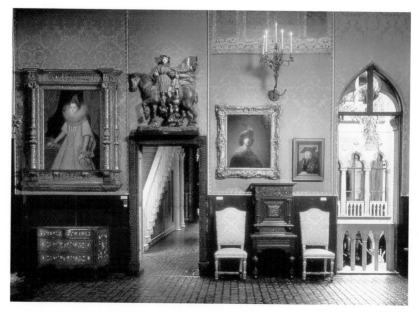

The Dutch Room of the
Isabella Stewart Gardner Museum.

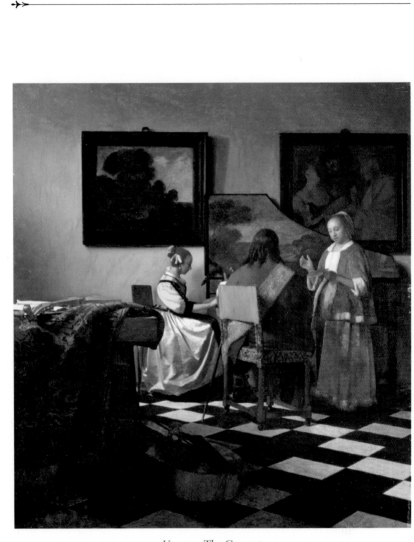

Vermeer, The Concert.

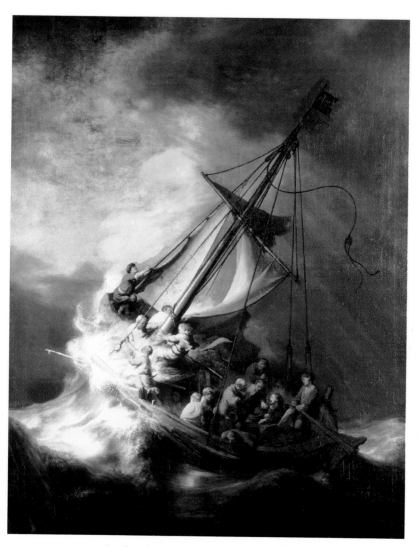

Rembrandt, The Storm on the Sea of Galilee.

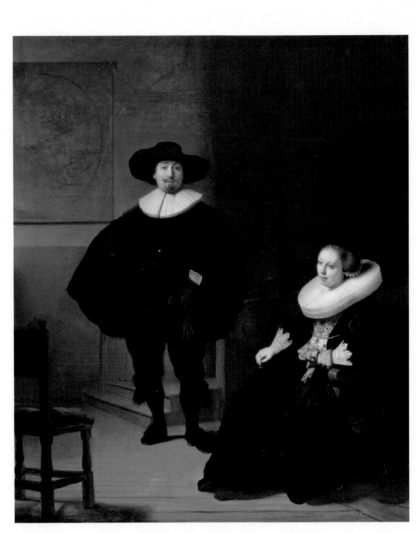

Rembrandt, A Lady and Gentleman in Black.

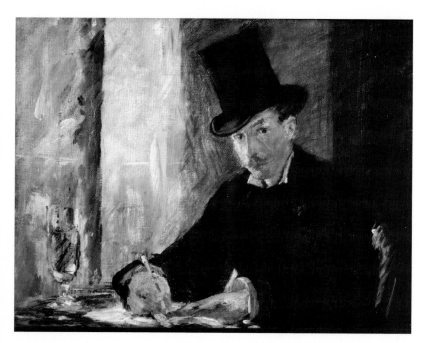

Eduard Manet, Chez Tortoni.

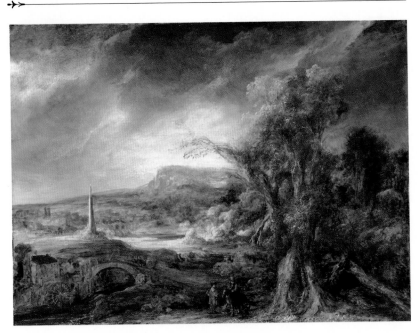

Govaert Flinck, Landscape with an Obelisk.

Degas, La Sortie de Pesage.

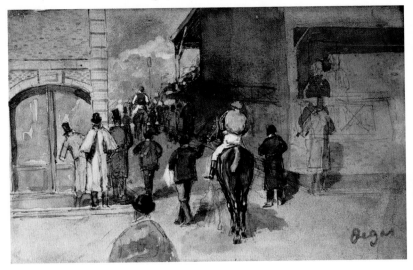

We soon stood up to leave. It was late. The restaurant had become loud and busy. Connor tried to find the door, but because of the effects of his stroke-like heart attack he could not recall the way out. He first walked toward the bathroom. Then he followed a waitress toward the kitchen. So I took his arm and slowly guided him out of the restaurant. I walked with him to his Dodge and watched him as he wheeled the car out of the parking lot. As he faded into the late-day traffic, I wondered about the thieves who looted the Gardner. They must have known Connor, they must have seen him as a sort of criminal hero. It occurred to me, too, that the men who robbed the museum must have been similar to Connor. Maybe they weren't as smart or as savvy as he, but they seemed like they were just as ambitious and just as evil.

WHILE CONNOR AND I TALKED THAT AFTERNOON, Leppo frequently dashed into the room. Standing behind Connor, he would add gritty details to an anecdote. "The code word for the stolen Rembrandt was Phyllis," Leppo told me. Or he would sharply tease Connor. "You realize all the criminals I have to deal with everyday to take care of you?" Then Leppo would announce that he had a conference call or a brief to write and hurry out again. But at the end of the day, once the team of secretaries and paralegals had all gone home, Leppo returned and sat down at the end of the conference table. He leaned back in his chair and put his fingers together in a little steeple and said that he wanted to talk about the Gardner case.

Leppo explained that Connor had recently recalled new details about the person who took control of the Gardner loot, and while Leppo would not tell me the particulars, he had been researching the tip, consulting his sources, and he thought that he might have a good angle on the person who controlled the art. "I confirmed the information. It's more than rumor," Leppo told me. "He is a person of interest, and I can tell you that I can do more with a private investigator than the FBI will ever do."

Leppo grinned and offered me a chance to get the inside story, to help them research their angle. "I'm not saying it's going to go anywhere," he said. "But I know how to investigate that person because I knew him." He laughed. "OK. I'm going to go further and say that he has a relative in the art business."

I looked at Leppo and then at Connor. The art thief nodded as if to say, *We're serious.*

Leppo pointed to a small ceramic bowl that sat in the middle of the conference table. The piece was brown and looked vaguely African, with three small heads surrounding the rim. I hadn't noticed it before, largely because it looked like someone had been using it as an ashtray.

"Where did this come out of? The Forbes?" Leppo said, looking at Connor.

"The Peabody Museum," the art thief said slowly. Connor explained that he would often pass himself off to museums as a wealthy collector of Asian art and antiques. The ruse gave him access to the warehouse of dozens of institutions, and he would regularly pilfer items from their storage shelves. The bowl, Connor explained, was one of the items that he had looted from the Peabody. "That was an inside sort of job." He shrugged.

I pressed Leppo for more details on his Gardner lead, and he told me that the person who took control of the paintings had deep connections to the Boston mob as well as ties to the art world. Leppo believed that the person had stashed the loot somewhere outside of Boston. "The paintings were cut from their frames. How far could they go in that condition?" he said. "But you have to go to the West Coast, you have to go to West Palm Beach, and you have to go to Israel."

"I don't think the person will just give up what they bought," Connor added. "They paid a lot of money for the paintings, and they could return it themselves for several millions. It's going to take some high adventurous escapades, situations that would technically be deemed illegal."

I must have looked skeptical. Leppo leaned over the table. "You want another hint?" he said. "Before the heist a guy came up to me, who was a well-known racket guy, a bookmaker, and said a lawyer is asking me for couple million dollars to buy into some artwork. What do you think?"

"And?"

"I have my own thoughts about what happened," Leppo said. "I continue to conduct my own investigation."

"But you won't give me details."

"I'm not going to divulge all of it," he said. "But I honestly believe that we might be on the right track. I'm going to be spending a lot of time on it and maybe solving the Gardner."

FROM HIS DECADES of experience as an art detective, Smith knew that there was no such thing as a perfect lead. People lie, evidence is inconclusive, memories are lost. He would often have to cut deals with unsavory characters—murderers, drug dealers—in order to move a case forward, and I tried to keep the same sort of dispassionate mind while considering Leppo's offer. I was sure that they had some solid information. Connor was after all a master art thief, perhaps the best in New England, and he had admitted to having scoped out the museum. Just as important, though, was the fact that Leppo had represented almost every major figure who had been accused of the crime. He had been the lawyer for golden boy gangster David Turner, mobster Carmello Merlino, antiques dealer William Youngworth, along with Stephen Rossetti and Ralph Rossetti, all of whose names have come up in the investigation. I had even come across some evidence that implied that Leppo himself could have helped to facilitate the return of the artwork. In an FBI report dated March 25, 1998, a confidential informant—most likely Richard "Fat Man" Chicofsky—told the bureau that Leppo would get $2 million of the Gardner's reward money if the paintings were returned. Leppo vehemently denied the account, calling Chicofsky, "a liar, one of the all-time great liars."

But there was plenty that spoke against getting involved—and I didn't really think that their effort would amount to much. Because if Connor and Leppo had such a powerful lead, why hadn't they tried to use it earlier? They knew as well as anyone how valuable a stolen masterpiece could be at a negotiating table. Plus, the information that Connor had provided so far had never fully squared up. The art thief had fingered David Houghton as the architect of the robbery, but people who knew Houghton thought that he was far too bumbling to have ever played a role in the heist. "When he was alive, nobody ever considered David Houghton a mastermind of anything—except, possibly, car repair and questionable disability claims," noted one *Boston Globe* article. But most importantly, there was a $5 million reward for the missing paintings, more than enough incentive to run down a quality lead without having to pull me in. Why did Connor and Leppo need my help?

Still, I wanted to run the angle out to its definitive end, and one afternoon, I drove down to Plymouth to meet with private detective Charlie Moore. He had known Connor and Leppo for years, and we met in his office overlooking Plymouth Bay. Moore was short and squat and sat in an office chair with a gun holster hanging from the back. His desk was littered with the tools of his private detective trade—binoculars, video cameras—along with a small metal replica of a hand grenade with a plaque that read: "Complaints Department: Take a Number."

Moore explained that he and Connor had struck a deal on the Gardner case almost a decade ago—if the private detective helped Connor recover his collection of art and antiques, Connor would give Moore everything that he knew about the museum robbery. They struck the deal years before Connor lost his memory, and the art thief had provided Moore with far more information than he ever offered me or Smith. Connor detailed all of the strategies of his stick-up crew; he gave up all the names of his old associates, Ralph Petrozziello, Osby DePriest, John Cericola. "We ran out all the relatives, brothers, sisters, kids. We looked at all the properties, to see if it was stashed some place," Moore said. The private detective even developed an informant within Youngworth's antiques store and searched through Connor's trailer to see if there might be any clues hidden there.

But it all went nowhere, and Moore concluded that Connor simply didn't have any good information. "Myles has zero idea where those paintings are," Moore told me. The private detective explained that it was possible that Connor may have had some sort of connection to the thieves, that he might have drawn up a plan for the robbery and given it to an associate or maybe one of his friends had committed the heist.

But now "Connor's long-term memory is gone. His short-term memory is not that much better," Moore told me. "The whole thing is a joke." And when I told Moore about Leppo's new information, Moore gave a hoarse laugh. He didn't think that I should spend any time pursuing the angle or otherwise get involved.

Moore and I talked for another hour that afternoon. The private detective still ran down leads in the case. A source would provide a new name or Moore would land a tip from an informant. The private detective had cracked other art heists—he once recovered paintings swiped from the home of the president of Harvard University—and Moore believed that someone would soon break open the Gardner caper. "It's just a matter of time," he said flatly. "All it takes is one good lead." Before I left, I asked Moore what he thought of the museum itself. I was curious to know what a hard-boiled gumshoe might think of such an intimate art experience. "Oh, I've never been inside," he said. "I'm looking for the reward and the paintings."

AS I LEFT MOORE'S OFFICE and drove back to Boston, I wondered who would be searching for the Gardner art if there weren't a $5 million reward. Is it even possible to separate art's fame and fortune from its beauty and truth? It didn't quite seem possible for Connor or Leppo or Moore. Even Isabella Stewart Gardner had a hard time. She enjoyed the gilded reputation that came with buying Old Master paintings, and she'd sometimes leak the news of a recent acquisition to the society pages, which grew to call her "Donna Isabella." Still, I knew that the missing paintings had a power that went far beyond mere human greed. I had seen it in Smith. I had seen it in Dan Falzon. I had seen it in security director Anthony Amore. I had begun to even see little glimpses of it in myself late at night as I lay in bed, the room dark and deep, the sounds of the world quiet and muffled, the images of the lost art flittering through my mind like hazy pictures from an old slide projector. The arching hand of a singer, a spumy wave smashing against a rock, the deep stare of the man in *Chez Tortoni*, my mind getting giddy as a drunk. Who has those paintings?

10. PROGRAM FOR
AN ARTISTIC SOIREE

Any News on Your Side

THE TRAIN SLID into Eastbourne with a sigh. It had been a three-hour trip from London's Paddington Station, a meandering passage through the hills of southeast England, and when the train finally came to a stop, I jumped onto the platform. The station was large and cavernous with a tall, vaulted ceiling that gave the ambient noise—the clang of locomotives, a squawking public address system—a hollow echo. Some pigeons flittered along the floor. The air smelled of stale cigarette smoke. In the far corner of the building, a few drunks shielded their eyes from the dirty afternoon light that stabbed through the arched and once grand Victorian windows.

During the nineteenth century, Eastbourne was a booming seaside resort, hailed as having the sunniest beaches in all of England, which is saying a lot in an island of almost constant rain. The town became the summer home of Charles Dickens and Lewis Carroll. Frederick Engels visited so often that he requested his ashes scattered along the shore. But over the past few decades, the British have been going to Spain and Portugal to get their annual dose of sun, and the boardwalks in Eastbourne have become old and rickety, the resorts half-empty, the town a distinctly British version of Coney Island. In the train station, there was a billboard for the Lifeboat Museum and a raft competition, and signs pointing toward Beachy Head, a set of chalky cliffs at the edge of town that are believed to be the most popular spot in England to commit suicide. Each year, about twenty people throw themselves off the bluffs.

At the far end of the platform, pacing back and forth, was Paul Hendry. A large man with rounded shoulders and a comfortable belly, he wore a double-breasted, pink-pinstriped suit. In one breast pocket was a matching pink handkerchief; in the other pocket was a gold Rolex pocket watch dangling from a thin chain. A cigarette hung rakishly from his mouth.

Hendry put out a large hand that enveloped mine like an oven mitt. "Turbo," he said in a deep Cockney accent. "Pleased to meet you." Hendry still goes by his underworld alias, the Turbocharger, and as we strode out of the train station, the inspiration for the moniker became obvious. He charged across the parking lot like a bull, his head tucked into his shoulders, arms swinging at his sides, body pushing ahead of his feet, puffing at a cigarette, all the while keeping up a constant patter. "How was your trip?" he asked, and before I could answer, he told me: "It was great that your train was late. I got me a cup of coffee and ran into this bloke who was an art thief. Worked out of Brighton. I knew who he was, but I'd never met him. And there he was in the station, buying a paper. Look, he gave me his card." Turbo slowed down to flash me the small piece of paper. "It's really quite lucky. He could be a great source."

When Turbo was fourteen he became a "knocker," slang for a person who knocks on the door of country estates to convince owners to sell their fine antiques—and then robs them if they don't. Turbo rarely filched works himself. "Oi, I was too big and noisy for breaking and entering," he explained. "There was one instance, I remember, where I went to go steal some jewelry. I had to creep into the house, while the occupant was downstairs. I got through the window and jumped down and went CRASH! The person came out, and I said to him, 'I will never do this again.' I let myself out the door and walked out. From then on, I said 'my role must be more as a handler.'"

Turbo boasted that he once was one of the biggest fences in England, with a half-dozen gangs working for him. "I would tell them where to go, what to steal, and then sit back at a nice hotel and wait for them to arrive and pay them off. Champagne, cocaine, a girl, anything they wanted." Turbo would typically give the stolen artworks a quick restoration and then draw up some false paperwork before filtering the items back into the open market. Sometimes he would get lucky and make a briefcase full of cash on a single score. In 1985 he bought a stolen Old Master for £10,000 on a Tuesday—"It was a beautiful painting, worth about $6 million now," he said—and by Saturday, he sold it for £50,000. More often, though, he would sit on stolen works for months, even years, before he would try to sell them. "You never want them to be able to trace the works back to you," he said. "That's how you get caught."

In 1993 Turbo's son, Oliver, was born, and he decided to go clean. He had two convictions, one in 1983 for handling a stolen eighteenth-century Dutch bureau, and another in 1990 for swiping a bronze sculpture. So, first with the Sussex County Police, and then later with Scotland Yard, he became a police informant and freelance stolen art broker. "I'm a liaison between the crooks and the coppers," he explained. "They both trust me, and I work to make sure that stolen art gets returned." Turbo will also tip off museums or galleries if he hears that they are being targeted for a big heist. "I can't afford a Picasso. I can't afford a Rembrandt. I can't afford iconic works of art, so the only way I can look at them and appreciate them is at a public gallery or museum," Turbo said. "I tell the thieves, stick to the little stuff. Stealing the big artworks is a headache."

As we walked to Turbo's car, he noticed that I was struggling to keep good notes. "I'll try and slow down, but I'm a bit of a quack-quack, someone who can't stop talking. That's what I am. It's very effective for dealing with people. When they talk to me, they think that they have everything, but they've got virtually nothing," he said. "But, really, this is me naturally. I used to go on speed and cocaine twenty years ago, and then I was completely crazy. People use to give me what I wanted just to get rid of me. It was a selling technique. If I was trying to sell you something, you'd say, 'Whatever price you want, just take it.'"

We pulled out of the parking lot in Turbo's lipstick-red BMW, and he explained that he needed to stop off at a shop and buy some shoes. It was a small boutique located on the northern edge of town, and Turbo waved hello to the saleswoman as we stepped inside. She was blond and young, no more than twenty-five, dressed in a stylish T-shirt and taut jeans. Turbo told her that I'd come from America to write a book about him.

"You really want a discount, don't you," she said, as she pulled a shoebox from under the counter.

"You couldn't do any reductions?" Turbo asked.

She raised her eyebrows.

"I always get 10 percent off," he added.

"Do you have a privilege card?"

"No. But my son always comes in for the latest T-shirts and things," Turbo said. Then he laughed. "Oh smile. Come on."

"Yeah, yeah," the saleswoman said, a slight flicker at the edge of her mouth. "OK, 10 percent."

"And how about if I buy two pairs?" he said. "How about 20 percent for two?"

She shook her head. "Awright, 20 percent."

As we walked out of the store, Turbo explained that the stolen Gardner artworks would go back to the museum if everyone proved as open to negotiation as the shoe saleswoman. In the months before he died, Harold Smith believed much the same thing, and I had come to England to see if I could pick up where he had left off. Later, much later, I would realize that there were leads that I could cross off conclusively. By the end, I could say with certainty that Youngworth seemed to have run some sort of hoax, that Connor didn't appear to have more information than what he'd shared already. But there would be leads that I would never fully resolve. The Irish lead, the Turbo connection, was one of them.

But I didn't know that then, certainly not as I struggled to keep up with Turbo. "Those pictures can be returned, but certain things have to be granted," he said. "You need a deal. I've been working on it, and sometimes, it feels really close. You feel like you have it. But then someone pulls the plug. Sometimes it's the authorities. Sometimes it's the bad guys. It's a very difficult situation. But I tell you, if a few people with enough power got together, the Gardner paintings could be returned tomorrow."

WHEN HAROLD SMITH first heard about Turbo, he flew to London to interview the reformed art fence. They met at a downtown hotel and over a cup of coffee Turbo told Smith that his business partner, Antonio Alberto Margiotta, was once offered the stolen Gardner paintings. It was in the early 1990s, and Margiotta was working at an antiques fair in Coconut Grove, Florida, when a man named Whitey Bulger approached him and asked if he wanted the Gardner loot for $10 million. Margiotta tried to bargain. He'd take all the stolen works for $1 million. But Bulger wanted the full amount—and Margiotta never heard from him again.

Turbo didn't think much of the story until a few years later when he heard that Bulger had shipped the art to Dominic McGlinchey, the head of an Irish paramilitary group. After McGlinchey was murdered with five shots to the head, the paintings fell into the hands of McGlinchey's crew. A motley assortment of ex-IRA hit men and bomb-makers, the group had strong ties to the republican movement and stashed the works in one of their safe houses, somewhere in the rural west coast of Ireland. "These are very dangerous people," Turbo explained. "They will go to Baghdad on holiday. They will steal the milk right out of your coffee."

Smith had heard of James "Whitey" Bulger before. At the time of the museum heist, Bulger was one of the most powerful gangsters in Boston, the head of the infamous Irish-American mob, the Winter Hill Gang, and during the 1970s and '80s, Bulger controlled the New England underworld with savage brutality. Calculating and cruel, Bulger was the avatar of the shrewd but ruthless mobster, a very modern, very Bostonian version of Al Capone. He was someone more than capable of masterminding something as big as the Gardner caper. "Bulger is a very dangerous man. Not just because he is a murderer, but because he is smart and sadistic," Smith once told me.

Earning the nickname "Whitey" for his shock of blond hair, Bulger started out as a brash small-time hood. He hotwired cars and got into fistfights and once was arrested for giving a police officer the finger. By his early twenties, he had graduated into armed robbery and loan-sharking, and spent more than a decade in prison for a spree of bank heists. In jail, Bulger devoured World War II biographies, examining the mistakes that had brought down Patton and MacArthur, and when he came out in 1965, he hoped to be a different type of thug, a brainy kind of criminal. He would be careful and cunning and present himself as a "good bad guy." He would hand out free turkeys on Thanksgiving. In his gangland territory, there would be no heroin dealers. Even as he hung out in underworld dives and beer halls, he would not smoke or drink. He was a workout fiend.

Still, Bulger could be brutally cruel. He was involved in nearly two dozen murders and would often torture his victims before killing them. When Bulger discovered that dope runner John McIntyre had become a police snitch, he interrogated him for hours. And then, after garroting McIntyre and shooting him in the head, Bulger had an associate yank out McIntyre's teeth with a set of pliers. Bulger's rise to power had the unlikeliest of allies, the FBI. The relationship began in 1975 when agent John Connolly persuaded Bulger to become an informant. The two men had grown up together in one of Boston's poorest neighborhoods, Southie, and for a while they had lived in the same housing project, just a few doors from one another. In a town like Boston, a place of families and clans, that counted for a lot. "You can't survive without friends in law enforcement," Connolly told Bulger during their first meeting, and the agent promised Bulger that the FBI would look out for him if he began snitching on public enemy number one, La Cosa Nostra.

At the time, Bulger's betrayal seemed like a major score, and Connolly became one of the stars of the Boston field office, the agent who convinced the city's biggest Irish gangster to turn state's witness. But it was Bulger who managed to wring the most out of the opportunity, and he snitched on his underworld competitors in order to expand his own criminal empire. He gave Connolly reams of information on the Italian mafia, and when the bureau arrested mob capo Jerry Angiulo, Bulger quickly took over his underworld business. Bulger also offered information on crime boss Howie Winter and dozens of other up-and-coming criminals, always making sure to snatch up their gangland operations after they'd been sent to jail.

Bulger's relationship with the bureau helped him become the incon-

testable king of the Boston underworld. Nearly all the major bookmak-
ers paid him a cut of their profits. Most of the major drug smugglers
gave him protection money. It helped, too, that his brother, William
Bulger, was the president of the Massachusetts state senate. The base
of Bulger's personal kingdom was Southie, where he served as the judge
and jury, the hometown hero who never left, and teenagers would sometimes scrawl on their school notebooks: WHITEY RULES. "The thing about
Bulger," longtime resident John Lyons told me one afternoon, as we
stood in Veteran's Park, overlooking the harbor, "was that he was our
justice of the peace. If you went to him, he would get things done. If
someone bothered your daughter, you'd tell him, and he'd go to the kid
and say, 'you put your hands on her again, you won't have any hands.' It
was like a code of the Old West back then."

The FBI grew dependent on Bulger, and in exchange for his underworld information, they squashed prosecutions against him for murder
and loan-sharking. Connolly also tipped Bulger off to stings and handed
him the names of other informants, essentially writing the death sen-
tences of police collaborators. Over time, Connolly and his FBI supervisor, John Morris, became so entwined with the organized crime figure
that they seemed to think that they were gangsters themselves, and they
would share long dinners with Bulger, exchanging bottles of wine and
hand-carved knives, the line between cop and criminal fading into gray
ambiguity.

The corruption of the Boston bureau went far beyond Connolly and
Morris. Eighteen agents were later implicated by the scandal, and some
believe that the double-dealing is one of the reasons that the bureau
has never been able to return the Gardner art. The most concrete evidence dates back to 1991 when a team of FBI agents snuck into Carmello Merlino's TRC auto body garage and installed a listening device in
the ceiling of his office, right over the spot where Merlino would usually
hold court. The state police ordered the wiretap just a few months
before the mobster began talking to authorities about returning the lost
Gardner paintings. But hours after the bug had been installed, Merlino
was having all his underworld conversations in the parking lot along
Dorchester Avenue, far away from the police's listening ear. "Looking

back now, Connolly must have been the leak," retired state police officer Eddie Whelan told me. "He made contact with Whitey, and Whitey brought it back to Merlino. There's not a doubt in my mind. How else would they have found out about the wire so quickly?"

Would the TRC bug have broken open the Gardner case? It seems possible. At the time of the wiretap, evidence that Turner was involved in the heist had just begun to filter into the FBI, and within the year Merlino came forward with his offer to return the paintings. If Merlino hadn't been tipped off, maybe the tapes would have recorded the mobster talking about who had the art or provided clues as to location of the stash. Either way, the corruption within the Boston bureau was pervasive—and perhaps reason enough to think that the museum's robbery investigation wasn't a prime concern. "I think that the whole FBI office was distracted by what was going on with Bulger, and they didn't make the museum investigation a priority," Gardner lifetime trustee Arnold Hiatt told me. "Morale was low, corruption was rampant. It wasn't the place to do any real detective work."

Bulger's criminal reign eventually came to a sputtering end, and federal prosecutors organized a case against the mobster, indicting him for money laundering, racketeering, and eighteen counts of murder. But before the FBI could serve the indictment, Connolly gave Bulger one last gift— he tipped Bulger off to the coming charges, and the mobster fled Boston in December 1994. Bulger was well prepared for life on the run. As early as 1977, he had created passports for himself under the name Thomas Baxter and Mark Shapeton. He also set up safe-deposit boxes all over the globe, from Montreal to Venice, each one containing large amounts of cash and jewelry. Bulger returned to Southie a few times before vanishing completely, and now despite appearing on *America's Most Wanted* twelve times and a $2 million reward for his capture, Bulger remains second only to Osama bin Laden on the FBI's Most Wanted list.

TURBO'S STORY FIT like a puzzle piece into Smith's other research. Shortly before Smith flew to London, he interviewed retired FBI agent Robert Fitzpatrick, who said that drug dealer Joe Murray claimed access

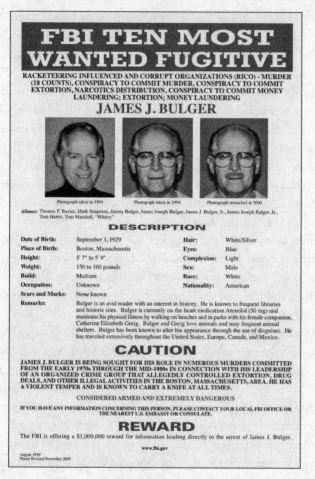

FBI wanted ad for James J. "Whitey" Bulger.

to the stolen art in early 1992. At the time, Murray was one of the biggest drug runners on the East Coast, regularly laying down $1 million for packages of marijuana, responsible for bringing more than a million pounds of drugs into Boston. Murray was tightly allied with Bulger's crew, and he called Fitzpatrick late one evening to say that he was sitting on paintings from "the biggest art heist ever" and promised that he would make Fitzpatrick a "hero" by returning the works.

But within weeks of the call, the Maine state police found Murray in the foyer of his summer home, his body slumped next to the front door like an old teddy bear. Murray's wife claimed that Murray attacked her with a fishing knife, and she shot him five times with a .357 Magnum in self-defense. But Fitzpatrick believed that Bulger might have been involved in the killing. Bulger knew that Murray had been talking to the FBI about his criminal operations, and there were some suspicious aspects to Murray's murder. Murray's wife weighed 125 pounds. Could she have been strong enough to shoot him five times with a gun as powerful as .357? Why had law enforcement never interviewed any members of Murray's family? Had Bulger perhaps sent someone to kill Murray and pocket the paintings?

Smith knew that Bulger was not the type of gangster to have organized the Gardner heist. A museum robbery would have been too public, too risky. Instead, Bulger would have made it his business to find out who committed the theft and gotten his cut. That was his criminal style. When Bucky Barrett tunneled into a bank vault in Medford and robbed hundreds of safe deposit boxes, Bulger visited him soon afterwards, demanding a portion of the more than $1 million in profits. Barrett resisted, and so Bulger lured him into a house in Southie, stuck a gun to his head, and forced Barrett to call up his associates and rustle up payment money. Then, after Barrett gave up thousands in cash, Bulger shot him in the back of the head. "I think Bulger probably had control of the paintings before he went on the run," Fitzpatrick told Smith. "He would be the type of guy who could keep something like the Gardner secret for all these years."

The Bulger lead also gave support to an Irish connection. During the 1980s, Irish-American mobsters provided extensive support to the IRA's effort to create a united Ireland—they would help republican agents go on the lam or smuggle guns to paramilitaries in Galway and Belfast. A Boston gang once heisted the National Guard Armory in Quincy, stealing dozens of belt-fed M-60 machine guns, and when the Irish police recovered the weapons three years later in a safe house in Dublin, the M-60s had been used to kill eleven people and wound nineteen others. The Boston mobsters earned their own dividends from the operations—they gained a powerful political veneer from supporting the IRA. They were sticking up banks, selling drugs, running gambling operations, not out of shameless greed but for a bigger, grander political cause. They were helping their Irish brothers back home.

Bulger saw himself as a chest-thumping Irish patriot, and when he heard TV news reports about IRA bombs murdering civilians, he would cheer and give hefty applause. Together with Joe Murray and mobster Patrick Nee, Bulger made his largest contribution to the republican cause in 1984, organizing a massive arms shipment to the IRA. The guns left the harbor town of Gloucester late one September evening on a boat called the *Valhalla*. Commanded by an old, grizzled fishing captain, the boat looked like any other commercial fishing vessel. It was a short, fat workhorse, loaded with fishing tackle and swordfish nets. But inside, just beyond the 7,000 pounds of mackerel bait, were seven tons of weapons, including Smith and Wesson handguns, .30 caliber sniper files, large-bore shotguns, and more than two dozen AK-47 machine guns. The boat sped across the Atlantic, and just off the coast of Ireland, it pulled alongside an Irish fishing trawler called the *Marita Ann*. The American crew quickly transferred the guns and ammunition to the IRA ship. The *Valhalla* turned south, and within the hour, the Irish Navy had seized the *Marita Ann*. An informant within the republican army had snitched. Worth more than $1 million, the 165 guns and 70 rounds of ammunition were believed to be the largest shipment of illegal guns in Irish history.

Turbo told Smith that the Gardner paintings had probably been shipped across the Atlantic in much the same way, tucked into the bottom of a fishing boat, with a quick transfer right off of the coast. Smith knew the IRA or an affiliated gang would want to take control of the paintings, that they understood how to turn stolen paintings into underworld commodities. Republican groups have been involved in dozens of art heists over the years, and they would occasionally bootleg looted canvases through the web of criminal channels that cross the Atlantic. When Montreal police staked out a group of Irish mobsters in order to recover a Goya stolen from a Quebec City church, they accidentally uncovered paintings swiped from Dunsany Castle, a burglary allegedly masterminded by the IRA.

The IRA also had a criminal sort of devotion for Vermeers, and they have swiped paintings by the Dutch Old Master on at least three different occasions. The biggest caper began late one evening in 1974, when a fervent nationalist named Rose Dugdale approached the Russborough House just south of Dublin. She rang the doorbell of the mansion, explaining that she had car trouble, and when the servant turned around to fetch some help, three thugs shoved their way inside. After tying up the owners, Dugdale and the group fled with nineteen paintings, including a Goya, a Gainsborough, and Vermeer's *Lady Writing a Letter with her Maid*. Valued at more than $20 million, the theft was hailed as the largest art heist in the history of the United Kingdom.

A week after the break-in, the Irish government received a ransom note. In exchange for the stolen paintings, the thieves wanted $40 million and the release of four Irish political prisoners. The police refused to negotiate and responded with a massive, door-to-door hunt for the missing art, promising to search every house in the country. A few weeks later, an Irish police officer was knocking on doors in County Cork, when he came upon a small, lonely cottage set back from the road, crouched against the ground, held together largely by the weight of its roof. The person who answered the door acted suspicious. She had rumpled hair and greasy jeans and couldn't quite explain why she had recently decided to rent the cottage. The police staged a raid within hours—Dugdale was inside with the Vermeer. The rest of the paintings were sitting in the trunk of her car, undamaged.

Smith noted the suspicious similarities between the Russborough theft and the Gardner heist. In both cases, the thieves used ruses to gain entrance to house museums that contained Vermeers. In both cases, the thieves appeared to take trophies. In Russborough, Dugdale filched a copy of Beit's diary. In the Gardner, they swiped the finial. The Gardner thieves also appeared to be looking for some sort of payoff. "Tell them they'll be hearing from us," the intruders told the guards. And during the theft of the Boston museum, one of the thieves used the word "mate." It was an offhand remark, said as a robber tied up a guard in the basement. But the expression is used almost exclusively by Irish, British, and Australian natives. For Smith, the evidence, taken together, was powerful, and it came at a time when he had already exhausted almost everything else. He had cleared Youngworth from his suspect list, he had run down the best tips from his toll-free line, and while Smith had his doubts about the Irish angle, it appeared to be his best lead yet. "I definitely believe that some of the paintings could be in Ireland," he told me shortly before he died.

SMITH'S FIRST CALL about the Irish lead was to Dick Ellis. The founder of Scotland Yard's Arts and Antiques Squad, he knew the Irish art underworld better than almost anyone. He had recovered scores of canvases stolen by Irish criminals, including a Vermeer stolen from the Russborough House, and after retiring from the Yard, he joined a private art-theft recovery business called Invaluable. Smith visited him in his London offices, a small, crowded garret, tucked away at the top of a four-story walk-up. Over a cup of tea, the British art detective told Smith that he had confirmed Turbo's information through other sources and approached a group of well-connected Irish mobsters about the possibility of returning the stolen paintings. "The good news is that there was a response, and the feedback that I'm getting is that they're interested," Ellis told Smith. The bad news was that the group was afraid of a sting—and highly skeptical of any reward offers. "What is in it for them is the big question that they have to ask," Ellis explained.

Turbo had devised an elaborate scheme for the recovery of the Gardner paintings. The plan was classic Turbo—thoughtful and informed, while being quixotic and conspiratorial. It called for a powerful American political figure, someone like Bill Clinton or Ted Kennedy, to reach out to another, equally high-level IRA politician, perhaps Sinn Fein's Gerry Adams or Martin McGuinness. The IRA leader would then turn to sources within the republican movement to find out who exactly had a controlling interest in the art. Those people would be compensated with the help of Irish-American fund-raising groups within the United States, and then the paintings would be flown to Boston and deposited in the confession box of a Catholic Church. "The confession box is key," Turbo told me. "It gives the symbol of absolution."

Turbo believed that Irish republicans would want to return the Gardner paintings to show that they had put their criminal past behind them. At the time, the political arm of the IRA, Sinn Fein, had just committed to a ceasefire and won some seats in the Irish parliament, and they were eager to distance themselves from the shoot-and-bomb elements within the movement. "Why should they return the paintings? First, they would get brownie points with Irish-America. A big thank-you for the help during the dark days of the struggle," Turbo told me. "Second, no one wants to be associated with terrorism anymore. The republicans knew that when they woke up on September 12, 2001, they needed a new angle, and sometimes when your name is in the frame, you have to pay up. Really, we should call the Vermeer, 'the Pork on the Irish Peace Process.'"

Smith had reservations. He knew that Turbo was prone to embroider stories and inflate facts, that the one-time art fence saw shadowy machinations and wild conspiracies in almost every corner. Turbo told Smith that he believed that George W. Bush had secretly set up the destruction of the World Trade Towers so that he would have an excuse to invade Iraq. He recounted long stories about how the FBI was helping Whitey Bulger stay on the run because the mobster held so much damning evidence against them. But really what concerned Smith was the lack of factual evidence. There was no proof of a connection between Bulger, the IRA, and the Gardner art. No photograph, no wiretaps, not even a money trail—and Smith made sure to tell Turbo as much.

Still, Smith believed that the pros of the lead outweighed the cons, and he began working with Ellis and pushing Turbo's plan. Smith wrote a letter to Senator Kennedy to see if he would be willing to kick-start the process. He reached out to high-level Sinn Fein politicians like Martin Ferris. He rang up the lawyers of imprisoned IRA operatives who might benefit by returning the lost paintings. "Interest continues to increase in regard to the Gardner case and the possibility of the republicans being able to help effect the return of the paintings to mankind," Smith would write in emails. "Any news on your side?"

As Smith plugged at the angle, he would sometimes uncover more evidence that the paintings were in fact in Ireland. An informant called Colin came forward and said that he had seen the lost Vermeer in a hotel room in Dublin. A longtime dealer in stolen art, Colin saw the front and back of the canvas, and he believed that it was the real thing, the painting nabbed from the Gardner museum. And at least for a while, Smith thought that he might actually recover the lost art, and when a BBC reporter contacted him about an interview in the summer of 2004, he denied the request because he believed the media attention might jeopardize the return of the paintings. "Discussions are going on and are often times laborious," he wrote. "An interview at this time could be detrimental to the cause of obtaining the return of the Gardner paintings."

But after working the Irish lead for more than two years, Smith never landed a solid, call-the-curators bead on the art. Politician Martin Ferris stopped responding to his emails. English defense attorney Giovanni Di Steffano told Smith that none of his gangland clients had anything to offer. Kennedy sent back a form letter. Smith didn't lose all confidence and remained exhaustively meticulous. In January 2005, he set up an afternoon conference call with Turbo and Gardner case agent Geoff Kelly. While Turbo had given his account to the FBI's London field office, Smith wanted to make sure that the Boston case agent also heard the informant's story. The conversation took less than an hour, and Kelly promised Smith that he would look into the tip. But Smith never heard back from the agent—Smith died three weeks later.

11. PROGRAM FOR AN ARTISTIC SOIREE II

Where's Whitey?

INCE SMITH'S DEATH in 2005, the British art detective Dick Ellis has been pushing the Irish lead, and at least from this side of the Atlantic, it seemed as if the police were on the verge of a major break in the case. Shortly after I joined the search, a London tabloid reported that a team of FBI agents had traveled to Ireland in search of the Gardner paintings. According to the article, the FBI believed that an IRA gunrunner was behind the robbery and that a group of republicans had stashed one of the paintings outside of Galway, somewhere in one of the western counties, Clare or Cork. FBI agent Geoff Kelly did not deny the account. "I can't comment specifically on an IRA connection," he told the reporter, "but I would not rule it out. We are considering all viable theories."

Ellis and I met at a restaurant in London's East End. It was a dark place, proudly out of date, sporting purple leather chairs and a low-hung ceiling. Insurance adjuster Mark Dalrymple had suggested the restaurant—he worked the Gardner case with Ellis—and when I arrived, the two detectives were already halfway through a bottle of Spanish red. Dressed in a sports coat and slacks, Ellis had a wide face and the thick, knobby body of an aging rugby player. If Ellis looked like the good cop, or at least a reasonable one, then Dalrymple was the bad cop. He was thin-framed and slump-shouldered. His yellow-stained fingers drummed a pack of Benson and Hedges.

I pulled out my voice recorder.

"No recording," Dalrymple said.

"It makes everything more accurate."

"No recording."

"Why not?"

"No recording."

I looked over at Ellis. He nodded his head. I put the device away.

"He's probably wearing a recording device under his shirt anyway," Dalrymple said, between long sips of wine. "Most of what you read by journalists is bullshit, made up, or a slant. The media jeopardizes art recovery. They force thieves underground with their headlines. The media should know what happened, but only after the recovery. If I were actually hired to work this case, I wouldn't be talking with you."

I pulled out my notebook. "So why are you talking with me?"

Dalrymple gave a soft chuckle. "You know what I want you to write about me. That I'm good-looking, I've got a big cock, old bills like me, and Americans think I'm part of the royal family."

"It's not that we don't like the media," Ellis explained. "It just doesn't help us do our work. Because for this to work, for us to return the Gardner art, there needs to be a media blackout. No stories. Nothing. For, I don't know, three months. There can't be any rumors about who did what when. There can't be any confusion. Look at company buyouts. You don't hear anything about it beforehand. Even if it's a hostile takeover. The news comes at the twelfth hour."

They had a point. Art thieves—all criminals really—spook easily. After a Rembrandt, a Delacroix, and a Gainsborough were stolen from the Montreal Museum of Fine Arts, a group of criminals tried to ransom the paintings back. The gang wanted $250,000 and returned one of the works, a Brueghel, to prove that they had access to the loot. But when the day of the buyback arrived, one of the thieves saw a police car and called off the deal. The paintings have never been seen by the public again.

"So are the paintings still in Ireland?"

"There is a lot of rumor going back and forth, a lot of speculation, and what we hear from our sources is that the paintings are in Ireland," Ellis said. "But we haven't seen any proof of life. When we see proof of life, we'll get excited."

"Do you know who has them?"

Dalrymple tapped a cigarette out of his pack, while Ellis swirled his wine around in his glass. There was a long silence. "We're not in the guessing game. That's just not what we do," Ellis said slowly. "We identify who matters most, who controls the works. We don't theorize. We don't reveal our information."

"Turbo says the works are in Ireland. He says he's negotiating to get them back."

Ellis arched an eyebrow. "Do you believe him?"

"Harold Smith seemed to believe him," I said.

"Turbo is a bit like following an English country lane that wanders this way and that, calling at every village along the way. He's got good sources, very good contacts, but he often speculates on the information and then it's bollocks," Ellis said. "You have to protect him from himself."

I asked Ellis how he planned to recover the Gardner paintings. "Not easily." He sighed. The problem was that the masterpieces appeared to have been collateralized, he explained, and a number of different groups now had a financial interest in the art. Ellis had seen this happen in dozens of other cases. So had Smith. A thief will steal an artwork and then use it as a type of underworld cash, trading the paintings for a stash of handguns or kilos of cocaine. Ellis once tracked a group of Old Master canvases that went from London to Antwerp to Luxembourg and back to Antwerp, each time used as part of an underworld deal. First it was drugs, then looted diamonds. The works were finally recovered in a sting. "You can't sell famous paintings like a Vermeer on the open market, and so they incur overheads," Ellis said. "They are used as bonds."

Dalrymple jabbed at me with his cigarette, underscoring Ellis's point. "We know that parts of the Gardner paintings have been sold as shares, as securities. But control of them changes as family relationships change, as people change. There is not just one group that we're talking with."

Ellis finished off Dalrymple's story. "To recover the Gardner paintings, you have to show the criminals respect and trust. Trust that is built up over time. Then you play a game. I'll show you mine, you show me yours, and then, hopefully, you meet the bad guys in a place like this and make the exchange."

"But why not just raid the gang? Just send in a SWAT team one morning?"

"Americans," Ellis said with a laugh.

Dalrymple leaned over the table, purring smoke out of the side of his mouth. "If it were gold bullion or a case of jewelry, we would just smack the bastards as hard as we can. But these are paintings, and the people who have them are criminals. Ireland is not a place to go gallivanting about. It is still a big village, and in some places, everyone is on the take. You hire a car to go to Limerick, and they'll know that you've hired the car and why you're there, before you're even at the foot of the driveway," he said. "What you need to understand is that these things are nicked for money. The thieves will give them up when someone gives them some money—and they know that they will not be arrested. Otherwise, they'll just sit there. They're long-term players."

Dalrymple sipped from his wine and gave me a sideways glance. "I mean really, why don't you just go up to Ireland and see if you can find the paintings? Go to a bar in Limerick and just ask for them. The best thing that could happen is they just ignore you. Or you might get murdered." He blew out a thin curl of smoke. "Come to think of it, maybe you should go up to Limerick."

A FEW DAYS LATER, I rode the train out to Eastbourne. When Turbo was a stolen art fence, he purchased a home a few miles east of the city. It was a small, boxy house, right along the beach with an expansive view of the English Channel. A few grounded trawlers and some old fishing gear sat in the front yard. Waves sucked at the beach in a low, constant murmur. "I wanted a place that would be quiet and protected," Turbo told me, pulling into the driveway. He pointed to a large brick house across the street. "The British security services used that place as a safe house for years. Agents would come back from Ireland and stay there to get debriefed. Salman Rushdie also lived there during the 1990s, while the Iranians were after him."

Turbo wanted to show me his collection of art, and I followed him inside, stepping into a house brimming with sculptures, ceramics, etchings, posters, illustrations, engravings. In the living room, there was a still life by Edward Ladell, a seascape by an eighteenth-century Dutch artist, a faded watercolor, the paintings hanging frame to frame from floor to ceiling. Turbo gestured to a gentle oil portrait of a woman and her cat. "This one is by Joe Maxwell. It was exhibited at the Royal Academy," he said. "I've got a big collection of Maxwells, actually. I got to know him many years ago. We just hit it off. We became friends. It's become powerful patronage now and all that stuff." Farther back, in the study, along the hallways, there were more prints and paintings, some of them hidden and half-forgotten. A small watercolor sat on the floor like a pair of sweaty gym socks. A cobweb the size of a dinner plate hung from a neo-Surrealist work. Many of the works were covered in a silvery sheen of dust. But, Turbo assured me, "None of it is stolen."

Turbo's interest in art didn't have family roots, or none that he knew of. He was adopted into a family of five shortly after his birth. His adoptive father was an accounts manager for a local newspaper. His adoptive mother worked on and off as a house cleaner. They beat him frequently, he said, and he recalled never wanting to take his shirt off in gym class because of the red webbing of welts that laced his back. "It wasn't an easy childhood. Nothing Norman Rockwell or anything like that," Turbo said. "In that situation, some kids would get lost in books. I would get lost in paintings. It was a form of escapism. It was my drug of choice. I was looking at Sotheby's catalogues at age twelve or thirteen. It was a way to get away from the awful terrible life that I was leading."

Turbo paused and said, "You thirsty? I'm thirsty," and I trailed behind him as he moved out of the house and into a pub across the street. It was a large, well-lit place with gilded chandeliers and vinyl booths and lots of soccer memorabilia hanging over the bar. We sat down at a table, and Turbo ordered a double espresso and a Red Bull—"this doesn't do much for me, really,"—and launched into his history of the stolen Gardner art. The account unspooled in a rush of names and places, secret hideaways, baroque plots, Whitey Bulger, South Boston, Patrick Nee, Galway, Joe Murray, Dublin, Dominic McGlinchey, until, eventually, Turbo explained that the fate of the paintings now lay with Thomas "Slab" Murphy.

I knew the name. According to British investigators, Murphy was once the IRA's chief of staff, a trained terrorist who had masterminded dozens of attacks on British forces, including the Warrenpoint ambush that killed eighteen. To help the IRA purchase guns and bombs during the height of the struggles, police believe that Murphy built a massive bootlegging empire, importing everything from pigs to drugs. After the IRA disarmed in the 1990s, Murphy kept up his illegal smuggling business and now heads a criminal empire worth more than $70 million, according to the BBC. "Slab is a lot like Carlo Gambino. He is king of the volcano, but you wouldn't know it. He looks like a simple Irish farmer, but he's one of the most powerful people in the country," Turbo told me.

"So how close did you and Smith actually come to the paintings?"

"Very," Turbo grinned.

He tapped a Marlboro out of his pack and explained that Smith's messages about the art eventually reached Murphy, and he reached out to the group that controlled the paintings. "In 2002, when we first got involved, Whitey Bulger went to a place called Bantry Bay, right down there at the bottom of Ireland, and attended a meeting at the country house of a high-valued stolen art fence and drug dealer. At the meeting, there was Slab Murphy, Whitey Bulger, and my man, who I can't name. There were negotiations about how to give the pictures back, but the problem was law enforcement. They didn't want it to happen. They wouldn't take yes for an answer. They didn't want the monies to be paid. Everyone was afraid of what would happen if a reward was paid to criminals."

"So who has the paintings now?"

Turbo didn't know for sure. "And if I did know, I don't know if I would tell you." But he believed that the paintings still sat with gangsters affiliated with the IRA, members of Dominic McGlinchey's old crew, and that the situation was growing more complicated as an increasing number of underworld figures purchased shares in the loot. "The McCarthy Dundons are now reputed to have some financial interest. As is another gangster on remand for the murder of a bouncer, who is a big-time antique dealer-cum-international drug smuggler. People have been lending money against certain things, and now that they're owed money, they want to be paid if the paintings are returned.

Turbo called over a waitress and ordered us a lunch of fish and chips along with an appetizer of whitebait and a Coke for me and a Coke for him and another coffee for him and said that he probably would have some dessert but he would order it only after he's eaten and had a cigarette and what was he talking about again? How to recover the Gardner pictures? "Really, you can run a banner headline tomorrow saying we know where the pictures are. The problem is going to be getting them back. It's my information that the people who have the paintings have been offered something by Murphy, but that they just haven't been offered the right deal, so you have to up the ante, you have to raise the stakes. We need to get those paintings back to the museum and on the walls again. I mean really we can do it. We can do it right now.

"I mean I've bugged everyone from George Bush to Tony Blair over those paintings. I tell them 'make the paintings a bit of pork, an earmark,'" he said. "We have people who have it and want to give it back. I've bugged Senator Hillary Clinton and Representative Peter King. They all know who Turbo is." The lack of any real response from the politicians—almost always form letters—had convinced Turbo beyond all doubt that there must be some sort of dedicated government cover-up. "The simple fact is that current FBI director Bob Mueller was the U.S. attorney in Boston at the time of the theft and had knowledge of Whitey Bulger and his murders before and during and after they happened. Mueller broke numerous laws, and that's half the reason the search for the paintings is so lukewarm." Turbo pointed his fork at me for emphasis. "You'll see. As you work on this case, you'll get to a crossroads, and you'll have to make certain decisions, and to go forward, you'll have to expose certain things that will be very uncomfortable to say the least."

Turbo paused for a moment to sip some coffee, and I asked him if we could go outside. I had to take a break. I felt hot and cramped. My mind was dizzy. We walked along the beach for a stretch. A slow, salty wind came in off the water. The ocean lapped quietly against the stones. "Bulger still has got an interest in the paintings," Turbo continued. "But there's no impetus to search for him. He's keeping a notebook about everything that happened in Boston, something that shows just how deep the corruption goes, and the FBI doesn't want to find him. I heard recently that every time that the Bulger squad leaves Boston, Bulger had been tipped off by certain members of that squad a week earlier."

"But do you actually know where exactly the paintings are, Turbo?"

He shrugged. "I've heard all sorts of places. Limerick. Galway. South America. The paintings might even still be in a bungalow in Boston. What matters is the person that can go like that"—Turbo snapped his fingers—"and release them. I've really only been interested in the Vermeer. That's really the Holy Grail, and we've had a confirmed sighting of that painting in Ireland. But I've also heard the paintings have been separated and that maybe the CEO of a Fortune 500 has some of the Gardner art."

"The CEO?"

"Yup, yeah, that's what my contact told me."

We walked a little farther. "Ellis warned me that you had a penchant for making up stuff."

Turbo laughed. "I've heard it before, that I can be a bit of a Walter Mitty, a fantasist, and to be honest with you, it's a necessary ingredient in this business. You see the arts and antiques world is filled with oddballs. We're round people that won't go into a square hole. People respond to art in different ways, and so you need to be imaginative, to really know art, to try and figure out what happened to stolen paintings."

It was getting late, and Turbo drove me back to the train station. We motored along a road next to the beach, passing old amusement parks and empty putt-putt courses. Turbo stared out the window. "I don't know what it is about this particular case, but you can just obsess about it. You hear those first lines—'In the early morning hours of March 18, 1990, two men dressed as police officers' and that's it. You're hooked," he said. "You'll spend the rest of your life thinking about it. You can't stop thinking about it. It will be just in the back of your mind always. It's more addictive than crack. It really is, isn't it?" Turbo blew out some smoke, the plume swirling past his head and out the open window. "That's what I think. This case is the crack cocaine of theft, and you know why? There's nothing. Here you have this massive theft, and you've got nothing substantial. No one's ever poked their head over the parapet and said, 'I've got it.'"

A FEW DAYS LATER, I booked a flight to Shannon Airport, just west of Limerick, Ireland. I was going to look for one of the world's most wanted men, Whitey Bulger.

I was some two hundred interviews into the case, the thin, Rubiconic line between passion and obsession had already been crossed. Back home, my Gardner files were taking over my office, spilling out of cabinets, growing on the floor like paper stalagmites. I had begun dreaming about the lost paintings regularly. The first dream occurred about a year into my research. I was staying at the home of retired robbery detective Sandy Guttman, and we spent the day discussing various leads and theories and suspects. That night, I slept in his guest room and dreamed about the Gardner art for the first time. Like most dreams, it was a little weird and very realistic—and it began with me stepping into a dingy hotel room and discovering some packages in the back of a closet. They were large and rectangular and tied up with twine and old newspaper. I was undoing the string, when someone stuck a gun under my ear. It felt hard and cold. I woke up, my heart rattling within my chest. Then, maybe two months later, I dreamed that I was walking through an empty mansion, looking for a painting to steal. I wandered through the vacant hallways and bare white rooms until I saw a Picasso over a fireplace. I put my hands on the sketch, my fingers wrapping around the gilded setting when a flashlight blinded me. It was the police. By the time I left for Ireland, the Gardner case was making a cameo in my dreams once every few weeks.

I had worked other big investigative projects. I had spent my whole career doing research of one sort or another. I had covered drug-fueled murders, the attacks on the World Trade Center, other art crimes. But the Gardner work wasn't like any of my previous reporting. The caper was so big, the suspect list was so long, that I had to draw up a database just to keep track of all the names. I didn't want to confuse Dickie Joyce (a friend of Carmello Merlino) with Bobby Joyce (a bank robber associated with mobster Patrick Nee) or William Joyce (a high school classmate of David Turner) or Louis Royce (a Boston area thief). The caper attracted the most slippery of characters. Everyone seemed to have some sort of angle. I once rang up an English stolen art fence who claimed that his name was Clive, but he wanted to be called Charley, although it seemed that he was actually the informant code-named Colin. When I first got him on the phone, he told me that he had never seen the Gardner art, not a single drawing. But as we started talking, his story began to change, and by the end of the interview, he was positive that he had seen the Vermeer. It was in a house west of Dublin. The painting was on the floor, and now that he thought about it, there was no way that he could be mistaken. He was 100 percent sure, absolutely certain, that he had seen the Old Master canvas. Then his cell phone cut out. I called him back a dozen times, but I never heard from him again.

I did my best to run every Gardner lead to the ground, and some of Turbo's information seemed plainly wrong. He told me, for instance, that FBI agent Mike Wilson had seen the stolen Vermeer in a hotel room in Dublin in early 2002. I contacted Wilson who declared Turbo's account "an utter fabrication." So did two other law enforcement agents. I also spoke with Patrick Nee. Turbo said that Nee was with Bulger when he tried to hawk the Gardner paintings in Florida in the 1990s. But Nee was in prison at the time and strongly denied the account.

But I was able to confirm some of Turbo's other information. Mark Dalrymple verified the role of underworld IRA groups. "I'll tell you that 70 or 80 percent of what Turbo says is fairly close to the truth," he told me. Dick Ellis maintained that a source had told him that he had seen the Vermeer in a hotel room in Dublin. Turbo also told me that he had good information that Bulger was currently in Galway Bay, posing as a retired doctor and traveling with his girlfriend Catherine Grieg. The tip fit together with the last confirmed sighting of Bulger. In September

2002, a British man strolling through London's Piccadilly Circus spotted an American whom he had met in 1994. The Brit approached the American and asked how he'd been. The American, shocked at being identified, brushed him off. The British man didn't think much of the incident until he watched the film *Hannibal* and recognized Bulger on the FBI's Most Wanted List. The man went to the FBI with the tip, and within weeks, the bureau uncovered a safe-deposit box in a London bank registered to Bulger. Inside the box was $50,000 and a key to another safe-deposit box in Dublin.

I didn't do much more with Turbo's tip until I was sitting in a pub one afternoon some two weeks into my visit to England. It was a dark, hovel-like place, and I sat at a table near the window, reviewing my notes with Turbo, when I realized that finding Bulger in Galway might be my best lead, my only chance at recovering the Gardner paintings, because if you found Bulger, you would uncover the art. That's what Smith had said. That's what Turbo had said, and as the thought flashed across my mind, I took a long slug of beer and pulled out my computer and booked the next flight to Ireland.

I BOARDED THE PLANE to Shannon a few days later. It was a bargain flight, and people piled onto the jet like it was a school bus, sitting in whichever seats they could find. A group of college students walked onto the plane singing songs; beet-faced men trundled down the aisles, their fists bulging with cans of beer, laughing and giggling like teenage girls. After the flight took off, the clamor of the passengers became noisier and more festive, and at one point, it seemed like the whole plane had turned into a rowdy, late-night pub. *I say no, nay, never!* the man in the seat in front of me slurred.

I asked the woman sitting next to me about the quickest way to get from the airport to Galway Bay. She gave me a quizzical look. I discovered later that bluntly asking the Irish for directions was considered gauche and graceless. It implied that the conversation was a transaction, a way for me to gain something from you. Apparently, the best way to get directions in Ireland was to start a sort of friendship. You approached the person, talked first about the weather, the food, anything really that was on your mind. You made the encounter into a conversation, sharing about yourself, asking queries about your newfound acquaintance, and then, eventually, you would find out where you wanted to go.

"American?" she said.

I nodded.

Her name was Audrey, and in the lyrical tones of West Ireland, she told me that she and her husband lived outside of Limerick with their five children and that she was coming back from a week's vacation in Monaco. She asked me why I was going to Ireland, and I told her about the Gardner theft and the potential Irish connection. I left out the Bulger angle—Turbo recommended that I not mention his name.

"Oi, I believe it. There used to be a lot of art thefts around here," she said. "The IRA, they loved that sort of stuff." Audrey explained that her grandfather had been a dedicated republican, and for a long time he helped smuggle guns into the country, hiding them on his farm in County Clare. "I remember he would put the shotguns under his apple harvest or secret them in the back of his outhouse," she said. "I wouldn't be surprised if he didn't have a few paintings. He was a loyal to the cause, and the Irish are a lot like leprechauns. We love to hide things like pots of gold, so that people will never find them."

I laughed. She shook her head. "Really, I mean the Irish seem so nice and friendly, if it weren't for the weather, everyone in the whole world would want to move here." Audrey then gave me a glance, her brow arched and furrowed. "But really the Irish, they are cunning, cunning, cunning people. Underneath it all, they can all do the devil's work. When you go into a bar anywhere in Ireland and order a pint, they ask 'so where are you from, what's your surname.' They're being friendly, but they really just want to know who ya are, what you're up to."

Audrey's words rang in my head as I motored toward Galway Bay. The area was wonderfully picturesque, craggy and green, dotted with sprawling farms, verdant hills, flocks of grazing sheep. Along the coast, mossy sandstone cliffs overhung the ocean, offering wide views of the blue-black water, and everywhere a wind blew loud and constant, beating the hedges into canted angles, pushing mists as thick as cotton across the heath.

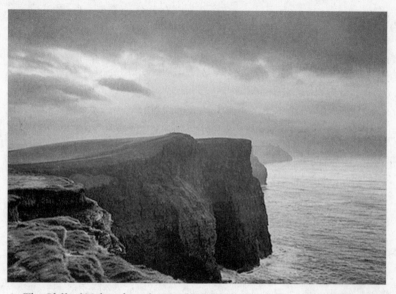

The Cliffs of Moher along the mouth of Galway Bay, County Clare, Ireland.

Depending on your viewpoint, the deep valleys, the soupy fogs, the remote villages could seem perfectly romantic—or darkly foreboding.

As I drove along the narrow roads, I passed dozens of places that seemed like the perfect hiding spot for a cache of stolen art. A lonely farmhouse tucked behind a grove of firs. Some broad fields of gorse and heather. A tall, tangled tree in the middle of a verdurous rise. I wanted to stop and investigate, search for signs of a concrete bunker or a man standing lookout. After all, Turbo believed that the paintings might be stashed in the area. So did Ellis and Dalrymple. But I stayed in my car. I didn't have a single clue as to where the paintings might be hidden, and as I drove along the winding streets, past tight stone fences and long fields, I reminded myself of investigative journalist Veronica Guerin. When she tried to interview Irish gangster John Gilligan on his rural country farm, he punched her in the face and ripped open her shirt to see if she was wearing a wire, and when she continued to write about the gangster over the following months, members of his crew ordered a hit on the middle-aged, single mother. Guerin was murdered in the spring of 1996. She was sitting at a stoplight in Dublin when a man pulled up next to her on a motorcycle and shot her in the head.

I hoped that hunting Bulger would be safer, much safer, and I sped toward the towns along Galway Bay. Turbo told me that Bulger would most likely be in a seaside village, a place where he wouldn't be noticed, and I moved from one small harbor town to the next, Liscannor, Doolin, Murrough. I would stroll the main streets; I would trundle along the beaches. Bulger looked more or less like your average American retiree. He was in his late seventies, with blue eyes, a bald dome, and a slightly stooped back. He stood about five feet eight, weighed 160 pounds; he had a wide gait and brawny arms. And I would stare at every older man that I saw. Did he have Bulger's eyes? His wide, rolling walk?

The work was unsparingly boring. I would perch myself on a park bench, my sunglasses tight around my head, watching and waiting, gazing at every new person that walked by, hoping for that sudden flash of recognition, that stomach-buzzing moment of identification. I thought I came close a few times. In the town square of Doolin, I saw a man wearing a driver's cap and sunglasses. He looked to be about Bulger's height, with the same meaty arms and square chest. I moved closer, my palms damp and heavy. The man stared at a cable-knit sweater hanging in the display window of a gift shop. I edged next to him, hoping to get a good glimpse of his face. "Ya don't think he'd actually like it," I heard him say. My body sagged. The accent was far too Irish. Then I spotted an older man walking along the shore. He had the stooped shoulders, the bald head. I jogged toward him. He seemed broody, a bit dangerous, and I ran faster, soon overtaking him. But when I turned around, I saw that he had green eyes.

Late on my first evening, I drove to the seaside hamlet of Lahinch and stepped into pub that looked like a place that Bulger might go for a nightcap. It was small and dark, the floors sticky with stale beer. A stuffed horse's head hung over the bar, the animal's stiff ear holding up a radio antenna. The place was empty except for two farmers sitting on barstools. One of them wore a set of overalls and a rumpled cardigan. The other had a long, white Santa Claus beard that hung down past his chest.

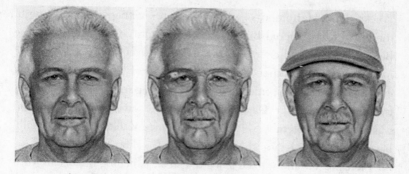

Age-enhanced photos of Whitey Bulger.

I slid onto a barstool and ordered a Guinness. The bar was quiet. No music played on the radio, no TV blared in the corner. The barwoman, a young, gap-toothed woman, poured half of my pint—a loud whooshing sound—and then let the beer stand. She didn't ask the usual questions. She just stood there, still as a statue, gazing at the bubbling glass. Then she poured the rest of the pint, while the bearded farmer continued telling a story about a man trying to steal some sheep from his farm.

"When he came to my house, I was ready for him," he explained.

"No?"

"I went into the barn and grabbed my gun. The single barrel. I pointed it right out the window. He came closer, and I watched him. I was standing on top of my bed."

"Well, did you shoot him?"

"Fecking yeah. Got him in the shoulder. That's what happens, when you go sneaking around my farm."

When I looked up, I found the bearded farmer glaring at me. His eyes looked red and glassy and mean. That's when it dawned for me—there was no way that I was going to find Bulger by meandering the Irish countryside. Even if Turbo's tip was accurate—a stretch by any account—it would take years to catch the gangster. It had been a wild, harebrained scheme from the start. My zeal had gotten the better of me. I felt stupidly naïve. There were never any concrete clues of an Irish angle. All of Bulger's old associates—Stevie Flemmi, Kevin

Weeks, John Martorano—had turned state's witness, and not one of them had ever fingered Bulger for the museum robbery. In all of the Bulger wiretaps and court documents and surveillance records, there had never been any mention of the paintings. I later discovered that even the Murray tip seemed doubtful. The drug smuggler was released from prison after the Gardner heist—in the summer of 1990—and was killed in September 1992, and it seemed unlikely that he would have been able to secure the art during such a short time period.

I left the bar and walked along the street, smelling the ocean, with its tangy mixture of salt and moisture. At the end of the town was a small, wooden pier, and I strode down to the end. In the distance, I could see the Atlantic shimmering for endless miles. It looked infinite, the water melting into the darkness. Some high-pitched laughter rose and fell behind me. An old sedan rumbled past. Everything seemed hollow and distant. Weightlessness settled into my body. I stared into the distance and wondered if I would ever recover the paintings, if their location would always remain unknown. I thought about it for a long moment and realized that no matter what happened, I would never comprehend some aspects of the caper; parts of the heist would always remain out of my reach. I lingered for a little while longer, turning the thought over in my head, and then walked back to my rental car and drove to the airport. Only later did I realize that my best lead was yet to come.

THERE WERE TOO many well-respected art detectives behind the Irish lead to ever dismiss it, and I kept in touch with the British investigators, Dick Ellis and Mark Dalrymple. I also spoke frequently with Turbo. While the art fence remained one of Ellis's best sources, I often feared that the Gardner caper had driven him into a sort of madness. We would talk on the phone, and sometimes he would imply that some of the works had already been returned. "If any pictures come back, it will be kept secret until they all come back," he said. "So, who knows, one may already be on their way, or even back in the Gardner, undergoing conservation?"

But, then, in almost the same breath, Turbo would tell me that the Gardner pictures had gone to Russia, purchased by a Dr. No—like mob figure, if they weren't in the hands of a French tycoon who stored them in the basement of his Paris mansion. It often felt as if Turbo could weave almost any story from the clues of the case, that he could build every sort of theory within the void of evidence. He once emailed me to say that he thought that the stolen Gardner paintings might kick-start a new Middle East peace deal. If Murphy returned the art, then the IRA leader could be sent to Libya to help their negotiations with Israel:

[Prime minister] Tony Blair wants to make progress in the Middle East, Thomas Slab Murphy should be used to negotiate with the leader of Hamas, Ismail Haniya, to discuss how Slab moved from being a Military general to peacemaker. At the moment no-one wants to talk to this bad guy, Ismail Haniya. What better way forward than Thomas Slab Murphy leading a delegation to Gaza, or even better Ismail Haniya leads a delegation to Ireland for talks with Slab, Martin McGuiness, and co on how to move the Middle East peace process forward.
I think this could be a stroke of genius.
They laughed at the Wright Brothers, they laughed at Einstein, they laughed at me, [they] are not laughing anymore.

I didn't respond to that particular comment. Nor did I reply when Turbo told me that a member of the Saudi royal family might have some of the Gardner paintings, or when Turbo began saying that the reward money was a bluff, a way to smoke out the thieves. A part of me was afraid that if I engaged him on these wild ideas, these uncoupled leaps of logic, that the darkness of the Gardner mystery might blind me too.

12. LA SORTIE DE PESAGE

Put My Picture on the Cover

VERY TIME I began running down a new angle on the Gardner case, I thought I might be holding the clue that would unravel the mystery. It was a powerful feeling. I would get an anonymous tip or an ex-cop would offer a promising item, and my mind would jump and buzz. I would feel an urge deep within my belly. *I need to run that down.* The conceit imbued everything with a generous sense of purpose; an intoxicating compulsion came with every clue. Because that was the thing about the case— it was unsolved, an unknown, a question mark. Would the next lead be the one? Or would it be the one after that? Would I wake up one morning to find out that someone else had recovered the paintings? While I could weigh the evidence, perhaps make a few predictions, I had no idea. None.

After spending so much time on the case, it was an odd and uncomfortable feeling not to know, not to have any idea. It seemed so unusual for our time and place. For the most part, our lives are filled with expert knowledge and cynical predictability. We have rote jobs and inevitable weekends. Within seconds we can access websites that explain how to make atomic bombs or list the names of all the actors who ever made a cameo on *The Simpsons*. Sometimes I would find myself frustrated at the case's unpredictability, the way it seemed to float above understanding, but at the same time I knew that the mystery of the case was its real attraction, the draw that kept me working.

AFTER I RETURNED FROM ENGLAND, I went back to my case files. I had been working the caper for more than three years and added hundreds of pages of documents, search warrants, informant reports, trial transcripts, and witness statements. I had uncovered snapshots of more than two dozen suspects. In a rural Massachusetts bookstore, I discovered a rare 1931 book that offered details about the paintings that helped me sort out the hoax tips from the real thing. And after a long, detailed search, I finally caught up with Ray Abell, the guard who let the thieves into the museum on the night of the heist. He had gone bankrupt, gotten married, and moved to rural Vermont. His mother told me that he had always been "awfully shaken up about the theft." But when I spoke to him on the phone, he seemed haughty and imperious, and after a short conversation, he said that he didn't want to ever hear from me again and hung up. Then a few weeks later, he left a bizarre late-night message on my voicemail. "I'm just calling to inform you that Tabor Dix and I weren't together when the museum was robbed. Your trick wasn't all that cute." Some minutes later, he called again and left a second voicemail. "Apologies. Something got attributed to you that you didn't do." I never heard from Abell after that. I never found out who Tabor Dix was; I was never sure who Abell's phone message was meant for.

I continued to run down the tips that came in on my website and toll-free number, no matter how wildly bizarre. It was a long string of dead ends. A retired FBI agent told me that British antiquities smuggler Michel van Rijn may have been behind the heist, and so I visited him in his London home. (In an apartment filled with kitsch—pink flamingos, glowing tiki torches, fake palm trees—van Rijn told me that he had been in Lebanon at the time and had the documents to prove it.)

I exchanged letters with a convicted child rapist named Rocco who said that the Rembrandt self-portrait was sitting in someone's wallet between two pieces of wax paper. (Rocco would tell me whose wallet if

I would make sure that his latest appeal was heard, and when I told him that I had no influence over the court, he called me a "total screwup.")

I received a letter from a jailed mob associate named Kenny. He wanted to send me the Flinck in order to earn his early release for an armed robbery charge. (I visited Kenny in a maximum security jail in upstate New York; I drove to New York City to meet with one of his associates; I talked to half a dozen lawyers to make sure that I could take control of the art without being arrested. Kenny never produced as much as a snapshot.)

I scraped bottom with a suspect named George Dempster. Deeply infatuated with Isabella Stewart Gardner, Dempster told friends that the Boston heiress was his patron saint, that her ghost would often give him spiritual guidance. In the 1980s, Dempster landed a job at the museum as a guard, but the staff supposedly caught him caressing one of the sculptures and fired him. Smith had nursed some suspicions about Dempster, that his obsession with the museum and its founder might have driven him to steal the paintings, and retired robbery detective Sandy Guttman recommended that I confront the ex-guard and follow him around for a few days. It was a time-honored law enforcement practice, Guttman told me, spook an uncooperative witness and see what happens. So I hired a young private detective named Chuck to help me, and sitting in the alleyway across from Dempster's house, I called him on my cell phone. "People think you have the paintings," I said, "that you stole the works because you were obsessed with the art."

"That's ridiculous," Dempster said, his voice high and sharp. "My life is that museum. I would never do anything to hurt Mrs. Gardner."

I told Dempster that I heard rumors that he had been near the museum on the night of the theft. "Palace Road late on a Saturday night?"

"I was going to visit a friend."

I talked to Dempster for another ten minutes, repeatedly accusing him of masterminding the theft. Then Chuck and I waited. People flitted in and out of the building, door open, door closed. And besides for a short break for sleep, I stayed there through the night and into the next day, until finally, just before noon, Dempster stepped out onto the street.

Chuck had gone home by that point, and I followed Dempster myself, staying a truck-length behind him, trailing him as he walked up the street. He was tall, maybe six foot two, with bottle-blond hair and a long face. I don't think he noticed me. I don't think he noticed anyone. As he strode along, he gazed at the sky daydreaming, humming a little tune. I followed him for another half a mile, before I turned around. I felt greasy and dishonest, a shady hack of an investigator. From the moment that I first talked to Dempster, I should have known that he wasn't the type of guy to steal a piece of candy, forget a Vermeer. I had wrongly accused him. I had openly misled him. I didn't tell him that I was sitting outside of his apartment or offer the truth about the evidence against him. I never felt as far away from the Gardner paintings.

AS I WORKED THE CASE, I would occasionally come across evidence that golden boy gangster David Turner was one of the men who looted the museum. The mentions would be random and brief. His name would surface in a news article, or a tipster would swear on his life that he was one of the thieves. I never put much effort into the lead, though. Smith told me that the men who robbed the Gardner had probably sold the paintings and had no idea where the art might be, and Turner had been convicted of plotting to heist the Loomis Fargo armored car depot and was sentenced to almost forty years in prison. If he had the paintings, why hadn't he tried to give them up in exchange for shorter jail time?

But as other leads dried up, I wrote Turner a letter. After being convicted of the Loomis heist, the gangster was sent to a maximum-security prison outside of Scranton, Pennsylvania. Turner granted me an interview on the condition that his lawyer could review his quotes and cut out anything that might be incriminating. His lawyer also approved my questions in advance, and I was not allowed to ask Turner about any other cases, like the murder of Charlie Pappas, the Bull & Finch robbery, or the Canton home invasion. It was a deal that I cut with no other source and suggested a lesson taught in Police Academy 101—if a suspect immediately asks for a lawyer, they're probably not going to tell you the truth.

When Turner came on the phone, he spoke slowly and carefully, like an actor reading from a script. In a thick Boston accent, he maintained that he was innocent, that the FBI had set him up for the Loomis heist in order to recover the missing masterpieces. "[FBI Special Agent] Neil Cronin testified that if I was facing serious charges, a lengthy sentence, that I would be motivated to help him return the Gardner paintings," he said. "Once they had arrested us, and the paintings didn't show up, they should have gotten reasonable."

"But why did they target you?"

"I don't know," he said. "I had nothing to do with the robbery. [The feds] have information from different sources, but it's all just rumor and conjecture, and how do you defend yourself against that? They sent my prints to the FBI, but they came back negative," he continued. "I could take a polygraph test—I would pass it."

We talked for an hour that morning, and Turner told me how he met Carmello Merlino, how he was innocent of the Loomis theft, how the witnesses against him were all liars and con artists. I kept asking Turner about the museum heist, and slowly, over the course of the conversation, his voice began to show a jaunty sort of pride. It's hard to describe exactly—it wasn't as if he were plainly bragging. But there was an undertone of vanity, of raw arrogance, like he couldn't help but gloat when he talked about the robbery. "I've seen memos that they sent directly to the director of the FBI, saying that they believe that I was participant," he told me. "I believe the Gardner is a big embarrassment. It was a major crime."

I found the tone intensely uncomfortable, and I quizzed Turner again and again about his role in the theft. But he wouldn't answer the most basic questions. He refused to say if he was in Boston at the time of the heist or speculate about who may have been involved or even tell me why his name had come up so often in the FBI reports. And when I got off the phone, I started to work the lead hard. I pulled the Loomis files from Moakley Courthouse and called some of Turner's old criminal associates. I landed the FBI files on Merlino's effort to return the art and made an afternoon visit to TRC, the body shop that served as the criminal headquarters of Turner's crew.

Then, a few weeks later, a source called and asked if I wanted to interview the last person to see the thieves before they entered the museum. The name of the witness was Jerry Stratberg, and on the night of the heist, he had attended a party in a dormitory across the street from the Gardner. At around 12:30, he left the party with a group of friends, and they stood on the street for a while, discussing what they were going to do next. One of his friends wanted to head home; someone else suggested visiting a bar. Stratberg then pulled a friend, Nancy, onto his shoulders and piggybacked her down the street. After a few yards, she pointed out some men dressed as police officers sitting in a hatchback. Curious, Stratberg walked up to the car and stared at the driver. "It was disconcerting. We were minors who had been drinking, and so Nancy and I just turned around and walked back to our friends," Stratberg told me. "I don't remember if I thought he was a real cop or not. I just knew that we should get out of there."

Stratberg heard about the theft on Sunday, and he and his friends went to the police the following morning. "The cops wrote everything down, but they didn't seem to take us too seriously. I mean they made it clear that they were talking to minors who had been drinking, and it seemed like they kind of discounted what we said," Stratberg told me. "I felt annoyed. I mean I had been drinking that night, but I wasn't sloppy. I was confident in what I remembered."

Stratberg now worked for Harvard University as a financial services manager, and while he often thought about the crime, he never heard from law enforcement again. No one asked him any follow up questions or showed him any mug shots, and so one afternoon, I presented him with an array of suspects who had been tagged as the thief over the years, including Bobby Donati, Brian McDevitt, Gerry Kaplan, and David Turner.

Stratberg examined the photos closely. "While my memory of the driver's face is foggy," he said, "the only photo that registers for me is that of David Turner."

I asked Stratberg if he was sure.

"I couldn't positively identify him," he said. "But I wouldn't have provided a description to the police in the days after the event if I had not been confident of what I had seen."

I asked Stratberg if he had ever heard of the name before.

"No. Nothing."

I'm not sure why—maybe it was the years of empty leads—but I hadn't really expected Stratberg to finger any of the pictures, certainly not with any confidence, and I sat there for a long while, gazing at the photograph of Turner, feeling suddenly like I was staring into the eyes of one of the Gardner thieves.

IF SMITH WERE STILL ALIVE, he would have thrown himself into the Turner angle, and so I did what he would have done. I reached out to Turner's family members, high school buddies, and old neighbors. I rang up cast-off lawyers, forgotten landlords, and distant underworld friends. I pulled Turner's Marine records, contacted Braintree High School alumni groups, and posted ads in South Boston newspapers looking for people who might have known the golden boy gangster. For years, I researched the Turner angle, and I began to know more about him than I do about most of my friends. I found out that he would buy lilies for his mother on Easter, that he had the *Boston Herald* delivered to his Braintree home, that he got arrested for shoplifting a few months after graduating from high school. I discovered that he played both ways on the high school football team, that he went skiing in Vermont, and that when he was robbing a house thirty minutes stretched into three hours. I eventually even landed a copy of his high school yearbook. His classmates voted him "most unique," and the editors featured an image of him wearing an ear-to-ear grin under the sixteen-point headline, YOU HAVE BIG DREAMS OF FAME. The Gardner theft occurred five years later.

As I talked to people who knew Turner, as I gathered wiretaps and court rulings and surveillance documents, evidence of his involvement in the caper became all but undeniable. I flushed out Jerry Stratberg's account and discovered that when he spoke to Boston police two days after the theft, he described the man in the hatchback as having "Asian" eyes. Stratberg was specific in his description, telling the officer that the man looked like he had one Asian and one Caucasian parent. And by all accounts, Turner's eyes fit that description. It was patently obvious in pictures, and people who knew Turner well—high school buddies, family friends—often remarked on the facial feature, telling me that his eyes were almond-shaped and slightly angled. "Oh yes, he had these narrow, sort of slanty eyes," neighbor Joan Moran told me. Turner's unusual eyes also appeared to be something that a witness would focus on when they came across the gangster engaged in a crime. When Andrea Freedman testified against Turner in the Canton home invasion case—he allegedly put a gun to her head and stole $130,000 in cash from her home—she described the thief as having "slanted" eyes. "When someone holds a gun to your head [for forty-five minutes to one hour], and you are looking at his face, which is not covered, you just don't forget it," she told the court.

Turner also showed suspicious behavior in the days before and after the robbery. Prior to the theft, he rented a home on Arborview Road in Jamaica Plain, about a ten-minute drive from the museum, and police surveillance teams often spotted underworld figures visiting the house

A mug shot of David Turner. A witness who saw the thieves before they entered the museum said one of the intruders had "Asian" eyes.

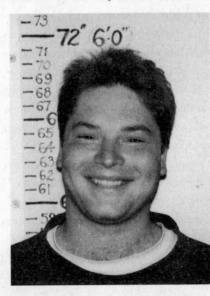

in the months preceding the heist. And then, on March 19, the day after the caper, Turner left Boston and drove his Corvette down to Florida, and when a police officer posed as a friend and called his house, a woman said that he "was on a mini vacation."

There were also important similarities between Turner's alleged robberies and the Gardner caper. Turner's heist of the Loomis depot was scheduled for Super Bowl Sunday. The robbery of the Bull & Finch bar took place on Labor Day. The Pappas murder was committed on Thanksgiving Eve. The Gardner heist happened on St. Patrick's Day. Investigators say that Turner would often wear disguises during his robberies, use handcuffs to secure witnesses, and bring along a police scanner to keep track of law enforcement. The Gardner thieves dressed up as police officers and used handcuffs to tie up the guards, and some believe that one of the intruders had a scanner hanging from his belt.

Turner's background also matched the profile of the Gardner thieves, a professional criminal who knew little about art. At the time of the heist, Turner had been arraigned eleven times, including once for theft, and no one could recall him as having any interest or experience with art. "I remember him, big, loud, dumb, and pretty," Braintree high school classmate Michael Waugh said. "He was a great athlete. He took the baseball team to the state champs," childhood friend Chris

Police sketch of the taller Gardner thief (left); mug shot of David Turner (right).

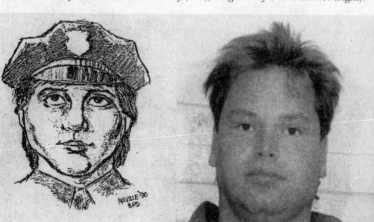

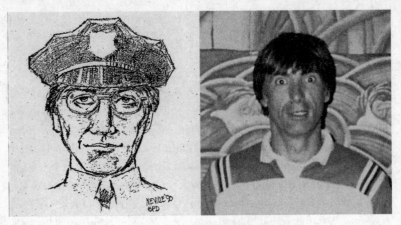

Police sketch of the shorter Gardner thief (left);
picture of George Reissfelder (right).

Ruggierio told me. "The Gardner heist definitely sounds like his MO," retired state police officer Eddie Whelan said.

A number of others have fingered Turner over the years, most notably FBI agent Neil Cronin, and Turner's own underworld boss, Carmello Merlino, twice tried to return the paintings, first in 1992 and then again in 1998, and each time the person who controlled the art appeared to be someone close to him. I eventually even discovered a document that seemed to have been written by Turner's own lawyer that argued that the golden boy gangster was behind the robbery. The text appeared to be the draft of a motion for a new trial and argued that law enforcement had little doubt that Turner controlled the masterpieces. "[The FBI] reports paint a very compelling picture that the government believed Turner had *direct* access to or was in actual possession of the paintings," the document concluded.

If Turner was involved, George Reissfelder was probably his main accomplice, the shorter thief. An associate of Merlino, Reissfelder looks jaw-droppingly similar to the police composite, with the same lined cheeks, snarled mouth, and angular chin. A close friend of Turner's told me that Reissfelder may have been killed over the paintings, and an FBI confidential informant report—most likely from Richard "Fat Man"

Chicofsky—said that Reissfelder was one of the thieves: "Source believes that the actual participants in the robbery of the GARDNER MUSEUM were possibly DAVID TURNER . . . [and] GEORGE REINSFELDER [*sic*]." Reissfelder also fits the profile of the Gardner thieves. He had little artworld experience and a long and violent criminal record, including convictions for passing bad checks and armed robbery. "George went insane about absolutely nothing, his eyes like red-and-white tops spinning in his head," his ex-wife Janice Santos recalled. "My nights were plagued with him waking me, choking me, calling me everything imaginable, punching me, accusing me of thinking of someone else."

Reissfelder might have been someone to keep the paintings—he had connections at some of the highest political levels. One-time Democratic presidential nominee John Kerry had served as Reissfelder's attorney for years, and he once pushed for Reissfelder to get an early release in a murder case. It was an event that made headlines across the state because Reissfelder bolted for Florida during the furlough, and when he was arrested outside of Jacksonville, he pulled a gun on a police officer. Reissfelder's case later inspired a Republican political attack ad, which painted Kerry as soft on crime. "After being paroled, Reissfelder immediately proved to everyone that Kerry exercised poor judgment in helping secure his freedom," wrote Stephen Marks, a former Republican operative who made the video slamming Kerry. "It wasn't long after his release that Kerry's 'poster boy' continued his criminal ways, quickly involving himself with a Mafia-controlled drug ring in Boston."

When I first began working the Turner angle, I would write letters to the golden boy gangster, asking general questions about his life, and in a round, sloping script he would reply to my missives, telling me how he left the Marines because of a back problem, that his one drug charge was for marijuana. But I stopped writing when the hard evidence began to filter in. I wanted to get a full understanding of his role in the heist before I continued communicating with him. Then one afternoon, weeks later, I received a short note from Turner. He hadn't heard from me in a while, he said, and he wanted to share a poem about how the FBI had wrongly prosecuted him for the Loomis heist. Titled "The Storm on the Sea of Galilee," the verse used the biblical tale as a metaphor for his life, portraying himself as one of the apostles, an honorable man swept up in a set of dramatic circumstances beyond his control. "David Turner cries out so desperately," the poem reads. "'Save me, Lord, Save me, for the ship is going down.'"

I read the poem a dozen times. Would a person innocent of the Gardner crime write verse like this? Did Turner think that it would convince me that he had not participated in the heist? I recalled detective Eddie Whelan, who told me that Turner would often taunt investigators, offering sly winks and prideful snickers as he was arrested for a crime, and that's when it dawned on me. Turner wanted his name placed squarely within the history of the caper; he couldn't resist bragging about his biggest heist. Turner and I continued exchanging letters, and he told me that he wanted to author an autobiography. "I think it would be a great read and best seller!" He also said that I should feature him prominently in this account. "I think if you put my picture on the cover, you would sell more books!" This was, I realized, the same jaunty arrogance that I heard during our phone interview—the mocking smirk of a crook who believes that he's committed the perfect heist.

I eventually wrote Turner one last letter, telling him about all the new information that I had uncovered about his role in the robbery, the eyewitness, the trip to Florida, the connections to other gangsters. I wanted to give him the opportunity to explain the weight of facts against him. But Turner never responded. He did not provide an alibi or address any of the new evidence or continue to proclaim his innocence. Instead, I received a note from his lawyer: "At my client's request, I am writing to ask that you have absolutely no further contact with him, via letter or otherwise. Additionally, he no longer provides you with his consent to attribute any statements to him." It seemed like my letter had been too close to the truth.

SO WHERE DID the paintings go? In the Byzantine ways of the Boston underworld—in the tricky ways of the Gardner mystery—it seemed that everyone was guilty and no one was. At one point, the FBI confidential informant reports indicate that Carl Benjamin—a friend of Merlino's—

was sitting on the masterpieces. But Benjamin died in 2005, and his wife has no recollection of him ever mentioning the lost art. Perhaps mob associate Robert Guarente was the mastermind? He was a friend of Turner's, a frequent visitor to Merlino's body shop, and had connections to Myles Connor. But Guarente died in 2004 without any sign of the paintings. The FBI confidential informant reports also imply that Turner himself had the loot. That seems nearly impossible. Turner would have almost certainly given up the canvases to get out of his thirty-eight-year prison sentence.

What about Bulger? Merlino was friendly with Bulger's right-hand man, Stevie Flemmi, and investigators believe that Merlino was paying tribute to the gangster. Turner might have known Bulger too. During the 1980s, Bulger would often spend the night at his girlfriend's place at 160 Quincy Shore Drive, Apartment 101. In 1998 Turner bought an apartment within spitting distance, at 166 Quincy Shore Drive, Unit 111. (Turner purchased the apartment from Marty Leppo. Turner paid in cash. No mortgage.) Turner also attended high school with Stevie Flemmi's nephew, and investigators have linked Turner to William Hussey, Flemmi's son. But there still wasn't any hard evidence of a Bulger connection, not a whiff.

Or Myles Connor? Merlino knew the art thief well. They had been in prison together, they traveled in the same underworld circles, and according to an FBI report, Connor once even asked Merlino to come to New York City with him to meet with a publishing house to discuss a book deal. Or how about Youngworth? Merlino knew him too. "Dirty motherfucker," he called him. So did Turner. "A real lowlife bottom feeder," he said. Maybe Joe Murray? The drug dealer knew Leppo who knew Merlino who knew Turner. There seemed endless links, highly speculative connections, and sometimes I would study my mess of FBI files and wiretap reports and feel like I was playing a high-stakes game of six degrees of Gardner separation, with Leppo serving as Kevin Bacon. The lawyer linked everyone—he served as counsel for Turner, Merlino, Youngworth, and half of the Rossetti clan.

Eventually, though, I found one plausible explanation as to why no one had ever come forward about the lost masterpieces—they had all been murdered. An FBI confidential informant report once fingered Lenny DiMuzio for the museum robbery, and in June 1991 he was shot to death and shoved into the trunk of his car. Investigators believe Turner was the triggerman. Bobby Donati was once believed to have raided the museum, and police saw him hanging out at Merlino's body shop at the time of the heist. He was killed in September 1991, his body also jammed into the back of his car. Turner's name was listed in prosecutor Sikellis's files as one of the possible killers. The FBI investigated Charlie Pappas as a potential thief. He was killed in 1995, and Turner, again, is widely believed to have been the gunman. In March 1991, a year to the month of the heist, George Reissfelder was found dead from cocaine poisoning. Merlino was the one to discover Reissfelder's body, and many believe that the death was a target killing. It reminded me of something that Manet once said. "The concise man makes one think," the artist told a friend. "The talkative man irritates." And the dead ones say nothing at all.

AS THE WEEKS turned into months, the months into years, I thought constantly about the person who took control of the Gardner art. After leaving the museum, the thieves would have most likely driven to a location outside of Boston, a quiet, tree-lined street in Weymouth or somewhere just under the freeway in Everett. In an empty parking lot or an old body shop, the thin fog still hanging in the air, someone would have taken control of the canvases. He might have been one of the thieves, he might have been someone else entirely. He would have probably handed the men a wad of cash and let them keep their gumball prizes, the finial and the ku. He would tell the men that if they ever told anyone about the heist, anyone at all, he would kill them.

Perhaps that night, perhaps as much as a year later, the works would come into the control of a man that I came to call G. He would secret the art away in a safe house, maybe in an old barn past Springfield or in a shed behind a gas station in Brockton. G had some power within the Boston underworld. He would know the big shots—Whitey Bulger, Frank Salemme—but he wasn't one of them. He took control of the art because it was valuable. He may have heard whispers of an art collector in Japan who would pay top dollar for a Rembrandt, or maybe he needed a bargaining chip, something to get him out of a legal jam. Perhaps he thought that if he waited long enough that he might be able ransom some of the works back to the Gardner.

G was a composite, a fiction, someone built out of all the rumors and whispers and half-truths. It was something Smith often did. In order to make sense of a vexing theft, he would write a barely fictionalized version of the caper, and I had found a half-dozen novelized heists among his files. The practice gave him a better perspective on a case, it knit all the loose investigative ends into a single, understandable whole. And by that point, I was consumed by the heist—it had wormed its way into almost every waking moment. Sometimes I would get up at four thirty in the morning to start chasing suspects, a quick break for lunch, a quick break for dinner, and when I went to sleep, I would try and calculate the hours that I worked that day. Was it seventeen or eighteen? Does eating lunch while reading a book on Bulger associate Kevin Weeks count? Had there been a time during the day when I wasn't thinking about the lost paintings? One evening, my wife pulled me aside. "You need to take breaks," she told me. "You need to shower every two days."

But as much as G was a fantasy, an imaginative by-product of all the hours I had put into the case, he was fully based in fact—there was plenty of precedence. In 1978 seven paintings, including a stunning Cezanne, were stolen from a home in the Berkshires. The works were worth more than $30 million, and the case stood for decades as the largest unsolved burglary from a private residence in the state of Massachusetts. It turned out that the thief had secreted the paintings in the attic of the law office of defense lawyer Robert Mardirosian. After the thief was murdered over a gambling debt, Mardirosian took control of the art, and according to investigators, he held onto the paintings for years, first moving them to Monaco and then to Switzerland. In 1999, almost twenty years after the heist, Mardirosian used a Panamanian shell company to attempt to arrange for the auction of the Cezanne at Sotheby's in London. Authorities stopped the sale—and the painting was recovered. In my mind, G was the Gardner's Mardirosian.

I would often fantasize about G. I would use off-the-record quotes, court transcripts, and wiretaps to fill out my conversations. I would recall Merlino and Connor as I thought of G as being of medium height, his once well-muscled body now soft and pillowy. In my dreams, G would need reading glasses, he would be almost bald. While he would have had a few convictions—firearms possession, breaking and entering—he would have largely retired from the criminal world. Living near the ocean, perhaps in Plymouth or Marshfield, he would own a small construction company or manage a few convenience stores. He would be with his second wife, his children grown and out of the house. But he could also be in prison, stuck in a cell without any way of getting access to the lost art, too smart to trust anyone else with his valuable stash. He could be on the run, hiding in Ecuador or Ireland, living like a man with only a few days to his life. He might be George Reissfelder or Bobby Donati or Whitey Bulger or someone else entirely. But if I tell myself what is most likely the truth, the most probable explanation, I realize that G is dead, murdered, his body moldering in the ground, the paintings abandoned.

Whether G was dead or alive, jailed or free, I thought so much about him that I began to imagine a meeting. We would get together for a drink in a restaurant somewhere just south of Boston, maybe in the back streets of Hyde Park or along the shore in Quincy. It would be a dark place with small, inky windows. The stools would be dotted with men with husky shoulders and callused hands: letter carriers, carpenters, perhaps a volunteer fireman or two. The place would smell of sweat and stale grease. Over the bar, there would be television flickering a Red Sox game. I would find G in the back.

"Ulrich, huh? What kind of name is that?" In a town of families, he wants to figure out mine. I tell him that I'm German, that I grew up just outside of New York City.

"Giants fan?" he asks.

I nod.

"I still think about that fuckin' Super Bowl."

"Brady didn't quite do it for you, did he?"

"Fuck awful," he says. "I lost thousands."

The waitress comes over. "Can I get you guys anything?"

"Tanqueray and tonic," G says.

"Sam Adams for me."

She leaves, and the sounds of the Red Sox fills the space between us.

"So do you have the art?"

He laughs. "Get down to it."

I smile. He pushes the plastic menu across the table. "Do I have the paintings? Does anyone have the paintings? I thought they were destroyed. Someone couldn't take the heat."

"Really."

He looks at me. His eyes are shiny and hard like little pennies. "Really, the paintings were burned up. You know the saying, 'Ashes to ashes, dust to dust.'"

"I don't believe it. It would be like burning money, putting a match to $5 million. Why do it?"

In my starry-eyed dreams, he ignores my question and starts to hunt. What have you found out? You speak to Turner? What ever happened to the guards? They still alive? I answer him honestly.

"Now, it's my turn," I ask, "why are you meeting with me?"

"That's a good question," he says. "Because I fucking hate reporters. The guys that come out of the joint, they want to go clean but not a single one of them can get a job. I hired one guy and then a reporter came asking questions. I had to let him go. So fucking stupid."

The waitress brings our drinks. G sips deeply from his glass and then wipes his mouth with the back of his hand.

"I heard you asking questions," he says. "I want to see what you got."

I nod.

"I hear people saying you have Turner."

"I don't have Turner. It was the feds that got him. Cronin was the first to come out and say that Turner did it. I just dug through their files and added a few things, found a few people."

In my dreams, G shakes his head, his jowls swaying loosely. "That Loomis thing was outrageous. Sending in a snitch to TRC with a wire and having an FBI agent pretend like he was guard. I mean they framed Turner. They hid evidence from him during the trial. They used Fat

Richie who was the biggest fuckin' con artist you ever met in your life. Davey had a job back then. He was working on the Big Dig. The feds put him on that score, because they wanted the paintings. They made that place irresistible—"

"—to a criminal."

G looks at me. He takes another sip of his drink.

"Davey stood tall. I'm proud of him," he says. "You write that down, OK? He stood tall. He's no rat."

"So you know Turner?"

"Not real well."

"But why didn't he roll?"

"He's a tough guy."

"Come on. Everyone rolls when they're facing forty years. All he had to do was give up some pictures," I say. "Really, why didn't he roll?"

"He probably thought he could get off. Remember—he beat the Pappas rap. He beat the *Cheers* rap. He beat the home invasion. He was—what did they call him, 'the Teflon don of South Boston.'" G smiles. "The thing is that Davey doesn't really know where the paintings are. He didn't know in '97. It's too late. He has nothing to trade—and everyone else is dead."

"Murdered."

G angles his head. "I'd be careful if I were you."

"I'm just doing my best to find out what happened."

"You have until 2036, I think. That's when Davey gets out."

I pause for a moment, a soft flutter in my stomach.

"And you?" I ask.

"Me?"

"What?"

"Why not return the paintings? There's a $5 million dollar reward."

"I have a family. Four grandkids. Jail is no place for an old man."

"But the statute of limitations has run out."

G gives a cold chortle that manages to prickle my skin even in my imagination.

"The FBI, they can catch you on something else," G explains. "Maybe the works crossed state lines or some shit. They can give you ten years just for lying to a grand jury. Think about that." He touches the straw in his gin and tonic. "Really, you have to remember that right after the Gardner theft, Janet Reno coined the term 'art terrorism.' The feds think the art is being held for ransom. They want someone for this. They want someone bad, and I tell you, it's not going to be me."

"So tell me, who was involved?"

He smiles.

"Connor?"

"An inspiration to us all," he says.

"What do you mean?"

"He showed us how easy it was, how art was a voucher, something to trade."

"Youngworth?"

He frowns. "A junkie and a rat."

"Turner?"

"I'm not saying anything."

"Reissfelder."

"I told you."

"Donati?"

"He's dead, right? Didn't someone smack him over the head?" he said.

"What about the guard?" I say. "The thieves had some inside angle."

"Sure, a guard made some money, I'll tell you that."

"And the paintings? Why cut the Rembrandt?"

"All these questions." He shrugs. "Someone saw a way to get something valuable. Maybe it would be worth some money, maybe it would get them out of jail. They had seen what Myles could do, and they were committing a lot of crimes at the time, so they figured, why the hell not. It would be an easy job, a cakewalk. But the paintings got ruined. They were stupid. Then came the heat, and people started dying, getting killed."

"But why did you do it? I mean why steal those paintings?"

"I didn't do it. You make sure to write that down too. OK?" He watches me closely as I scribble the words into my pad in large block letters.

"But listen, two guys go in and get $200, $300 million in paintings. What's better than that? Right? No one gets hurt. No one gets caught. You know, I'm not saying doing armed robbery is the right thing to do. Because it's not," he says. "But this was the perfect heist."

I want to argue the point, I want to tell him he's wrong, but I know better. We listen to the sounds of the game for a moment.

"You afraid of getting caught?"

"They still don't even know how many people were in the museum that night—and almost everyone is dead. Dead or too smart to say anything."

"And the paintings?"

"Tucked away for a rainy day."

"Will you ever return them?"

"They'll come back, when they come back."

I hear his cell phone. It's on vibrate. He answers. "Yeah."

I hear someone talking on the other line, a baritone.

"No, not on the phone," he says. "No, No. OK. Sure. I'll be right there."

He throws a $20 bill on the table.

"It's been nice talking with you, kid. I got some business I gotta take care of. You'll be hearing from me."

But I never do.

13. FINIAL

Like a Spiderweb

I WAS DIALING THE NUMBER of Kevin Vermeërsch, a props handler for the popular TV show *Monk*, to see if he might be sitting on the stolen Gardner paintings when I realized that my obsession needed to come to an end.

Even as I thought of G and Turner and finding the paintings hidden in a storage unit somewhere in the South Shore suburbs, I was running down other leads. They were wild tips, crackpot angles that seemed as likely to produce the paintings as proving the existence of Sasquatch. Smith had done the same thing, and shortly before he died, he thought that the thieves might have stored the paintings within the museum itself. He had received a number of letters saying as much. "The artworks were hidden in a secret safe in the walls," wrote one group who called themselves "God is Sovereign." "The safe is under a flower vase that is beside furniture that has a green colored seat and back rest."

The lead didn't make much sense—why would someone break into the museum and not take anything out? But Smith wanted to make sure that he could cross it off of his list, and in December 2004, three weeks before he died, he emailed the museum to see if he could walk through the building and look for a secret passageway or compartment. The museum responded quickly. A visit wouldn't be necessary. They had recently installed a new heating and ventilation system, and as part of the construction work, almost every wall had been opened up and renovated. There was no way that the paintings could still be within the building.

The Vermeersch tip seemed just as bizarre. It began with a call from journalist Dary Matera. He told me that he had been watching the television show *Monk* when he caught a glimpse of the Vermeer in the background of two different episodes of the show. Matera knew that one of the early Gardner suspects, Brian McDevitt, had worked as a screenwriter in Hollywood, and so he began calling the show's production staff to see if he could learn more about the canvas that was being used in the set. But Matera was never able to get a straight answer. "I think that they're hiding it, that's why they won't tell me what's going on," he told me. "But we have to be careful. We don't want to spook them and make the painting vanish."

Matera had written a book on art theft together with retired FBI agent Tom McShane, and so I followed up on his tip. I called NBC Universal, the company that produced the show, to see if they might know more. I rang the props studio, and then, as I was scrolling through the show's credits, I noticed that one of the prop handlers was named Kevin Vermeersch. Vermeer, Vermeersch. Maybe he had the canvas? Within minutes, I found a phone number for him in Cambridge and began dialing. But as I listened to the ringing of the phone, I thought—what am I doing? The only evidence is the lack of evidence. *Monk* is a nationally syndicated TV show. Why would anyone with a stolen painting show it to millions of people every week?

I placed the phone in the cradle and backed away from my desk, like a drunk who realizes that he needs to go home and get a long night's rest.

SINCE THE GARDNER THEFT, much has stayed the same. Museum security remains lax, galleries continue to be such easy targets that thieves will hit them again and again. In August 2007 five men strolled into the Musee des Beaux-Arts in Nice, France, late on a Sunday afternoon. While one intruder pulled out a handgun and subdued the staff, the other men stole four paintings. Two of the works—a Monet and a Sisley—had been pilfered from the gallery in 1998. The Sisley had also been swiped from the gallery in 1978. The museum had not taken any extra security measures since the 1998 heist, and there were no cameras to record the entrance and exit of the thieves. "We will however make a point of looking at security in the city's museums," the city's deputy mayor in charge of culture sheepishly told reporters the next day.

At the same time, art prices continue to soar, making the theft of paintings and sculptures more attractive than ever. In November 2006, Christie's sold more than $490 million worth of art in a single evening, the largest sale in auction history. The next year, the market shot up even higher, and Christie's posted worldwide sales of $6.3 billion. Indeed, almost every major sale seems to break some new market record. In May 2008 Christie's sold a Lucian Freud canvas titled *Benefits Supervisor Sleeping* for $33.6 million. It was the most expensive work ever sold by a living artist. The next day, Francis Bacon's large three-panel canvas *Triptych 1976* landed more than $86 million at Sotheby's, the largest amount ever spent on a postwar artist.

But a few things have changed, and there have been some positive outcomes of the Gardner caper, most notably the Theft of Major Artwork law. At the urging of the museum, Senator Edward Kennedy added an art theft provision into the 1994 Crime Act. At the time, the five-year statute of limitations on the two federal charges in the case—interstate transportation of stolen property and the receiving of stolen property across state lines—were set to expire. The new law changed that, extending the statute of limitations to twenty years. The law also made it a federal crime to steal, receive, or dispose of any cultural object worth more than $100,000, and while Congress passed the law after the heist, it could be used to convict someone who handles the masterpieces today. "The crime is handling the stolen works or concealing them and that can happen at any time," art theft lawyer Bob Goldman told me. "If someone buys the Gardner Rembrandt fifty years down the road, they can still be prosecuted under this law."

The heist also prompted the American Association of Museums to revamp its security guidelines, and the group now recommends that its member institutions have a fully enclosed control room and run background checks on all potential guards. "The Gardner theft was a big shock, and it gave security some new respect," security expert Stephen Keller told me. "The event was one of the driving factors in moving museum security from a bunch of retired cops who slept during the rounds to a trained force." Keller, though, is the first to admit that the changes haven't been nearly enough. "It's the same problem for so many museums. They're strapped for funding, and they still don't believe that it can happen to them. I have museum directors who still say to me, 'Why do I need a panic button?' And I tell them, because of the Gardner case."

Today, the Gardner museum has a balanced budget, and the building has been fully renovated, complete with a new roof and improved lighting. It has also become one of the most well-protected art institutions in New England. During the day, video cameras manned by trained guards watch every corner of every gallery. During the evening, night-vision cameras track the surrounding streets. The museum also stations a guard in every room, has a hidden control room, and requires everyone in the museum to regularly revalidate their key cards. The reforms have been expensive. In order to attract better staff, the Gardner raised the starting salary of a third-shift guard to $13 an hour. That's more than $4 above minimum wage and almost 10 percent more than the national average. Security is now one of the largest budget items—guards constitute more than one third of the staff. "If you work at another museum, you might think, 'a theft will never happen here,'" security director Anthony Amore told me. "But at the Gardner, a theft may never happen again, but everyone who works here is reminded every day that it could happen, that it did happen."

I BELIEVE THAT the Gardner paintings will reappear. Maybe not next week, maybe not next year, but someday. How they're returned, who will recover them, is like asking what will happen next in Vermeer's *The*

Concert. You can stare at the canvas for hours, you can make a well-reasoned guess, but, really, you have no idea. Perhaps it will be the investigative work of Anthony Amore, or maybe a son will hear his father's deathbed confession, or a couple will be emptying out their basement in Braintree and find the canvases hidden in an old cardboard box. It often takes decades for stolen artworks to find their way back to their owners. In 2002 the Tate Museum in Britain recovered two Turner paintings that were stolen in 1994. In 2005 authorities discovered Pablo Picasso's *Woman in White Reading a Book*—the work had been nabbed from the home of a collector in 1940. North Carolina waited more than 140 years to get back its copy of the Bill of Rights. A Union Army soldier stole the artifact in 1865, and the playbill-sized piece of parchment floated around the art underworld for decades until the FBI recovered the work in a sting in 2005.

If the masterpieces are returned tomorrow, Gardner conservator Gianfranco Pocobene is the person who would confirm their authenticity and work to restore them. I visited him one afternoon in his studio, and when I explained my interest in the lost paintings, he moved to the set of conservation files that lined the back wall of his office and pulled down the binder devoted to Vermeer's *The Concert*. It was as thick as a telephone book, and Pocobene flipped through the pages and showed me X-rays of the painting, snapshots of the back of the stretcher, curatorial scribblings from the 1930s about a scrape in the varnish. "What we have here is a lot like a doctor's notes on a patient," he said, "and in a way, it's really almost all we have left of the work."

The detailed notations would make it nearly impossible for someone to try and scam the museum with a fake. "If someone were really good, it might take us a few days to figure out if their painting was a hoax," Pocobene said. "But there's too much information in the binder. We know what the edges of the canvas look like, the craquelure over the surface, the abrasions. The painting has aged over four hundred years, and you just can't replicate that too easily." If someone claimed to have one of the stolen paintings, Pocobene would also examine the oil pigments and thread count to see if they matched up with the original. "Would someone know about the underdrawing of the Vermeer? Precisely what it looked like and replicate it?" He shook his head. "No way."

Pocobene often thinks about the moment that the missing masterpieces are recovered. "I wonder about getting the call. Will it come in the middle of the night? What will I bring?" Pocobene's main priority would be to protect the works from further damage, and perhaps the first thing that he would do is adhere a thin tissue paper to the front of the canvases in order to secure any loose or flaking paint. What happens next would depend on the type of damage. If the stolen paintings were stored in a damp basement, Pocobene would probably dry the works out in a special chamber that slowly sucks the wetness out of a canvas. If one of the paintings developed a mold, he would place the work under an ultraviolet light, which kills most types of fungus and dry rot. Once a painting was stabilized, Pocobene would clean it, gently scrubbing off dirt and grime. The work is slow and careful—washing one square foot of canvas can take a whole day. If Pocobene finds a rip or cut in a canvas, he would reattach each of the torn threads using tweezers and a microscope. Then he would fill in the missing paint, replicating the exact colors and brushstrokes of the original. Had the artist used impasto and thickly layered the paint? Or was there a scumble or glaze covering the area to make a duller, softer effect? He would try to make the restoration look as authentic as possible—and it might take him as long as a year to fix a small tear. "We can't get the work back to its original state," he said. "I mean someone could make a really good copy of a Vermeer. I mean really good. We know so much about the painting, the techniques, the materials, the underdrawing. But that's not enough. The brushstrokes have everything to do with Vermeer being a genius and everyone else being a copyist."

The one thing that Pocobene knows for sure is that the stolen paintings have suffered some irreversible harm. The thieves knifed the two Rembrandts from the frames, and although Pocobene might be able to repair some of that damage, he will never be able to fully restore the canvases. The paintings will always show some sign of desecration. And the potential for far greater damager remains unnervingly real. If the thieves ever dropped one of the works, the stretcher would most likely shatter, leaving the loose canvas to turn and twist, the paint falling from the surface like crumbs from a piece of burned toast. "If you have a tear and 20 or 40 percent loss of paint from rolling and unrolling, there's probably not a lot we can do. I'm not saying that the painting will be ruined. But you'll always see that damage."

Until the art is returned, Pocobene recommends that the paintings be kept in conditions that do not allow for large fluctuations in temperature or humidity. Ideally, the art would be stored in a quiet room at a steady 70 degrees and 50 percent humidity. That means that your typical Boston-area house might be one of the worst places in the country to stash one of the stolen Gardner masterpieces. Without any effort to protect the painting, the dry winters and warm summers will cause the canvas to bend, warp, and eventually splinter and crack. Pocobene also advised that the art be kept out of direct sunlight, and if the paintings are in a tube, keep them in the tube. If they're laid out flat, keep them laid out flat. "Really, the less the paintings are handled, the better."

HAROLD SMITH'S SEARCH for the paintings was stopped by death; mine was stopped by life. My wife and I were expecting our second child, and I knew I couldn't continue to spend my days visiting prisons or calling up members of Braintree High School, class of 1985. It had started to seem selfish—and I missed my family. It was time for me to put the case away for a while. I was sure that I could come back, that the Gardner case would be waiting for me, a book without an ending, a puzzle forever without its last piece. I felt some resolution: David Turner was in jail, George Reissfelder was dead. In a brutal, ugly way, I felt like some of the criminal debts had been paid.

I had come to terms with the fact that the Gardner heist would always live beyond my comprehension, that it was ultimately like the Vermeer itself, a narrative mystery. Critic Wendy Lesser argues that this is the very nature of our fascination with true crime: "Murder is an inherently frustrating subject because it keeps moving away, evading us. We want to ask the big questions; more than anything else, we want to get the answers to the big questions. Yet all we can get at, finally, are the details. That's why the enjoyment of murder . . . always consists of wallowing in the gory details. The details are all we can grasp."

My dream, though, was not to understand the theft—it was to return the lost art. But that too remained a mystery. The paintings were still missing, hidden away in some dark corner, imprisoned without food and water, a set of dissidents in a cold, concrete cell. I had all sorts of emotions about leaving the case: anger, disappointment, regret, sadness, grief. But sometimes there was a small part of me that was happy that the paintings hadn't been returned. The art would always be something to look for. The word "search" comes from the Latin *circus*, or circle, meaning to go around, and it has an extraordinary power. It gives people a direction, a compass by which they can orient their lives. Searchers— once you start searching—seem to be everywhere, beachcombers and buck hunters, armchair historians and storm chasers, art detectives and dumpster divers, anyone who stares at a Rembrandt.

I came to believe that searching was a deep part of our nature, a way for us to find order and meaning in the world, and at the top of the list of masterpiece hunters might be the museum's Anthony Amore. He recently took a new approach to solving the crime, drawing up a massive database of suspects and their associates, listing all their addresses, telephone numbers, places of employment, and criminal records in a large spreadsheet. Sifting through the information, looking for links, Amore hopes to catch a connection that might have otherwise escaped notice. Right now, the database has more than 1,000 names and more than 2,000 addresses. "It's already proven its worth," he said, "because it makes it much easier to figure out what leads just aren't credible."

I would occasionally hear from others. Private detective Charlie Moore made a visit to the museum. "It's pretty impressive. A lot of nice stuff. I can see now why they robbed the place," he told me. Charlie Sabba and Youngworth still spoke regularly—and Sabba continued to "paint like a madman who is crazy about painting." I saw Marty Leppo one last time in the Norfolk Superior Court in Dedham. He was defending a man accused of keeping a cache of nearly one hundred guns and four homemade pipe bombs, and during a break in the trial, we met in the narrow hallway outside the courtroom. "Yeah, that Jewish lead didn't work out," he told me, "but listen, I got a new angle on the case. I've been talking to some mafia guys in New York, and I'm matching it up with some stuff that Judy Youngworth told me. I think, finally, that we're getting close to finding the stuff."

Perhaps the only place that the investigation did not appear pressing was the Boston FBI office, and agents continued to overlook leads, or at least take an awfully long time to chase them down. After witness Jerry Stratberg's account tagged David Turner as one of the thieves, I emailed the lead case agent Geoff Kelly and told him about the development. I thought that Kelly would want to talk to Stratberg. He was the last person to see the thieves before they entered the museum, and Stratberg said that no one from the bureau had ever showed him photos of the suspects. But six months later, Stratberg told me that he had yet to hear from Kelly. "It's fairly outrageous when you think about it," he said.

Then, in December 2007, the *Boston Globe* reported that two FBI agents served a grand jury subpoena to one of the guards that worked the night of the theft. The agents told the guard—presumably Abell— that they hoped that the grand jury would "shake things up." But most Gardner observers, including myself, reacted with impatient frustration. Abell had let the thieves into the museum. His account of the night of the heist had a number of holes. He was unable to pass a polygraph. Why did it take almost two decades to put him in front of a grand jury?

I RETIRED MOST ASPECTS of my Gardner hunt. I mothballed my tape recorder. I stopped posting advertisements in suburban Boston newspapers. But I couldn't surrender everything. I still wanted the paintings back. My Gardner theft website would stay up. So would the toll-free number. My Rembrandt and Vermeer posters would remain hanging in my office, placeholders until the originals came home. One afternoon, late in my search, I met up with Harold Smith's grandson Rich Mancuso. It was a dark, rainy day. Water fell from the sky in gray sheets. I waited for him in a coffee shop near Copley Square, and when he stepped through the door, I could tell immediately that he was Smith's grandson. He had the same broad eyes and almost military bearing. Rich shook off his umbrella and apologized for being late. The day before, he had been called to New York to work a jewelry heist. A gang of thieves had broken into a store in Harlem and pocketed about $500,000 worth of diamond rings and necklaces. Rich had joined the family business some six years earlier. He always loved art. He drew constantly as a child, landscapes, portraits, murals, and majored in fine arts in college. After graduating, he worked as a general claims adjuster for a few years, before he signed up with Greg Smith's company handling fine arts and jewelry losses. "I didn't want to have the life of a struggling artist," he said, "and I knew the job. When I was growing up, I had seen my grandfather working constantly. I watched him take calls at the beach, at the golf course, at five in the morning. I knew that it was a job that you devoted yourself to."

When Harold Smith was alive, Rich heard a lot about the Gardner robbery, but he had never helped with any leads or interviews. He was still learning the basics of the job back then, and his grandfather didn't want to distract him. Recently, though, Rich had been talking with Greg about the theft, and they had decided that it was time to get back into the investigation. "It seemed like such a shame to let a case like this fall to the back burner, especially after my grandfather did so much work on it."

Rich had just started to research the robbery, reading back issues of the *Boston Globe*, meeting with Dick Ellis on a recent trip to London to discuss the Irish angle. He planned to start digging into his grandfather's files in the coming weeks. "The case is remarkable, it spreads out like a spiderweb going in all these different angles and directions," Rich told me, "and I could see the case developing into a real passion. I think that is what happened to Harold. You start on this case, and it becomes much more than a hobby." As I listened to Rich, I felt for a moment like I was talking to an earlier version of myself, when my younger ears—as Rich's did now—rang with Smith's powerful words: "When art is stolen, there are hundreds of thousands of people who would be deprived of seeing it. Art theft isn't just a crime against the owner. It's a crime against the American people."

Rich and I talked for another hour, and when we stepped outside, the rain had slowed to a drizzle. The sun had come out from behind the woolen clouds. A golden light blanketed the streets. Rich had a client from Lloyd's of London that he planned to meet for dinner. He was running late, and I watched him as he hurried to his car. I knew that I would be hearing from him soon.

ABOUT A YEAR AND A HALF after the Gardner heist, two thieves slipped in through the back door of the Bull & Finch pub on Beacon Street. Tucked into the basement of a five-story Georgian revival town-house, the basement bar is narrow and cramped, a warren-like place with oak-paneled walls and an exposed wood ceiling. Stained-glass windows filter in splinters of afternoon light, well-worn stools surround the U-shaped bar. The pub was the inspiration for the hit television series *Cheers*, and over the years it has become one of the most visited sites in the city, a symbol of warm and cozy New England, ranked alongside Faneuil Hall and the Freedom Trail as one of the area's top tourist destinations.

The thieves were well prepared. A few days before the heist, they scoped out the bar, looking for alarms, examining the best entry and exit routes. They planned their robbery for the evening before Labor Day when the safes would be bulging with receipts from the long weekend. One of the bartenders promised to help the men in exchange for some of the stolen cash, and just after closing time he walked over to a Ryder truck that was parked outside the back entrance. The bartender told the thieves that he'd prop open the door on his way out. "You're all set," he said. "We're leaving now."

The intruders wore gloves and ski masks and carried a duffle bag filled with tools. They eased into the bar through the rear entrance and came up behind late-shift janitor Altair DeSouza. One of the thieves—a heavyset man with almond-shaped eyes—hoisted a bottle of Midori liquor and cracked it over DeSouza's head. The janitor slumped to the floor, unconscious, and the men handcuffed him to a food preparation table in the kitchen. The thieves then found the bar's manager, Tracy Kozelek. They threatened him with a crowbar and handcuffed him next to DeSouza. Then, using bolt cutters and a sledgehammer, the robbers smashed open two large safe-deposit boxes and escaped with nearly $50,000 in cash.

Two weeks after the heist, the *Herald* ran a front-page story about the break-in: FEW "CHEERS" AT HUB BAR AFTER ROBBERS TAKE $50G. That evening, David Turner called one of the thieves, Gray Morrison, to discuss the score.

"Did you read the paper?" Morrison asked.

"Yup," Turner said. "Front page."

The heist bore Turner's distinctive criminal fingerprints—it showed a powerful resemblance to the Gardner caper. The thieves had inside information, they struck on a holiday weekend, they used handcuffs to secure the employees. A number of witnesses fingered Turner for the crime. A bouncer told police that he had seen the golden boy gangster plotting the heist together with the bartender. Morrison confessed to investigators that he and Turner were behind the heist and provided details that no one else would have known, like how Turner had purchased the bolt cutters in a store in Chinatown and used a black gym bag to carry the tools into the bar.

Prosecutors charged Turner with the Bull & Finch robbery in 1993, but he was acquitted. The problem was that Morrison and the bouncer had been offered generous plea deals, and the jury didn't believe their testimony. "It was a great trial, it was a fun trial. I turned them inside out," recalled Leppo, who served as Turner's defense lawyer. "Turner had a tape of my final argument, and he used to play it in his car as he used to ride around. The clerk told me, 'Marty, you used the term rat bastards, informants, calling them rats, a hundred times in that trial.'"

Turner continues to haunt Boston. He attacked some of the city's most beloved institutions; police believe that he was involved in more than a half-dozen murders. People still nurse a bottomless terror of his underworld power, and in whispered tones, they would remind me of how the gangster had murdered Charlie Pappas blocks away from where the two used to play touch football together. They recalled Andrea Freedman, the victim of the Canton home invasion. After she agreed to testify, Turner would sit in a Ford in front of her house, while his associates called her and said that if she fingered Turner for the robbery, she would be killed. Even the *Cheers* bar—the place where everyone knows your name and they're always glad you came—now has armed guards to safely shuttle receipts out of the bar. "Turner is not someone you forget that easily," former assistant attorney general Bob Sikellis told me. "He robbed this place of too much."

I RETURNED to the Gardner museum on a recent October morning, and the first thing to greet me was the smell, deep and earthy, a raw mixture of well-polished antiques and blooming orchids. It's like nothing I've smelled before or since, and I lingered in the cool darkness for a long moment, before moving down a tight corridor and into the courtyard. A fireworks flash of color and light, the verdant garden radiating with lush tulips and sweeping palms. The Roman fountain bubbled quietly under the double staircase. Sparkling sunshine danced along the walls. In the middle of the greenery, a large Ptolemaic urn was tucked under a lily, as if Dionysus had left the vase behind the night before. It was hard to imagine a more beautiful crime scene.

A tour guide led a group of students up the main staircase and toward the Dutch Room, and as the sounds faded, a man sat himself Buddha-style along the ledge of the courtyard, meditating next to the Roman sarcophagus. Walking along the arched hallway, a visitor whispered reverentially to his partner, tugging his arm, begging for the opportunity to show off his favorite painting. The flowers in the garden still rotate according to Gardner's wishes. Orange trees in March, delphiniums in June, poinsettias at Christmas, and on April 14, her birthday, a celebration of large, hanging nasturtiums. The museum was still what Gardner hoped it to be, a refuge from the ordinary and prosaic, a world of aesthetic creativity and artistic surprise, a building "to have [your] own personal encounters with beauty in a domestic setting."

It would be my last visit for a while, and I studied the airy watercolors in the Yellow Room, the Matisses, the Degas, the Whistlers. I strolled through the Chinese Loggia, gazing at the pieces of Asian sculpture, the Song Dynasty wood Guanyin, the remarkable temple stele of the Eastern Wei Dynasty. On the first floor, Gardner built an entire room around John Singer Sargent's masterpiece *El Jaleo*, a massive oil painting of a flamenco dancer. To highlight the visual motifs, she framed the work within a Moorish-style arch, a set of floor lights, and hundreds of blue and white Mexican tiles. The design gives the painting a vibrant, cinematic vitality, and I stood in front of the canvas and felt as if I could hear the flamenco dancer *click, click, clicking* her heels on the floor, while the band stomped and hollered their way through a fiery love song. When Sargent first saw his painting within the setting, he told Gardner that she had done more for the artwork than he ever had.

Eventually, I moved up the stairs and into the Dutch Room. Nothing had changed, everything stood the same, the empty frames, the roped off Victorian chairs, the slash of brown velvet encased by a gilded setting.

"Do you think the paintings will come back?" a woman asked the guard.

He nodded. "Oh, yeah. For sure, they'll come back. Hope will never die here," he said, "and when they do return, I tell you, we will have a line from here to downtown. Everybody will want to come and see those paintings."

The woman moved out of the room. The sounds of the museum— the soft shuffling of feet, the hollow gurgle of the fountain—became muffled and distant. A gentle light sifted through the bamboo shades, the room felt warm and languid and hazy. I stood in front of the missing Rembrandt seascape and stared into the silk green-gold wallpaper, and slowly my vision began to blur and narrow. There was canvas and underdrawing. Clouds, wispy and golden, drifted through the frame. The sturdy mast, the billowing sails, the plaintive looks of the sailors pulling at Jesus, begging to be saved. The colors flashed and dimmed, ochers and blues, olives and yellows. Holding his cap tightly on his head, Rembrandt gazed out, his eyes looking deep and wise. We stared at each other for a long moment, me and the Old Master, a gesture that seemed to cross all eternity. And then, as quickly as it came, the image faded away, more than just a wish, because for there to be beauty or love or truth, there must first be hope. The emotion filled my chest as I walked out of the room, padded down the stairs, and headed all the way home.

Want to know more about the case? Have information on the whereabouts of the paintings? The identities of the thieves? Please visit www.thegardnerheist.com or call 1-888-292-9380.

SOURCES

1. THE STORM ON THE SEA OF GALILEE: A DISTURBANCE IN THE COURTYARD

My account of the theft relied on a variety of sources, including Boston Police Department reports of the robbery and the FBI's "Letterhead Memorandum" released on March 21, 1990, which offered a detailed account of the heist. I also interviewed Anne Hawley, Lyle Grindle, Geoff Kelly, Jerry Stratberg, Dan Falzon, John Eglehof, Anthony Amore, Tom Cassano, Bob Fitzpatrick, Scott Melinchionda, and Barbara Magnum, as well as other persons who worked at the museum at the time of the theft. The names of Ray Abell, Ralph Helman, and Jerry Stratberg are pseudonyms.

Many of the details of Abell's experience were drawn from Stephen Kurkjian's "Secrets Behind the Largest Art Theft in History," *Boston Globe*, Mar. 13, 2005. The article is an excellent account of the theft, and Kurkjian is the only reporter that I know of who interviewed Abell at any length.

The detail about a motion detector that goes off when visitors get too close to the art first appeared in Kurkjian's "Secrets," as did the information about the data from the motion detectors still being on the computer in the security director's office.

The quote from Helman ("why are you arresting me?") on page 4 was also from the 2005 *Globe* article.

The exact order in which the paintings were stolen is not known. But investigators have been able to make some inferences because of the way that the frames lay on the floor of the Dutch Room. For instance, the empty frame of *A Lady and Gentleman in Black* was tucked under the frame of the Vermeer, suggesting that the thieves stole the Rembrandts before they stole *The Concert*.

Investigators are also not 100 percent confident that the thieves had a second car. In a 2001 speech in front of the International Foundation For Art, FBI agent Tom Cassano said: "We don't know if there were other people outside or not. We have reason to believe that there were probably at least one, maybe two, and probably they made a getaway in a van or larger vehicle or some sort of truck." See *IFAR Journal,* vol. 4, no. 1, 2000, 24. It also stands to reason that the Gardner loot, which included a large wood panel painting, would not have fit into a hatchback and that the thieves would have needed a second car in order to escape with all of the stolen art.

2. CHEZ TORTONI: THE ART DETECTIVE

The magazine article that inspired me to reach out to Harold Smith was by Adam Laukhuf and ran in the December 2004 issue of *Vanity Fair.* I am indebted to University of California, Berkeley, English professor Mary Koory, who walked me through the literary history of mysteries. She also introduced me to the idea that there are two kinds of mysteries: mysteries with a little m and mysteries with a big M.

The Berry-Hill Galleries scandal was well-covered by the media. See, for instance, "Gallery Under Legal Fire Declares Bankruptcy," Carol Vogel, *New York Times,* Dec. 22, 2005, and "Berry-Hill Galleries: Bankruptcy's Tentacles Spread," David Hewett, *Maine Antiques Digest,* Feb. 2006. Berry-Hill Galleries did not return calls for comment. The anecdotes about Ed Kienholz and Richard Wollheim came from *Pictures and Tears: A History of People Who Have Cried in Front of Paintings* by James Elkins (London: Routledge, 2001).

The quote from Breitwieser on page 17 ("I was fascinated by her beauty . . . ") came from "Art thief jailed for four years," BBC, Feb. 7, 2003. The second Breitwieser quote ("Whether it was worth a thousand euros or millions . . . ") came from "Court Jails Art Thief, Girlfriend and Mother," Amelia Gentleman, *Guardian* (Manchester, UK), Jan. 8, 2005.

The recounting of the Houston Museum of Fine Art heist drew upon "The Adventures of Harold Smith, Art Supersleuth," Sandy Granville Sheehy, *Town & Country,* Oct. 1991, 118. I also consulted a variety of articles from the *Houston Chronicle.*

Smith's quote regarding the melted gold on page 20 was from "Arrest, Not Ransom, Goal for Reward at Museum," Kim Cobb and James Campbell, *Houston Chronicle,* June 2, 1989, sec. A, 21.

The data from the Art Loss Register on page 21 was current as of June 2008.

Smith's estimate that stolen art is a $4 to $6 billion industry appears to have come from Interpol. It is a widely cited number.

Smith's quote on page 22 ("If it became known . . . ") came from "Art Museum Uninsured for Major Theft," Christopher Dauer, *National Underwriter Property & Casualty-Risk & Benefits Management,* Apr. 9, 1990.

The story about the Hammer Gallery theft first appeared in Thomas McShane and Dara Matera's *Stolen Masterpiece Tracker: The Dangerous Life of the FBI's #1 Art Sleuth* (New York: Barricade Books, 2006). I interviewed Thomas McShane and added more details to the account.

My account of the Golden Door heist relied on a number of sources, including interviews with Harold Smith, Greg Smith, Tara Smith, Sandy Guttman, and Bob Lee. I also had the case files on the robbery from the Miami police department. Smith also wrote a lightly fictionalized version of the case that gave helpful details.

3. A LADY AND GENTLEMAN IN BLACK: IT WAS A PASSION

The account of the Walters theft came from numerous sources, including Greg and Harold Smith and "Art Objects Are Pilfered from a Baltimore Gallery," *New York Times,* Aug. 21, 1988.

More information about the movie *Stolen* can be found at www.stolenthe-film.com. Smith's website for the Gardner case was: www.find-the-art.com. That site is now defunct.

The quote from Smith on page 32 ("Wives become ex-wives. Girlfriends become ex-girlfriends") was from "Filming an Art-Heist Mystery and Hoping for a Happy Ending," Ralph Blumenthal, *New York Times,* May 6, 2002.

Descriptions of Smith's Gardner tips came from numerous sources, including Smith's notes and interviews with Dee Markijohn, Tara Smith, Greg Smith, and Sandy Guttman.

My description of Rembrandt's life and work relied upon Simon Schama's *Rembrandt's Eyes* (New York: Knopf, 2001) and Charles Mee Jr.'s *Rembrandt's Portrait: A Biography* (New York: Simon and Schuster, 1998). My account of Vermeer's life relied on Anthony Bailey's *Vermeer: A View of Delft* (New York: Henry Holt, 2001). I also spoke at length about Vermeer and Rembrandt with various scholars, including Arthur Wheelock of the National Gallery, Jørgen Wadum of the Royal Cabinet of Paintings, and Alan Chong of the Gardner Museum. I'm also deeply indebted to Jacquelyn Coutre, who read this section over for accuracy.

The anecdote about the yellow tulips came from "Gardner Patrons Show Their Support," Desiree French, *Boston Globe,* Mar. 1990, Arts sec., 11.

Daniel Falzon's quote on page 40 came from "The Great Art Caper," Steve Lopez, *Time,* Nov. 17, 1997.

The potboiler is Brian McGrory's *Deadline* (New York: Atria, 2004). The animated video was made by multimedia artist Ezra Johnson and titled "What Visions Burn." It was shown in December 2006 at New York City's Klagsbrun Gallery. John Updike's poem "Stolen" ran in *The New Yorker* on Apr. 14, 2003, 66.

4. THE CONCERT: THE PICTURE HABIT

My account of Gardner's life and work relied on Douglass Shand-Tucci's *The Art of Scandal: The Life and Times of Isabella Stewart Gardner* (New York: Harper-Collins, 1997), Louise Tharp's *Mrs. Jack: A Biography of Isabella Stewart Gardner* (New York: Little, Brown, 1965), and Morris Carter's *Isabella Stewart Gardner and Fenway Court* (Boston: Houghton Mifflin, 1925). I also interviewed Douglass Shand-Tucci, Anne Hawley, and Alan Chong to flush out certain details. The Gardner's Kristin Parker was also very helpful in helping me run down specific queries, including information on the provenance of the stolen artworks.

The quote on page 43 ("have a house . . . like the one in Milan") came from Carter, *Isabella Stewart Gardner and Fenway Court,* 15.

The "pray who undressed you" anecdote on page 45 came from Tharp, *Mrs. Jack,* 43.

The quote on page 46 ("Mrs. Jack Gardner is one of the seven wonders . . . ") was from Hilliard Goldfarb's *Isabella Stewart Gardner Museum* (New Haven: Yale University Press, 1995), 8.

The Boston Red Sox anecdote on page 46 came from Tharp, *Mrs. Jack,* 290.

Gardner's keeping a scrap book of her media mentions was discussed in the Shand-Tucci book (*Art of Scandal*) and in "Mrs. Gardner Gets a Makeover," Christine Temin, *Boston Globe,* Apr. 30, 2003, Arts sec., C1.

The anecdote about Crawford's Notch came from Tharp, *Mrs. Jack,* 134.

The quote from Gardner on page 49 ("Downstairs . . .") came from Rollin Hadley, *The Letters of Bernard Berenson and Isabella Stewart Gardner 1887–1924,* (Boston: Northeastern University Press, 1987), 120.

The account of the purchase of the Vermeer came from Carter, 134.

The quote from J. Paul Getty's diary came from Werner Muensterberger's *Collecting: An Unruly Passion* (Princeton: Princeton University Press, 1994), 142. I first saw this anecdote in Edward Dolnick's excellent book *The Rescue Artist: A True Story of Art, Thieves, and the Hunt for a Missing Masterpiece* (New York: HarperCollins, 2005).

Gardner's purchase of fake antiquities came from Tharp, *Mrs. Jack,* 164.

The anecdote about the Havemeyers drew upon Frances Weitzenhoffer's *The Havemeyers: Impressionism Comes to America* (New York: Harry N. Abrams, 1986), 139. I first came across this anecdote in Shand-Tucci's *Art of Scandal*.

My account of Bernard Berenson's life and work relied on Meryle Secrest's *Being Bernard Berenson* (New York: Holt, Rinehart and Winston, 1979). The list of Berenson's visitors came from Secrest, 3.

The Berenson quote on page 51 ("How much do you want . . . ") came from Hadley, *Letters,* 39.

The anecdote about Gardner sending a Pissarro as a thank-you gift was from Shand-Tucci, *Art of Scandal,* 172.

Peter Sutton's comment about the Titian appeared in "Vermeer Painting,

One of 32 in World Called Greatest Loss," Christine Temin, *Boston Globe,* Mar. 19, 1990, 1. The Rubens quote came from Shand-Tucci, *Art of Scandal,* 175.

The Berenson quote on page 51 ("A glance at the . . . ") was from Hadley, *Letters,* 149.

The Gardner quote on page 51 ("Let us aim awfully high . . . ") came from Hadley, *Letters,* 66.

The Gardner quote on page 51 ("I've got the picture habit.") came from Hadley, 69.

The Berenson quote on page 51 ("You know that Gainsborough . . . ") was from Hadley, *Letters,* 51.

The Berenson quote on page 52 ("It will require cunning . . . ") was from Hadley, *Letters,* 52.

The most detailed account of Berenson's duplicitous double-dealing is Colin Simpson's *The Partnership: The Secret Association of Bernard Berenson and Joseph Duveen* (London, Bodley Head, 1987). The Gardner quote on page 52 ("Tell me exactly . . . ") was from Hadley, *Letters,* 177. Also see Meryle Secrest's *Being Bernard Berenson,* 148–49.

The information about the cost of a Vermeer in 1816 came from Dolnick, *Rescue Artist,* 64.

The menagerie anecdote was from *Time,* Aug. 24, 1936.

The press release from the fifteenth and sixteenth anniversaries are the exact same, except for one paragraph.

Information on the museum's financial health on page 57 came from the Gardner museum's IRS Form 990 for Tax Exempt Organizations, 1984.

Hawley's quote on page 57 ("overzealous . . . ") came from "Dances with Trustees," Anne Hawley, *Museum News,* Jan./Feb. 1998.

The anecdote about *America's Most Wanted* and the quote came from "Show Reenacts Art Heist," Susan Bickelhaupt, *Boston Globe,* May 2, 1990, Living sec., 65.

The information regarding the percentage of unreported art thefts comes from Jane Stapleton of the art insurance firm Huntington T. Block. Others believe that that figure may be too high. Noah Charney, director of the Association for Research into Crimes Against Art, told me, "there simply aren't good enough statistics to say a percentage of unreported cases, though it's certainly substantial (my guess, 20–30%)." The story about the Andy Warhol paintings and the Museum of Modern Art appeared in a number of outlets, including "U.S. Museums Meet the Challenge of Theft," Jason Edward Kaufman, *Art Newspaper,* Sept. 1997. When I contacted MOMA for more information, a press officer refused comment, saying that no one at the museum could recall the event.

The information came about the $50,000 spent on heist research came from the Gardner museum's IRS Form 990 for Tax Exempt Organizations, 2005.

The Gardner quote on page 60 ("I am breathless . . .") was from Hadley, *Letters,* 66.

5. CORTEGE AUX ENVIRONS DE FLORENCE: THE ART OF THE THEFT

The account of the Chagall robbery came from my interview with Harold Smith, Greg Smith, Rich Mancusso, and Neil Lieberman. I also relied on news accounts, including: "Museum's Stolen Chagall, or a Good Fake, Turns Up in Topeka Mail," Thomas J. Lueck, *New York Times,* Jan. 23, 2002; "Ransom for a Stolen Chagall: An Israeli-Palestinian Peace," C. J. Chivers, *New York Times,* Aug. 20, 2001; "Expert Says Topeka Postal Item Is Stolen Chagall," Carol Vogel, *New York Times,* Feb. 15, 2002; "Reward Is Offered in Theft of Early Painting by Chagall," William K. Rashbaum, *New York Times,* June 16, 2001. The account of the Vermeer theft from Brussels' Palais des Beaux-Arts relied upon Milton Esterow's *The Art Stealers* (London: Weidenfeld and Nicolson, 1973), 13.

Details of the Feller case came from interviews with Harold Smith and news reports, including "The Trusted Museum Insider Who Turned Out to Be a Thief," William Honan, *New York Times,* Dec. 19, 1991, and "The Adventures of Harold Smith, Art Supersleuth," Sandy Granville Sheehy, *Town & Country,* Oct. 1991, 118.

The account of the stolen Chinese vases came from interviews with Smith and a number of news articles, including Andrew Yarrow's "Man Tied to Art Thefts in Northeast Is Arrested," *New York Times,* Mar. 10, 1989, and "The Adventures of Harold Smith," Sheehy, *Town & Country,* Oct. 1991, 118. Smith's quote ("Right in broad daylight . . .") on page 66 came from Sheehy's article.

The account of the da Vinci heist came from press reports. Others, including Edward Dolnick, have wondered why thieves steal anything beside Old Master paintings.

Ralph Curtis's remark about the value of the Vermeer came from Carter, *Isabella Stewart Gardner,* 135. According to a search of news sources, the sale of the Manet made headlines in New York, Los Angeles, and Boston. The Robert Hughes article appeared under the headline "A Boston Theft Reflects," *Time,* Apr. 2, 1990.

The *Boston Herald* article listing the values of the works appeared on Mar. 18, 1998, 6. The Cassano speech was detailed in "FBI Provides Update in Gardner Art Heist Case," Bob Jackman, *Antiques and The Arts Weekly,* Nov. 21, 2000, and the *IFAR Journal,* vol. 4, no 1, 2001, 24. I also interviewed Cassano about the incident.

It's unlikely that anyone will know the true monetary value of the lost Gardner art. The paintings haven't changed hands for more than a century, and the only way to get a reliable figure for their total value is to sell the works, which Gardner's will prohibits. But recent comparable auction records show a demand for Old Masters paintings that makes $500 million seem ballpark. In January 2007 a questionable Rembrandt canvas, a portrait of an apostle, sold for $25 million, and in 2002 a stunning painting, *Massacre of the Innocents* by Peter Paul Rubens, went for $76 million. Even questionable Vermeers rake in enormous sums. The last painting by the Dutch Master to go to auction was a small, dark canvas called *Young Woman Seated at the Virginals*. When Sotheby's sold the work in 2004, they claimed it was a genuine Vermeer. Many experts disagreed. They argued that the work was too dark, too sloppy, to be genuine. Still, the painting sold for $42 million, more than five times the pre-sale estimate, and it became the fifth most expensive Old Master ever sold at auction. And all these values exclude the fact that when paintings are stolen and subsequently recovered, they experience significantly higher market values. See, for instance, Clemens Bomsdorf's "Munch Prices 'Driven Up By Thefts'" *Art Newspaper*, July 15, 2008, no. 193.

The *Boston Globe* story cited on page 71 was by Peter S. Canellos and ran under the headline, "$200M Gardner Museum Art Theft / Secret Collector's Passion or Ransom Seen as Motive," Mar. 19, 1990, Metro sec., 1. Gardner's quote comes from "Boston Museum Says It Was Uninsured for Theft," Fox Butterfield, *New York Times*, Mar. 20, 1990.

The Gardner quote "beyond question the finest of [Rembrandt's] landscapes" on page 74 was from Hadley, *Letters*, 200.

My discussion of Flinck's *Landscape with an Obelisk* drew upon Cynthia Schneider's "A New Look at the *Landscape with an Obelisk*," Fenway Court, Isabella Stewart Gardner Museum, (1985), 7–21.

The discussion of Rembrandt's *A Lady and Gentleman in Black* relied upon a number of sources, including interviews with Alan Chong, Arthur Wheelock, and Ernest van de Wetering. I also consulted *A Corpus of Rembrandt Paintings*, vol. 3, 1635–42, Rembrandt Research Project Series: vol. 3, Bruyn, J.; Haak, B.; Levie, S. H.; van Thiel, P. J. J.; van de Wetering, E., eds., 1990.

The anecdote about a group of men beating up a young man outside the museum first appeared in Stephen Kurkjian's "Secrets Behind the Largest Art Theft in History," *Boston Globe*, Mar. 13, 2005. I also interviewed Lyle Grindle about the event.

Smith's quote on page 75 ("the actual thieves to me sound like down-to-earth burglars . . . ") came from Rochelle Steinhaus's "The Isabella Gardner Museum heist," *CNN.com*, Nov. 26, 2002.

6. LANDSCAPE WITH AN OBELISK: SOMETHING THAT BIG

The account of the security of the Jewish Museum came from my personal reporting. I also interviewed Al Lazarte, Director of Operations, at the Jewish Museum, via email.

My description of the theft from the Kunsthistorisches Museum comes from media accounts.

The best account of the various Russborough House heists might be Matthew Hart's *The Irish Game: A True Story of Crime and Art* (New York: Walker and Company, 2004). I also relied on Mairead Carey's "An Artful Dodge," *Time*, Dec. 8, 2002.

The anecdote about fund-raiser-sponsored toilet paper came from "Hard-pressed museums in Revolt Over Government Funding," Fiachra Gibbons, *Guardian* (Manchester, UK), Nov. 22, 2003. I first saw this anecdote in Dolnick, 15.

The Smithsonian security issues were detailed in a Government Accounting Office report titled "Funding Challenges Affect Facilities' Conditions and Security, Endangering Collections" from Sept. 2007.

FBI special agent Bob Wittman provided me with the figure on the percentage of insiders involved in art heists. He said that the data came from the FBI's art theft database. Some believe the estimate is too high. Noah Charney of the Association for Research into Crimes against Art told me: "I'd say 25 percent have an insider involved in some way. For most art theft you don't need an insider to be able to pull it off, alas."

My description of thefts that occurred in the years leading up to the Gardner theft relied on "Hot Art: With Picassos Going For $38 Million, Art Theft Has Become a Booming Billion-Dollar Illegal Business, Second Only to Narcotics," Daniel Golden, *Boston Globe*, Feb. 12, 1989, Sunday sec., 16. I also drew on "$200M Gardner Museum Art Theft," Canellos, *Boston Globe*, Mar. 19, 1990, Metro sec., 1. The anecdote about a man stealing the Rembrandt self-portrait and its subsequent recovery first appeared in "Secrets Behind the Largest Art Theft in History," Stephen Kurkjian, *Boston Globe*, Mar. 13, 2005. I also interviewed Lyle Grindle about the event.

Information on the museum's financial health came from the Gardner museum's IRS Form 990 for Tax Exempt Organizations, from 1984 to 1989. Hoving's account about the building's condition appeared in *Connoisseur*, July 1990. It was substantiated by contemporary accounts in the *Boston Globe* and *Herald*.

7. KU: UNFINISHED BUSINESS

My account of the morning after the theft relies on a variety of sources. I examined Boston Police Department reports and interviewed Anne Hawley, Lyle Grindle, Dan Falzon, John Eglehof, Tom Cassano, Bob Fitzpatrick, as well as other persons who worked at the museum at the time of the theft. The names of Edgar Queensbury, Fred O'Shea, and Kelly Sanmarino are pseudonyms. I also relied on dozens of *Boston Globe* and *Boston Herald* articles that ran in the days after the heist, most notably "Gardner: Masterwork of Crime Retracing the Steps of Robbery's Twisted Trail," Elisabeth Neuffer, *Boston Globe*, May 13, 1990, which provided the details about Paul Crossen and Karen Haas. I also drew upon other Neuffer's articles from the *Boston Globe*, "FBI Is Said To Have Suspects Worldwide in Gardner Theft," and "Inch by Inch Hunt For Clues Goes On." The quotes of Debora Schwartz were from "Museum's Loyalists Stunned, Angered By Its Violation," John Ellement, *Boston Globe*, Mar. 19, 1990, Metro sec., 22.

Information on insurance costs at the time of the heist relied upon interviews and "A Lucrative Crime Grows Into a Costly Epidemic," Andrew Yarrow, *New York Times*, Mar. 20, 1990.

Hawley's quote on page 92 ("No questions asked") came from an article by Andy Dabilis, Kevin Cullen and Tom Coakley, headlined "$1M Reward Offered for Trail to Stolen Art, *Boston Globe*, Mar. 21, 1990.

My description of Bostonians flocking to the museum's galleries came from news accounts in the *Globe* and *Herald*, including Desiree French's article "Gardner Patrons Show Their Support," Mar. 1990, *Boston Globe*, Arts sec., 11.

My account of Daniel Falzon and his early work on the Gardner case came from a variety of sources, including "The Great Art Caper," Steve Lopez, *Time*, Nov. 17, 1997; "Secrets Behind the Largest Art Theft in History," Stephen Kurkjian, *Boston Globe*, Mar. 13, 2005; "Missing: Priceless Art, Reward: $5 million," Melinda Henneberger, *Reader's Digest*, May 2003. The *Time* article was particularly helpful in flushing out the details of Falzon's early work on the case and was the source for the information on his salary and first assignment. The anecdote about the ex-guard named Jeff was drawn from Henneberger's article. Retired FBI agent Bob Fitzpatrick once represented Jeff and offered other details on that particular lead. The anecdote about Rollin Hadley first appeared in Melinda Henneberger's *Reader's Digest* article. Information about Hadley's divorce comes from Norma Nathan's "The Eye," *Boston Herald*, Jan. 11, 1989, 6. I interviewed Gerry Kaplan in the summer of 2007. Details about his case came from myriad sources, including the *Reader's Digest* article.

The anecdote about Mireille Ballestrazzi and the signs of conflict and confusion came from "A Tangled 2-Year Inquiry Yields Few Answers in Boston Art Theft," William Honan, *New York Times*, June 2, 1992.

The anecdote about the letter-writer lead came from interviews with Lyle Grindle, Dan Falzon, and other museum officials. The anecdote first appeared in "Secrets Behind the Largest Art Theft in History," Stephen Kurkjian, *Boston Globe*, Mar. 13, 2005.

The anecdote on McDevitt relied upon FBI memos and news reports in the *Boston Globe*, *New York Times*, and *Reader's Digest*. Two accounts were particularly helpful: "A Tangled 2-Year Inquiry," Hoonan, *New York Times*, June 2, 1992, and "Gardner Art Theft Suspect Is Study in Intrigue," Brian McGrory, *Boston Globe*, June 3, 1992.

My account of David Turner's life and criminal career relied upon interviews with dozens of people, including Rob Goldstein, Joe Flaherty, Bob Sikellis, Chris Ruggiero, Eddie Whelan, Joan Moran, Mark Moran, Deborah Moran, Michael Waugh, Janice Santos, Sylvia Benjamin, Martin Leppo, and David Turner, among others. There were a number of people that I wanted to reach, but they did not respond to requests for comment. They include Turner's family members and Stephen Rossetti.

I also drew upon on various court cases. They included court-approved taped conversations as well as confidential informant reports, which became the basis for some of the conversations within this book. The cases include:

United States District Court vs. David Turner, et al. U.S. District Court, District of Massachusetts, criminal docket 99–10098.

Commonwealth vs. David Turner. Suffolk County Superior Court, criminal docket number 93–10603.

Commonwealth vs. Charlie Pappas. Norfolk County Superior Court, civil action number 93051–93055.

Commonwealth vs. David Turner. Norfolk County Superior Court, criminal docket number 94511–94513.

I also relied on various news accounts, most notably Michael Blanding's excellent article, "FBI: the Set Up," *Boston Magazine*, Nov. 2003, and "One Step Ahead Braintree Suspect in Thefts, Slayings Eludes Prosecutors," Anthony Flint, *Boston Globe*, Jan. 20, 1996, Metro sec., 1. Blanding's article was particularly helpful in detailing the morning of Turner's arrest for the Loomis heist and how Cronin interrogated Turner. It was Flint's well-reported, well-written article that described Turner as the Teflon Don of South Boston. Other articles provided details and help supplement my understanding. They include: "Police Probe Gardner Museum Ties; Drug Ring May Be Linked to Art Heist," Charles Craig, *Boston Herald*, May 27, 1992, 1; "Bail Revoked as Court Fears for a 2d Witness," David Arnold, *Boston Globe*, Nov. 28, 1995, 1; "Reports Say FBI Targeted Trio in Gardner Art Theft," Shelley Murphy, *Boston Globe*, June 13, 2000, Metro sec., 1; "Search for Gardner Heist Informants Turns Sour," Tom Mashberg, *Boston Herald*, June 14, 2000.

The Merlino quote on page 105 ("Very big and international . . . ") came from a Bob Sikellis memo dated June 10, 1992. The event occurred about a month after news reports surfaced that Merlino was trying to negotiate the return of the Gardner art.

The details about the return of the George Washington portrait came from a memorandum by Rolf Diamant of the National Park Service dated Jan. 27, 1995, titled "Recovery of Longfellow Paintings."

The Merlino quotes on page 106 ("Do I have a problem?") and the associated anecdote came from an FBI report by Neil Cronin dated Nov. 13, 1997.

The Merlino quotes on page 106 ("What the fuck is this . . . ") came from a wiretap dated Nov. 27, 1998.

The account of Neil Cronin's investigation of Turner and of Merlino's effort to return the Garner art was drawn from government documents and evidentiary hearing testimony from *United States District Court vs. David Turner, et al.* U.S. District Court, District of Massachusetts, criminal docket 99-10098. I also interviewed Cronin's supervisor at the time, Tom Cassano. The Morrison quote on page 107 ("No matter who you go with") came from a wiretap dated Sep. 17, 1991.

8. THREE MOUNTED JOCKEYS: INFILTRATE AND INFATUATE

A number of articles helped me flush out my account of Wittman. They include Roxanne Patel's "To Catch A Thief," *Philadelphia Magazine*, Mar. 1, 2005, and Jori Finkel's "Is Everything Sacred?" *Legal Affairs*, July/August, 2003.

The anecdote about the recovery of the Rufino Tamayo relied upon "One

Person's Trash Is Another Person's Lost Masterpiece," Carol Vogel, *New York Times,* Oct. 23, 2007.

The anecdote about McShane's stings first appeared in Thomas McShane and Dara Matera's *Stolen Masterpiece Tracker: The Dangerous Life of the FBI's #1 Art Sleuth* (New York: Barricade Books, 2006). I interviewed Thomas McShane and added fresh details to his account.

For more on Bamford's priorities, see "FBI's Top Man in Boston Returns to Roots," Dennis Shaughnessey, *Sun* (Lowell, MA), Oct. 26, 2007, 1; "Lowell Native Steps Up as FBI Head" Hillary Chabot, *Sentinel & Enterprise* (Fitchburg, MA), Jan. 13, 2007; "New Boston FBI Boss 'Won't Stop' Until Whitey Bulger's Behind Bars," Laurel Sweet, *Boston Herald,* Mar. 8, 2007, 16.

The Youngworth-Mashberg incident has been written about at length. During the summer of 1997, articles appeared in Boston newspapers almost every day. I relied heavily on Mashberg's early accounts, including "We've Seen It," *Boston Herald,* Aug. 27, 1997, 1, and "Lookin' Good," Tom Mashberg, *Boston Herald,* Aug. 30, 1997, 1. Mashberg also wrote a detailed account of his experience in a *Vanity Fair* article titled "Stealing Beauty," published in March 1998, that provided helpful details on Youngworth's early life, including the death of his mother. I also flushed out my account with *Boston Globe* articles written by Judy Rakowsky, Shelley Murphy, Daniel Golden, and Stephen Kurkjian. Dan Kennedy's article "Deal of the Art" appeared in the *Boston Phoenix,* Sept. 4, 1997, was also very helpful. I communicated with William Youngworth via email. I also asked him questions through Charlie Sabba. To fill out Youngworth's story, I also spoke with Martin Leppo, Tom Mashberg, Michel van Rijn, Diana Sandgren, Rocco Ellis, Charlie Moore, Myles Connor, Barbara Magnum, Anne Hawley, Lyle Grindle, Arnold Hiatt, Donald Stern, Mark Gentile, Mary Gentile, and others.

Youngworth's quote ("I am leading you ... ") page 117 came from a Randolph Police Department Report dated Aug. 8, 1997, written by Detective William Pace.

The McCrone quote ("Everything is ... ") on page 118 came from "Art Experts Say Paintings Are Rembrandts," Tom Mashberg, *Boston Herald,* Oct. 15, 1997.

Details about the meeting in the Plaza first appeared in "New Clues in Art Heist Mystery" Brian Ross and Jill Rackmill, *ABC News,* Mar. 11, 2004, and "Gardner Makes Pitches for Art," Tom Mashberg, *Boston Herald,* Oct. 3, 1997, 6. I also discussed the meeting with Hiatt and Mashberg.

Youngworth's quote on page 119 ("snap the olive branch ... ") came from "Antique Dealer Has New Demand for Return of Artwork," Tom Mashberg, *Boston Herald,* Sept. 8, 1997.

My account of the interaction between Smith and Youngworth came from interviews with Harold Smith, Greg Smith, Tara Smith, Dee Markijohn, and Sandy Guttman, among others. I also relied on the two documentaries made about Smith and the Gardner case. The first film ran on CourtTV and was titled

The Great Gardner Art Heist. A slightly different version was released theatrically and featured on the PBS series Independent Lens and was titled *Stolen*. I also had an unpublished transcript of Smith's interview of Youngworth for the documentaries. This document provided the quotes between Smith and Youngworth, including ("It made it very romantic . . . "), ("We're not the police . . . "), and ("The Boston FBI orchestrated . . . ").

Youngworth's boast of his skills at hawking sham Shaker furniture came from Mashberg's *Vanity Fair* article "Stealing Beauty," Mar. 1998.

Smith's quote on page 120 ("Youngworth claims he can . . . ") came from "The Isabella Gardner Museum heist," Rochelle Steinhaus, *CNN.com*, Nov. 26, 2002.

The information on Youngworth's aliases and arrest record came from his state Criminal Offender Record Information report. The quotes from Youngworth's email on page 122 ("couple days of hard travel . . . ") came from Rebecca Dreyfus's CourtTV documentary *The Great Gardner Art Heist*.

Youngworth's interview with ABC News aired Mar. 11, 2004. Produced by Brian Ross and Jill Rackmill, it was titled "New Clues in Art Heist Mystery." Gentile's account about the forged Rembrandt self-portrait was first detailed in two articles "Pal Says Scam Artist Pulled Fast One On ABC," Tom Mashberg, *Boston Herald*, Mar. 13, 2004, 8, and "Doubt Cast on Copy of Stolen Art," Stephen Kurkjian and Shelley Murphy, *Boston Globe*, Mar. 13, 2004. Information on the Youngworth lawsuit against Gentile and Youngworth's sister came from *William P. Youngworth III vs. Mark A. Gentile, et al.* U.S. District Court, District of Massachusetts, civil action number 05–30108-MAP.

Gardner's quote on page 127 ("I am now as a tramp . . . ") came from Hadley, 153.

9. SELF-PORTRAIT: I WAS THE ONE

The anecdote about a federal investigator visiting Myles Connor in prison came from interviews with Leppo and Connor. I also confirmed the broad outlines of the story with Dan Falzon. The *"kah-dah-tay"* anecdote first appeared in "The Great Art Caper," Steve Lopez, *Time*, Nov. 17, 1997.

My account of Connor's life relied on interviews with dozens of people, including Al Dotoli, Martin Leppo, Charlie Moore, Lenny Biondi, Arnie Ginsburg, Dan Falzon, Jack Zalkind, Tom Mashberg, Diane Sandgren, Rocco Ellis, and Myles Connor, among others.

I pulled too many articles about Myles Connor from the archives of the *Boston Globe*, *Boston Herald*, and other publications to cite each and every one. A few bear specific mention. The details of the rooftop gun battle came from: "From Hobbies to Theft, the Saga of a Fugitive," *Boston Globe*, Apr. 26, 1966, and "Officer, Fugitive Shot in Gun Duel," Louis Kaufman, *Boston Globe*, Apr. 26, 1966. The description of the items found in a Revere safe house relied on "2 Men, Stolen Antiques Seized," *Boston Globe*, Jan. 12, 1966. Details of the theft of the Rembrandt came from "Gunmen Flee Museum with Stolen Rembrandt," Robert Anglin, *Boston Globe,* Apr. 15, 1975, and "Stolen Rembrandt Safely Returned," Tom Sullivan and Bill Duncliffee, *Boston Herald,* Sunday, Jan. 14, 1976. Information from the Lexington stings were from personal interviews and "Easel Pickings: For This Art Collector, Priceless Paintings are Get-Out-of Jail Cards," William M. Carley, *Wall Street Journal,* Sept. 29, 1997. The detail about the 1982 raid came from "Hot Art with Picassos Going for $38 Million, Art Theft Has Become a Booming Billion-Dollar Illegal Business, Second Only to Narcotics," Daniel Golden, *Boston Globe,* Feb. 12, 1989. There were a few other sources that were particularly helpful: "Art of the Steal," Pam Lamber, *People Magazine,* Apr. 7, 2003; Forest Sawyer's ABC News documentary from June 25, 1998, titled "Master Thief: Art of the Heist"; "Stealing Beauty," Tom Mashberg, *Vanity Fair,* Mar. 1998.

Connor's quote on page 139 ("cipher that will lead . . . ") came from Forest Sawyer's "Master Thief: Art of the Heist." Connor's quote ("a life of opulent solitude . . . ") came from "Boston Art Caper (cont'd): The Art of the Deal," Carey Goldberg, *New York Times,* Jan. 13, 1998.

My description of the meeting between Smith and Connor came from interviews with Smith, Connor, and Al Dotoli. The following quotes ("How old are you?") page 140 and ("[Houghton's visit] was the last contact that I had in any way with the Gardner") page 141 and ("These robbers, two of them are dead now?") page 141 were drawn from Rebecca Dreyfus's documentary *Stolen.* Details on Donati's death comes from a letter from a Revere police detective to the FBI on Sept. 21, 1991, requesting an investigation of latent fingerprints. The name of the Revere detective was redacted from the document.

The quote on page 142 ("I think I can use my connections and powers of persuasion to make the case that has to be made") came from "Art Thief Released from Prison," Shelley Murphy and Stephen Kurkjian, *Boston Globe,* Dec. 8, 2005.

There is some evidence to the assertion that Connor had a $5 million art collection. In 1982 federal authorities searched Connor's East Boston home and confiscated more than 5,000 items. After Connor proved that he had either bought the items or inherited them, authorities gave most of the items back. A number of items were found to be stolen, to be sure, including a small statuette, which had had been pocketed from the Higgins Armory Museum in Worcester, Massachusetts.

I found other evidence supporting Connor's recollections about the rape case. Connor's Criminal Offender Record Information report shows that he was found guilty of unnatural acts in 1974. I also spoke to Jack Zalkind, the prosecutor in the case, who confirmed the broad outlines of Connor's story. I was not able to find much legal documentation for *Commonwealth vs. Myles Connor,* Suffolk County Superior Court, criminal docket number 573181ZZ. The court told me that the material was either lost or thrown out. The name Halloway is a pseudonym.

The anecdote on page 151 that Leppo would get $2 million of the Gardner's reward money if the works were returned comes from an FBI confidential informant report dated Mar. 25, 1998. The source is almost certainly Chicofsky. The report was part of the trial against David Turner: *United States District Court vs. David Turner, et al.* U.S. District Court, District of Massachusetts, criminal docket 99-10098.

The quote on page 152 ("When he was alive . . . ") came from "Unlikely Suspect Connor Crony Was No Art Expert, Others Say," Daniel Golden and Ric Kahn, *Boston Globe*. Sept. 23, 1997, A1.

10. PROGRAM FOR AN ARTISTIC SOIREE: ANY NEWS ON YOUR SIDE

Any serious account of James "Whitey" Bulger's criminal career must rely on the racketeering case of *United States v. Frances P. Salemme, James J. Bulger, Stephen Flemmi, et al.*, U.S. District Court, District of Massachusetts, No. 94–10287. As part of the case, U.S. District Court Judge Mark L. Wolf heard the testimony of forty-six witnesses and released a 661-page memorandum and about Bulger and his relationship with the FBI. I also relied heavily on *Black Mass: The Irish Mob, the FBI, and a Devil's Deal*, Dick Lehr and Gerard O'Neill (New York: HarperCollins, 2000); *The Brothers Bulger*, Howie Carr (New York: Time Warner, 2006); *A Criminal and an Irishman: The Inside Story of the Boston Mob-IRA Connection*, Patrick Nee, Richard Farrell, and Michael Blythe (Hanover, NH: Steerforth, 2006); and *Brutal: The Untold Story of My Life Inside Whitey Bulger's Irish Mob*, Kevin Weeks and Phyllis Karras (New York: HarperCollins, 2000).

I drew upon on numerous other sources, including more than two hundred pages-worth of FBI documents on the *Valhalla* gun-smuggling effort and interviews with other key sources. They included Patrick Nee, Phyllis Karras, John Connolly (who answered questions through his lawyers), Michael Sullivan, Donald Stern, Bob Fitzpatrick, Joe Flaherty, Kathleen Murray Locke, Tom Cassano, and other retired state and federal law enforcement officers. Requests to talk to Stephen Flemmi were denied.

The detail about a teenager scrawling "Whitey Rules" in a notebook comes from Michael Patrick Macdonald's *All Souls: A Family Story from Southie* (New York: Ballantine Books, 2000), 170. Susan Orlean's "The Outsiders," *New Yorker*, July 26, 2004, helped focus my reporting on Southie. The detail about Bulger cheering IRA bombs came from "Valhalla's Wake; Mob Tale of Intrigue, Betrayal, Death," Jack Sullivan, *Boston Herald*, Jan. 23, 2000, 1. The detail about the raid on the National Guard Armory came from "Suspect Is Reportedly IRA Member," Andrew Blake, *Boston Globe*, Jan. 12, 1991. The information about how the IRA uses the North Atlantic to launder stolen art and the detail about the Montreal sting came Hart's *The Irish Game*, 117. Information about other IRA-linked art thefts, including the Dugdale heist and Dunsany Castle thefts drew upon interviews with Hill, Ellis, as well as Hart's book.

The account of Smith and his work on the Irish angle drew upon Smith's notes as well as interviews with Harold Smith, Greg Smith, Tara Smith, Deadra Markijohn, Sandy Guttman, Giovanni Di Steffano, Martin Ferris (through his publicist), Rebecca Dreyfus, Susannah Ludwig, Colin McBride, Gil Dix, Derek Milner, Dick Ellis, and Paul Hendry, among others. I also relied on the two documentaries made about Smith by Rebecca Dreyfus, and Ellis's quotes on page 167 ("The good news is that there was a response . . . "; "What's in it for them . . . ") came from Dreyfus's documentary *Stolen*.

11. PROGRAM FOR AN ARTISTIC SOIREE II: WHERE'S WHITEY?

The London tabloid that reported on the FBI visit to Ireland was *The News of the World*, "FBI Hunts Euro 300M Provo Art Haul," Martin Breen, Nov. 12, 2006. In an email, Breen told me that he didn't actually write the article, that the byline was a mistake and the article was by Ciaran Barnes. I later interviewed Barnes, who helped flush out my account.

The anecdote about the last confirmed sighting of Bulger in London in 2002 has been mentioned in numerous news reports. Perhaps the most detailed account was Howie Carr's *The Brothers Bulger*, 316.

I found out that asking directions of the Irish was considered gauche from Pete McCarthy's deeply funny book, *McCarthy's Bar* (London: Hodder and Stoughton, 2000).

12. LA SORTIE DE PESAGE: PUT MY PICTURE ON THE COVER

George Dempster is a pseudonym.

For a discussion of sources on the life and career of David Turner, see notes for chapter 7.

Freedman's quote ("When someone holds a gun to your head . . . ") page 196 comes from *Commonwealth vs. David Turner*, Norfolk County Superior Court, criminal docket number 94511-94513.

Marty Leppo was the source for the information on Turner driving down to Florida the day after the heist. Leppo was in a good position to know this information. Leppo represented Turner in the Canton home invasion trial, and one of the issues in that case was whether Turner was in Boston during the winter and spring of 1990. I asked Turner if he drove down to Florida the day after the heist on two occasions. He did not respond to either query.

Neil Cronin's belief that Turner was one of the Gardner thieves came from transcripts from the evidentiary hearing for the Loomis trial. Cronin says "I believed [Turner] may have been a participant in the robbery" (64). In his "Memorandum and Order on Defendants' Motion for a New Trial," Judge Donald Stern writes in a footnote that Cronin "did believe that Turner had participated in the Gardner robbery" (17).

The document that appeared to be written by Turner's lawyer, Rob Goldstein, was discovered in the court files for the Loomis heist at Moakley Courthouse. On one side of the document was what appeared to be a letter from Stephen Rossetti to David Turner. On the other side was what seemed to be a draft of an appeal written by Goldstein. I sent the document to Goldstein and asked for his comment more than a dozen times. I also sent the document to the U.S. attorney's office. Neither would confirm what exactly the document was. I suspect that the document is a draft—or perhaps even the final version—of David Turner's appeal for a new trial.

The quote on page 199 ("source believes . . . ") is from an FBI confident informant report, dictated on Jan. 7, 1998, and signed by Neil Cronin. The source is almost certainly Richard Chicofsky.

The quote on page 199 ("after being . . . ") comes from Stephen Marks's *Confessions of a Political Hitman: My Secret Life of Scandal, Corruption, Hypocrisy and Dirty Attacks That Decide Who Gets Elected* (Naperville, IL: Sourcebooks Trade, 2008). In the book, Marks contends that Reissfelder "was wanted for questioning by the police in regards to the Gardner Museum heist." I emailed Marks and asked for evidence on this point, and he sent back a number of *Globe* and *Herald* clips. None of them indicate that Reissfelder was in fact called in for questioning for the heist.

Turner sent me three poems and said that a fellow prisoner friend named Ronnie Doe had written the works. I asked Turner to put me in touch with Doe, but he did not. The poems go on at length about how Turner was wrongfully accused and contain specific details about his trial that had not been written about in the press, such as the name of the prosecutors. Turner granted me permission to print the poems, and I came to believe that Turner wrote the poems, not Doe.

The information on the apartment on 166 Quincy Shore Drive came from information in Massachusetts Deed Transfer Records. The information was confirmed in an interview with Martin Leppo.

The person I call G is fictional. The anecdote about Robert Mardirosian relied on interviews with Julian Radcliffe, Charles Moore, and articles by Stephen Kurkjian and Shelley Murphy in the *Boston Globe*.

13. FINIAL: LIKE A SPIDERWEB

The full text of the Theft of Major Artwork law can be found online at: www.law.cornell.edu.

The quote on page 211 comes from "Priceless Paintings Stolen at Gunpoint from Nice Museum," Kim Willsher, *Guardian* (Manchester, UK), Aug. 7, 2007.

The quote on page 215 from Wendy Lesser came from *Pictures at an Execution: An Inquiry into the Subject of Murder* (Cambridge, MA: Harvard University Press, 1998).

The article mentioned on page 217 is by Stephen Kurkjian, "Grand Jury to Hear Art Theft Case," *Boston Globe*, Dec. 17, 2007.

As this book went to press in the summer of 2008, Greg Smith decided to leave G. J. Smith and Associates and start his own underwriting firm. Rich Mancusso will take over the family company. He plans to change the name of the firm to RCM, Inc.

Details about the *Cheers* robbery came from a variety of sources, including interviews and court documents. I was not able to contact Stanley Travers or Gray Morrison, despite repeated efforts. Thomas Kernshaw, the owner of the pub, refused an interview. To re-create the heist, I relied on newspaper articles, most notably "Few 'Cheers' at Hub Bar after Robbers take $50G," Jonathan Wells, *Boston Herald*, Sept. 17, 1991, as well as court documents, including *Commonwealth vs. David Turner*, Suffolk County Superior Court, criminal docket number 93–10603. The conversation between Morrison and Turner came from a wiretap that was part of that case. For more information on Turner, see the notes for chapter 7.

The anecdote about Sargent telling Gardner that she had done more for *El Jaleo* than he had came from David Park Curry's "Sargent's 'El Jaleo,'" *Burlington Magazine*, vol. 134, no. 1073 (Aug. 1992), 552–54.

BIBLIOGRAPHY

Atwood, Roger. *Stealing History: Tomb Raiders, Smugglers, and the Looting of the Ancient World* (New York: St. Martin's Press).

Dolnick, Edward. *The Rescue Artist: A True Story of Art, Thieves, and the Hunt for a Missing Masterpiece* (New York: HarperCollins, 2005).

Elkins, James. *Pictures and Tears. a History of People Who Have Cried in Front of Paintings* (London: Routledge, 2001).

Hart, Matthew. *The Irish Game: A True Story of Crime and Art* (New York: Walker and Company, 2004).

Houpt, Simon. *Museum of the Missing* (New York: Sterling, 2006).

McShane, Thomas, and Matera Dara. *Stolen Masterpiece Tracker: The Dangerous Life of the FBI's #1 Art Sleuth* (New York: Barricade Books, 2006).

Orlean, Susan. *The Orchid Thief: A True Story of Beauty and Obsession* (New York: Random House, 1998).

Shand-Tucci, Douglass. *The Art of Scandal: The Life and Times of Isabella Stewart Gardner* (New York: HarperCollins, 1997).

Tharp, Louise Hall. *Mrs. Jack: A Biography of Isabella Stewart Gardner* (New York: Little, 1965).

PHOTO CREDITS

ACKNOWLEDGMENTS

MY DEEP GRATITUDE goes to the many people who contributed to this book and whose names do not appear in its pages or appear only briefly. In particular, I would like to thank Anthony Amore, Katherine Armstrong, Deadra Markijohn, Nate Katz, Chelsea Stover, Jacquelyn Coutre, April Yee, Noah Charney, Jill McLaughlin, Bob Fitzpatrick, Chuck Moore, James Burleigh, Krystle Strand, Rebecca Dreyfus, Susannah Ludwig, Emily Olmo, Julian Radcliffe, Beth Py-Lieberman, Frank Apicella, Derek Shaffer, Bonnie Magness-Gardiner, Theresa Hernandez, Sara Sklaroff, Steve Fritsche, Holly Salmon, Peter Egan, Bob Harnett, Paul Smith, Semir Zeki, Maja Bernard, Bill Seeley, Joe Gross, Anne Scher, Al Dotoli, Gail Marcinkiewicz, Smokey Harnett, Josh Landis, Neil Lieberman, Alan Chong, Kristin Parker, Arthur Wheelock, and the many people at Lloyd's of London who sat through interviews.

Special thanks go to Sandy Guttman, who was an excellent host and helpful every step of the way.

I owe an enormous debt to Tara Smith and Maureen Egan, who read drafts and provided feedback. All errors are, of course, mine.

I would also like to extend my deepest appreciation to the source. I have relied on much of your hard work and diligent research—and I am enormously grateful.

A number of other journalists have pursued the Gardner story, including Tom Mashberg at the *Herald*, Shelley Murphy and Stephen Kurkjian at the *Boston Globe*, and filmmakers Rebecca Dreyfus and Susannah Ludwig, who made two excellent Gardner documentaries. They have all made powerful contributions to the understanding of the museum heist—and helped keep the paintings in the public eye. I'm a dwarf, in other words, who stands on the shoulders of giants.

Gillian MacKenzie is an agent without peer who gave constant advice. Kathryn Antony was always there to answer my questions—and there were many. Tom Ward spent hours reviewing the manuscript for legal concerns. I'm sorry about the cauliflower ear. And my profound gratitude goes to my editor, Elisabeth Dyssegaard. She brought major improvements to the text, and really, how many other editors would ask: "How is Sonja's big sister feeling?"

I could not have completed this project without the encouragement of friends and family. I had a wonderful set of critics including Daniel Belasco, Rich Shea, Ruth Boser, Brian Felder, Caitlin Kelly, Justin Ewers, and Craig Jerald. My brother Markus offered fine lodging and boozy encouragement ("Go to Ireland, young man!"). My sister also gave artistic good cheer. My father is a role model of powerful curiosity—and my mother led the way as a person and a writer. I'm still waiting for cookbook number two. Finally to my wife, Nora. This book could have not been finished without your unending love and patience. Thank you for the years of enduring, heartfelt support.

INDEX